Welcome, HOLY SPIRIT

*How you can experience
the dynamic work of the
Holy Spirit in your life*

BENNY HINN

Author of *Good Morning, Holy Spirit*

Ms. Sonia Raezak
306 S. Charleton St.
Willow Springs, IL 60480-1330

Publishers since 1798

THOMAS NELSON PUBLISHERS
Nashville • Atlanta • London • Vancouver

Published in Nashville, Tennessee, by Thomas Nelson, Inc., Publishers, and distributed in Canada by Word Communications, Ltd., Richmond, British Columbia, and in the United Kingdom by Word (UK), Ltd., Milton Keynes, England.

Unless otherwise noted, Scripture quotations are from the NEW KING JAMES VERSION of the Bible. Copyright © 1979, 1980, 1982, Thomas Nelson, Inc., Publishers.

Scripture quotations noted KJV are from The Holy Bible, KING JAMES VERSION.

Scripture quotations noted NIV are taken from the HOLY BIBLE, NEW INTERNATIONAL VERSION®. Copyright © 1973, 1978, 1984 by International Bible Society. Used by permission of Zondervan Bible Publishing House. All rights reserved.

The "NIV" and "New International Version" trademarks are registered in the United States Patent and Trademark Office by International Bible Society. Use of either trademark requires the permission of International Bible Society.

"Spirit of the Living God" by Daniel Iverson © 1935, 1963 Birdwing Music (a division of The Sparrow Corp.) All rights administered by The Sparrow Corporation. All Rights Reserved. Used by Permission.

"How Great Thou Art" by Stuart K Hine © 1953, 1981 Manna Music, 35255 Brooten Rd., Pacific City, OR 97135. All Rights Reserved. Used by Permission.

"He Is Lord" © 1986 WORD Music (A Division of WORD, Inc.) All Rights Reserved. Used by Permission.

Library of Congress Cataloging-in-Publication Data: 94–73956

ISBN 0-7852-7945-8 (pbk)
    0-7852-7982-2 (hb)

Printed in the United States of America

2 3 4 5 6 7 — 01 00 99 98 97 96 95

Dedication

Dedicated to my darling daughter,

ELEASHA,

whose gentle spirit brings me such joy.

I pray that she will experience the glorious touch

of the Holy Spirit upon her life at a very early age,

and that Jesus Christ will always be magnified

in and through her life to draw others

to the cross of Calvary.

Acknowledgments

My thanks to Rick Nash and Sheryl Palmquist for their editorial assistance in developing this manuscript, and to my friends, associates and staff for their support and encouragement with this project.

Contents

A New Day Dawning

Atlanta is a beautiful city, the heart and crown jewel of the South, but make no mistake, in August it's hot and humid! And when you're on Interstate 75 right in the middle of a massive traffic jam, with cars in front of you, cars behind you, and cars on every side as far as the eye can see, with the late afternoon sun shining overhead, it's really hot!

So there we were: in Atlanta, in August, surrounded by all sizes and shapes of vehicles, inching along on Interstate 75. Our van felt like a sauna on wheels due to the humidity. And to make matters even worse, *I was about to be late for my own crusade.*

"Why aren't we moving, Gene?" I inquired. "Where are all these people going?"

As we inched along, Gene Polino, my administrator and right-hand man, informed me that because of the miracle crusade and a pre-season football game the roads in downtown Atlanta were in complete gridlock.

We're headed for the Omni Coliseum in downtown Atlanta where our miracle crusade was scheduled to begin at 7:00 P.M. Although the seating capacity of the

Omni is 18,500, all advance information indicated a good turnout tonight. Based on advance reservations for buses and groups, along with the choir, partners, ushers, guests, and general public estimates, we would need every seat and more. And from the traffic surrounding us, it was clear that many more are streaming to the coliseum than we had projected.

"How much longer, Gene?" I asked.

"It's hard to say, but the traffic is moving along a little better now."

"I hope so. It's getting late."

Gene saw that I was deep in thought, and as he does so often, he anticipated what I was thinking, "Pastor, Charlie said that the fire marshal is working with us to help us get as many people in as possible. We've done everything we can to prepare for the crowds."

As we continued along the crowded freeway in the oven-like vehicle, the cellular phone rang—it was Charlie McCuen, my crusade coordinator.

"Hello, Charlie. What's happening at the Omni?" I asked.

"Pastor, miracles are happening already! The place is packed and the power of God is everywhere! People are coming out of wheelchairs and the atmosphere is charged with God's power inside and outside! We've never seen anything like it! The Holy Spirit is already at work, even before the service begins! God is doing something here far beyond anything we had prayed for! There is excitement in the air, Pastor! The service tonight is going to be awesome!"

"To God be all the glory, Charlie. We'll be there in a few minutes. See you shortly."

As I hung up the phone and thought about what Charlie had just said to me, the Lord reminded me of the scripture, "Now to Him who is able to do exceedingly abundantly above all that we ask or think, according to the power that works in us, to Him be glory in the church by Christ Jesus to all generations, forever and ever. Amen" (Eph. 3:20, 21).

I whispered a prayer of thanksgiving to the Lord for His faithfulness. "Thank you, Lord, for what you are doing. This is truly Your doing, and not mine. Lord, you're so wonderful and I love you so much." I began to reflect on everything Charlie had said and was filled again with awe and wonder at God's grace and mercy.

(As you read this book, dear reader, my prayer for you is that you will discover that "It's not by might, nor by power, but by my spirit saith the Lord." If you are hungry for the power of God, keep reading this book for in it I will share with you what I have learned from the Holy Spirit concerning His marvelous miracle-working power available to you and me.)

Gene interrupted my thoughts and said, "We're almost there, now, Pastor. I can see the Omni up ahead."

We drove in the back entrance to the coliseum and stopped. As the big door closed behind us, I got out of the van and made my way to the room which had been prepared for me. The television monitor was already on when I entered the room. I walked over to the monitor to turn up the volume. People were applauding and shouting everywhere! And there was a commotion in the wheelchair section! Miracles were happening! I could see them on the monitor! And I could feel God's presence in such a strong way right there in my dressing room. It was glorious!

My eyes were glued to the monitor. I was amazed at the power of God that was being displayed even before the service began. It was exciting! Miracles were taking place before my eyes!

"What an awesome God we have," I thought. As I continued to watch the monitor, I began to weep. I was overwhelmed by God's love and faithfulness. I was amazed by what was happening! A close-up shot of several sections in the arena allowed me to look into the faces of the people. I beheld a variety of emotions on the faces, from laughter and excitement to tears of joy and adoration—but the one common emotion I saw depicted before me was hunger, hunger to experience the glorious touch of the Master.

As I continued to stare at the monitor, I thought, "I know better than anyone else here that they are not coming to see Benny Hinn. Why, I would not go hear Benny Hinn myself. I would not even walk across the street to hear me preach. I know better than anybody else here tonight that these people are not coming because I'm here; they're coming because the Lord Jesus is here!"

The scripture from Isaiah came quickly to mind where God said, "I will not give My glory" (Isa. 48:11). I've learned over the years that's one thing God will not share.

Some may ask, "What motivates someone to travel a great distance and come to a crusade hours early?"

For me the answer is easy, because it wasn't that long ago that I, too, stood waiting to go into a service of Kathryn Kuhlman's, believing and expecting to receive from God. It was hunger that drew me, a hunger I still have today, and a longing to experience the glorious touch of His presence. I'm more hungry today than I have ever been. And that hunger and that longing to know Him and the glory of His presence only intensifies. The more I know Him, the more I want to know of Him.

Yes, I do identify with these wonderful people who attend our crusades, because I, like them, was so spiritually hungry that I thought nothing of traveling a great distance or arriving hours before the meeting began just to experience a visitation of God's presence one more time.

The thousands who fill these auditoriums and stadiums around the world come from different backgrounds and have different needs, but they come united by one thing: a profound desire to be lost in the power and wonder of the work of the Holy Spirit.

Only Yesterday   You see, it seems like only yesterday when I, too, stood outside the doors of the First Presbyterian Church in Pittsburgh, Pennsylvania, at 6:00 A.M. one morning in December of 1973, waiting for the doors to open for a service that would change my life completely.

If you have read *Good Morning, Holy Spirit,* you already know some of my story. A friend of mine by the name of Jim Poynter had invited me to travel with him by bus from our home in Toronto to Pittsburgh to a service by the famous healing evangelist Kathryn Kuhlman, and there we were that cold morning in Pittsburgh.

The image of that day is indelibly printed on my mind. The air was so crisp and cold, so cold, in fact, it almost hurt to breathe. The people around me were dressed in their warmest coats, heads protected by hats, feet covered with large boots. We stomped our feet, rubbed our hands together, pressed our arms tightly against our bodies to keep the cold, harsh wind out, even huddling together in groups, all in a futile attempt to get just a little warmer.

With great reluctance the night yielded to a steel-gray dawn that loomed menacingly over the city of steel. The light revealed the large buildings, blacktop, and concrete that surrounded the church on all sides, as if the city itself had grown up around the church much the way a corn field grows up around an Indiana farm house. The church itself looked at times like a cathedral and at other times like a fortress, with its ascending spires, elaborate edifice, and imposing doors. The light-colored stone of the church was stained a sooty black from pollution and age, giving the church an especially severe look.

Jim Poynter had told me a few things about Kathryn and her ministry—enough to convince me to go, but not enough to cause me to expect much to happen in her meeting.

Yet I was searching for something. In my heart I was starving, longing for more—and oh, how I needed it in those years.

Tradition and Transition

You see, I was born and spent my childhood in the coastal city of Jaffa, Israel, where the rugged shore of the Holy Land meets the turquoise Mediterranean beneath cloudless sky and warming sun.

Along with my five brothers and two sisters, we grew up as part of an international family and experienced a multicultural childhood in this cosmopolitan city. It was exhilarating and at times confusing. My mother, Clemence, was of Armenian descent. My father, Costandi, came from a Greek family. I was christened in the Greek Orthodox Church, but attended a Catholic elementary school. I spoke French at school, Arabic in our home, and Hebrew in the community.

But I didn't speak well. From earliest childhood, even the smallest amount of social pressure or emotional stress would bring on severe stuttering.

The other children made fun of me. My teachers thought I was a hopeless case. Worse yet, as the eldest son, I felt I was a tremendous disappointment to my entire family.

And even though my father was a fine man who loved me, he said things that wounded me to the core. "Out of all my boys," he used to say, "you are the one who will never make anything of yourself." Now please don't misunderstand, my father was a *wonderful* man, kind and generous, and I loved him—but that's what he said, and worst of all, I believed him!

Can you imagine how that wounded me? As my sense of self-worth withered, I withdrew from the world and those around me. I avoided being rejected by the children at school in any way I could. I still have vivid memories of hiding in a far corner of the playground day after day while the other children played. I did whatever I could to avoid rejection.

Although I was very young, I immersed myself in religious devotion to the Catholic faith as this was the only thing that brought me any solace. Many were the hours I spent kneeling on familiar stone floors, reciting the Hail Mary, the Apostle's Creed or the Lord's Prayer. I gave myself to prayer and study and to becoming a good student. Everything attached to my Catholic education became my focus. I spent so much time at the convent where I attended school that I practically lived there. But this didn't take away the empty, lonely feelings—it only camouflaged them, but not for long.

Throughout my childhood in Israel the threat of war was constant. I can vaguely remember my parents talking about it at times. But in 1967 the threat became a reality with the "Six-Day War." Don't think because of its brevity that those days were easy to live through; I assure you, they weren't. I can remember running to school the day the news broke out that the war had begun. As I look back now, I realize that the war was quick and decisive, but the build up to war was long and bitter, and full of anxiety. Israel's neighbors joined hands against her, expelled the UN peace keepers, and massed troops—particularly in the Sinai. Public and private diplomacy were employed—to no avail. The whole experience was terrifying.

A New Beginning

The next year, 1968, we emigrated to Canada. Up to this time I had only known life in warm, sunny Israel and felt secure in the religious life of the Catholic schools. Yet, I was suddenly uprooted from my somewhat predictable lifestyle and thrust into a world of unknowns. I had to adjust to something I wasn't accustomed to or prepared for. I moved to a new country, not knowing what awaited me.

The move couldn't have been more difficult for me, for in moving to Toronto, I had to adapt to a new continent, a new country, a new culture, and even a new climate. Suddenly I was faced with a new language, new surroundings, a new home, and different clothing to help me cope with the months of cold and snow. I was confronted with a new school and all the courses associated with my new culture. Suddenly, I was studying about a new form of government and learning about new holidays and traditions in a new society. *Everything* was so different!

Needless to say, the move to Toronto only increased my sense of loneliness and alienation. But God had a much better future for me than a past, much better than I had expected, for it was in Canada that I was born again. It was in this new country that I came into a relationship with Christ Jesus. Like Paul I said, "I count it all but loss for the excellency of the knowledge of Christ Jesus." God brought me all the way to Toronto so I could find His Son and changed my life forever.

The Ultimate Change

For it was in February 1972 when some fellow students at Georges Vanier High School invited me to a morning prayer meeting. For the first time, I saw people praying and praising God with real power and joy. I began to feel the same sensation I had experienced when as a child of 11 years of age I saw the Lord Jesus in a vision. That day is still so vivid in my mind . . . I can still remember feeling a powerful current like electricity rushing through my entire body.

I can still remember with vivid clarity the majestic appearance of the Master in that vision of the night, wearing a robe so white it glowed, and the crimson red mantle that draped it. And His eyes—they seemed to pierce right through me, embracing me with a love that is indescribable—and a smile that I shall never forget. And as He stood there, looking straight at me with His arms outstretched toward me, I saw the nail prints in His hands, and I knew it was the Lord. For it was in that experience that I knew there was a plan for my life.

And that day as I watched those students in 1972, hands uplifted, praying and praising God, not understanding everything I saw, yet I felt the same sensation and the same joy and the same love I felt that night I saw the Lord. And the only words I could utter were, "Come in, Lord Jesus, come in, Lord Jesus."

New Hope for Me

Becoming a "born-again" Christian brought new hope to my life, but it didn't make things any easier for me at home.

Almost immediately, my family began to ridicule and belittle me. To someone from the Middle East, breaking tradition is almost an unpardonable sin, and they felt my conversion had brought shame on the entire family.

Once as I witnessed to my family, my father slapped my face and said, "You mention the name of the Lord Jesus one more time and you'll wish you hadn't." For almost two years after that, my father and I seldom spoke. He even ignored me at the dinner table, and although his approval was important to me, we had no real relationship.

At 21 years of age, my life seemed like it was in shambles. I had very few friends, and my relationship with my family was strained to the breaking point. I had no career and no real purpose or prospects for my life.

But I did have the Lord, and an abiding faith in the supernatural power of God, and a desperate longing to experience His wonder-working touch upon my broken life.

The Power and Presence   Could Jim Poynter's invitation to attend a Kathryn Kuhlman service be that opportunity? His invitation couldn't have come at a better time.

Our journey to Pittsburgh was difficult. A snowstorm turned the seven-hour bus ride from Toronto to Pittsburgh into a trip twice that long. But the delay was providential. During that long ride, Jim and the others on the bus inspired me with stories of miracles from some of Miss Kuhlman's past services. Within me a sense of excitement and enthusiasm began to build. By the time we arrived at our hotel, it was one o'clock in the morning.

We wouldn't have long to sleep, Jim said. We must be at the church by six A.M. if we wanted to get a good seat.

This lady evangelist must be something special, I thought, *if people will get up before dawn and wait in the freezing cold to get into her meetings!*

When we arrived at the First Presbyterian Church, hundreds of people were already waiting in the darkness. Some had even brought their sleeping bags and slept on the front steps. I was small enough to slip through the crowd closer to the church doors, pulling Jim along behind me.

As we waited in the cold, something began to happen inside of me. The stories Jim had told during the bus ride, the excitement of the growing crowd, the incredible testimonies I overheard from people around me—all began to build a sense of expectancy in my own heart. I noticed I was trembling but dismissed it from my mind because I was so cold waiting in the winter air.

With every conversation, my faith grew stronger. *Today,* I thought, *on the other side of those doors, I will meet God.* The anticipation was nearly unbearable.

About an hour before the service, the crowd had grown so large we scarcely had room to breathe. "Benny," Jim said, "when those doors open, run as fast as you can."

"Why?" I asked, still trembling.

"They'll run right over you," he replied.

When the moment came, I dashed down the aisle toward the front of the church—with the crowd hard on my heels. The front pew was reserved, but Jim and I found excellent seats on the third row.

As I took my seat, my body was still shaking. By this time I had been trembling uncontrollably for two hours while I waited outside. I was glad to get into the warm sanctuary. But as I waited for the service to begin, even though the sanctuary was warm and comfortable, I continued to shake. At first the experience frightened me, but the longer it continued, the more pleasant it became. *What's happening to me,* I thought. *Is this the power of God?*

One hour later, almost out of nowhere, a radiant redhead wearing a yellow chiffon dress walked onto the platform. It was Kathryn Kuhlman, wearing the biggest smile I had ever seen.

Filled to Overflowing

From the moment she welcomed the Holy Spirit to the meeting, an atmosphere of pure exhilaration permeated that auditorium. As she led the people into worship, singing "How Great Thou Art," we entered into the very presence of God, and began to sing from the depths of our souls

> *Then sings my soul, my Savior God to Thee,*
> *How great Thou art, how great Thou art.*
> *Then sings my soul, my Savior God to Thee,*
> *How great Thou art, how great Thou art.*

As we continued, Miss Kuhlman led us in "Jesus, Jesus, There's Just Something About That Name" and "He's the Savior of My Soul." My hands were lifted to heaven, tears streaming down my cheeks, I worshiped God from the depths of my being, something I had never experienced before as a Christian.

It was at that moment that I became so aware of my faults and failures and felt so unworthy of God's blessing. "Dear Lord Jesus," I prayed, "Please have mercy on me."

Then, as clear as any voice I have ever heard, I heard Him speak these words to my heart: "My mercy is abundant on you." And at that moment I experienced such a closeness with the Lord beyond anything I had ever known, an experience that continues to this very day to impact my life.

The service continued for more than three hours, and I had never before witnessed such miracles. Tumors and arthritis disappeared. The deaf regained their hearing. People discarded their wheelchairs and crutches.

Hundreds streamed forward to the platform to tell how the Master had touched their lives.

As I sat there, my face wet with tears, I knew the Master had touched me too. I had come to the meeting psychologically scarred and emotionally crippled. But now I was transformed by His spirit, filled with a peace and joy that surpassed all understanding.

The Keys to Power

That day in Pittsburgh, a thirsty young man was filled to overflowing with the spirit of life. I was transformed in a moment by His touch, never to be the same again.

I see that same thirst and that same longing in the eyes of the people who attend our crusades.

A Passion for His Power

That longing is *very* important. In fact it's the first key when it comes to experiencing the work of the Holy Spirit: *You must have a passion for His power.* You must have a starvation in your heart that causes you to search and search until you experience in your own life the miracles recorded in the Bible, the very same miracles that are available today.

As we open our hearts to the Holy Spirit, He will pour His presence out upon our thirsty souls like torrential rains upon the parched earth. His presence will become so real and so tangible. Broken lives are healed because of this presence and lives are changed forever.

Here's one of the most powerful lessons I've learned about the work of the Holy Spirit: He manifests His presence and power to those who yearn for His touch upon their lives. Spiritual thirst draws His anointing like a siphon draws fluid from a full container to an empty one.

That is why the Lord promised through the prophet Isaiah when He said, "I will pour water on him who is *thirsty,* and floods on the dry ground; I will pour My Spirit on your descendants, and My blessing on your offspring" (Isa. 44:3, emphasis added).

Many people are spiritually empty, their lives barren and dry. But only those who are truly thirsty for His presence will be filled to overflowing. Only those who yearn to know the Lord and who yield to Him in faith will experience His power and His work in their life.

An Understanding of His Personhood

The second key in experiencing the work of the Holy Spirit in many ways is even more important: *You must understand that the Holy Spirit is a person.* He's not a force or an influence. He is a person, and only when we understand that can we appropriate His work.

While the Scripture plainly tells us that the Holy Spirit is a real Person with an intellect, emotion, and will, many Christians live their lives as if He were a force instead of a Person. They will never advance beyond a certain level in their Christian life until they truly come to grips with the fact that the Holy Spirit thinks, feels, communicates, perceives, and responds. He gives and receives love. He grieves when He has been wounded.

The Holy Spirit is so beautiful, so precious, so gentle, and so loving. But it wasn't until that memorable meeting in Pittsburgh that I truly realized that He is a *person* Who wants to relate to *me*.

The Most Wonderful Person

Right in the middle of that 1973 service, Kathryn Kuhlman stopped speaking and a hush fell over the auditorium.

Bowing her head, she began to weep. For several minutes, the only sound in that building was her deep sobbing. (Years later, her staff told me that nothing like that had ever happened in her meetings, before or after that service.) As she wept, I was glued to her every move, my hands clenched on the pew in front of me.

When she lifted her head I could see the fire in her eyes. *"Please* don't grieve the Holy Spirit," she pleaded, her voice quaking with emotion. "Don't wound the One I love. He's more real than anything in this world. He's more real to me than you are."

Then Miss Kuhlman described the extraordinary relationship that had developed between the Holy Spirit and herself. He was her intimate Friend and constant Companion, as well as the Source of God's power in her life.

I'd never heard anyone speak of the Holy Spirit in this way. As a new Christian I had a confused, clouded image of the Holy Spirit. I knew about His *gifts,* but I did not really know *Him.*

Until I attended that meeting in Pittsburgh, no one had ever fully explained to me that the Holy Spirit is a Person I could truly know. I had never heard Him described as someone's intimate and beloved Companion.

As Miss Kuhlman talked about the Holy Spirit, an inexplicable longing gripped my heart. That was it! That was the secret, I had to know the Person. *I've got to know Him,* I cried to myself.

Returning to Toronto on the chartered bus, I was

still overwhelmed by the experience. Little did I realize what was in store for me back home.

Can I Meet You?

I was physically exhausted when I got home, but still so excited I could hardly sleep. As I lay on my bed, I felt as though someone was pulling me off the mattress and onto my knees.

Kneeling in the darkness, I said the words that had been stirring in my heart all day. "Holy Spirit," I said, "Kathryn Kuhlman says you are her companion. I don't think I really know You. Before today I thought I did, but after this morning's meeting, I realize I really don't know You."

Like a little child, I said: "Precious Holy Spirit, I want to know You. Can I meet You? Can I really meet You?" I knew I had met God in faith in the Lord Jesus and that He had changed my life. But could I really know the Holy Spirit like Kathryn Kuhlman did?

Nothing happened for ten long minutes. No angels, no trumpets, no majestic voices. Disappointed, I started to climb back into bed.

Suddenly every atom of my body began trembling, and I felt a wonderful warmth envelop my body as though someone had wrapped me in a thick blanket. An incredible sensation of ecstasy flooded my being. A love so indescribable began to flood my soul. I didn't understand what was happening to me, yet I knew deep within my being God's plan for my life had begun to unfold.

The experience was so glorious that I wasn't sure if I was in heaven, Pittsburgh, or Toronto. When I finally opened my eyes, still tingling with the power of God, I looked around and discovered I was still in my bedroom in Toronto.

The next morning, the first words I uttered, not knowing why, were "Good morning, Holy Spirit."

Instantly, His presence filled my room, enveloping me in a heavenly warmth once again. For the next eight hours, my Bible was open as the Holy Spirit taught me about Himself from God's Word.

When I asked why He had come, He led me to the words of Paul: "Now we have received, not the spirit of the world, but the Spirit who is from God, that we might know the things that have been freely given to us by God" (1 Cor. 2:12).

He also showed me why I could never understand the deep things of God without His help: "Eye has not seen, nor ear heard, nor have entered into the heart of man the things which God has prepared for those who love Him. But God has revealed them to us through His Spirit. For the Spirit searches all things, yes, the deep things of God" (1 Cor. 2:9,10).

That morning, the Holy Spirit became as real to me as anyone I've ever known. At daybreak every day after that, as soon as I said "Good morning" to Him, He was there by my side, helping me understand the Bible, helping me pray, and enabling me to draw closer to my precious Savior and my wonderful heavenly Father.

I sensed His presence everywhere I went, but my bedroom was our special meeting place. I would race home from work and dash up the stairs to spend time alone again with Him.

There were times when that fellowship was so great that the Holy Spirit would say to me, "Please don't leave, stay with Me, even if it's just five more minutes."

It wasn't long after that I began preaching the gospel and was completely healed of my stuttering, all because of the power and presence of the Holy Spirit. One by one, the members of my family gave their hearts to the Lord as they saw the wonderful things the Lord was doing in my life.

From that day to this, the Holy Spirit has been my constant Companion and my mighty Helper. There isn't a time when I walk on the platform to minister to the thousands in the crusades we hold that I don't whisper, "Holy Spirit, walk out with me. This is Your service, not mine."

When the Spirit Comes

Without question, the reason so many wonderful miracles take place in these great crusades is because of the work of the Holy Spirit, and you only begin to understand His work when you begin to understand His personhood.

The Holy Spirit wants to anoint you with His power, to give you victory over temptation, to instruct you in God's Word, to fill you with wisdom and revelation, and to equip you for ministry. *But above all, He longs to have fellowship with you and to bring you into the very presence of God Almighty.*

And it is the Holy Spirit Who makes the Father and His Son, the Lord Jesus, so real in our hearts and lives. That's why the apostle Paul so earnestly wanted the believers to experience "the fellowship of the Holy Spirit" (2 Cor. 13:14 NIV). For the more we know Him, the more we know the Father and the Son. And the Holy Spirit never exalts Himself but always glorifies and magnifies the Lord Jesus.

The Lord Jesus said of the Holy Spirit: "He will glorify Me, for He will take of what is Mine and declare it to you" (John 16:14). The Holy Spirit does not seek His own glory, nor does He want to draw attention to Himself, but to Jesus.

How rich are these truths! How marvelous is the mystery of the Trinity! When I speak of such things, my mind instantly goes back to the ancient Nicene Creed which I learned as a child at the College de Frere, in Jaffa, Israel. It sums up so majestically my understanding of the Trinity:

> I believe in one God, the Father Almighty, maker of heaven and earth, and of all things visible and invisible;
>
> And in one Lord Jesus, the Son of God, the Only-Begotten, begotten of the Father before all worlds, Light of Light, Very God of Very God, begotten, not made; of one essence with the Father; by Whom all things were made: Who for us men and for our salvation came down from heaven and was incarnate of the Holy Spirit and the Virgin Mary, and was made man; And was crucified also for us under Pontius Pilate, and suffered and was buried; The third day He rose again, according to the Scriptures; And ascended into heaven, and sits at the right hand of the Father; And He shall come again with glory to judge the living and the dead; Whose Kingdom shall have no end.
>
> And I believe in the Holy Spirit, the Lord and Giver of Life, Who proceeds from the Father, Who with the Father and the Son together is worshipped and glorified, Who spoke by the prophets.

And I believe in One Holy Catholic and Apostolic Church.

I acknowledge one baptism for the remission of sins. I look for the Ressurrection of the dead and the Life of the world to come. Amen.

This same Holy Spirit longs to reveal Jesus to you and empower you to love Him with all your heart, soul, and strength. But for that to happen, you must welcome Him into your life.

Surrender to the Blessed Holy Spirit

There is no greater way to express our love to the Lord than to surrender to His Holy Spirit every day. In fact, it is absolutely *essential* if you are to know the person of the Holy Spirit intimately and experience His work profoundly. But surrender is only possible through prayer and brokenness before the Lord.

People often ask me, "Can everyone experience the Holy Spirit like you do? Can everyone see the Holy Spirit do the things that you've experienced?" The answer is absolutely *yes!* There is no special gift involved, only brokenness and surrender. So the question is not, "Do I have the gift?" The question is, "Can I surrender all to Him?"

Here's how the process begins. As you get to know the Lord, it is then that He begins to manifest Himself and His love to you. And a fellowship begins that grows and intensifies until you get to the place where you will say, "Lord Jesus, I give You my life, my mind, my heart, my dreams, my emotions, my thoughts; I give them all to You. I surrender spirit, soul and body. Do with me as You will."

And as you surrender to Him, it is then that the Holy Spirit begins to teach you, not just about yourself, but about all that the Father has for you (John 14:26). It is then that He imparts to you His strength and His living faith. For as Isaiah declared, "In quietness and in confidence shall be your strength" (Isa. 30:15).

Everything about the Word of God now becomes stronger, and everything about prayer now becomes richer. A passage of Scripture you have read 10,000 times becomes more powerful than ever because of the presence of the Holy Spirit. Your communion with God is richer than you've ever known, all because of the presence of the Holy Spirit. And a peace will come and a tranquillity will come into your life, and for the first time you will understand what the Lord Jesus meant when He said, "My peace I give unto you." All that becomes yours because of the Holy Spirit.

A Welcome Guest

Dennis Bennett, the Episcopal priest who helped introduce charismatic renewal into the mainline denominations, often compared the Holy Spirit to a guest who comes to your home:

While you are in the kitchen preparing refreshments, Bennett said, your guest sits quietly in your living room waiting for you to come and talk with Him. He doesn't barge into your kitchen and say, "I am waiting for you." Instead, he may wait for hours until you sit down and talk with him. He is a total Gentleman and does not force Himself on anyone.

The Holy Spirit is just such a Gentleman. He will not intrude into our lives or force His presence upon us. *But He will stay ever so close to those who desire His company.*

We need to welcome the Holy Spirit into every area of our daily lives by allowing Him to do His work in us and through us—at home, on the job, in school, at church, wherever we are. His wonderful presence should grace our prayer closets, our Bible studies, our worship, and our relationships with other people.

He longs to become *your* closest Companion and Helper. But it's up to you to extend the invitation. He is waiting for you to say, "Welcome, Holy Spirit."

Come with Me on a Journey

From the earliest days of my ministry I have dreamed of placing this book in your hands. *Good Morning, Holy Spirit* introduced you to the *person* of the Holy Spirit. Now you are about to discover the remarkable *work* of the Holy Spirit.

Now what any person *does* flows from and reflects who they *are*. In fact, we can't truly appreciate a person's work until we understand who they are. The same is true of the Holy Spirit. The better you understand who He is as a Person, the more you'll be able to understand, experience, and appropriate His work.

So this is how we're going to begin. We're going to look at who He is, what He's done in history, and what He wants to do today.

This book is going to help you understand His person and appropriate His power. And I pray as you read the following pages of this book, He will empower you with His presence and His power and reveal to you "It is not by might, nor by power, but by My Spirit." And when you have read the final page of this book, you will say, "Welcome, Holy Spirit."

2

The Unique, Divine Person of the Holy Spirit

Nearly seven hundred people filled the Greek Orthodox church in Toronto in the fall of 1982. It was a beautiful sanctuary; richly decorated with colorful icons and sacred art.

The priest in this beautiful church was a magnificent embodiment of this great religious tradition with his long beard and decorated flowing robe. Hanging from his neck were three jeweled crosses.

He looked very dignified—and *very nervous*.

Seated at the front of the church was the entire Hinn family—my mother, my brothers and sisters, aunts, uncles, and a host of cousins—along with a few close friends.

Before us was the casket of my father, Costandi.

At the age of only fifty-eight he had died of lung cancer. Daddy had been a smoker since he was a teenager. Even after giving his life to Christ several years earlier, smoking was a habit he struggled to break.

Since my parents were raised Greek Orthodox, my mother insisted that the funeral service be held in that particular tradition. In making the arrangements she told the priest, "I have only one request. I want my son, Benny, to conduct the service."

The priest was extremely upset. "No," he told her, "it cannot be."

She looked at him and said sternly, "This is our funeral and you will do what we tell you."

Surprised by her firmness, he reluctantly agreed. "Yes, Mrs. Hinn. What do you want me to do?"

"Well, you just begin the service," she told him. "Do whatever you have to and then let my son take charge."

As the service began I looked around and realized that the church was filled with people who knew our family but had never experienced a personal relationship with the Lord Jesus.

The priest walked from side to side, sprinkling incense from the censer—an ornamental container suspended from a small chain in his hand. The casket, which had been open earlier, was now closed.

The atmosphere was one of great sadness. People were openly crying at the loss of their friend and relative. After conducting a few ceremonial duties, the priest walked over to his special chair and motioned for me to come forward.

"He's Not Here!"

I walked over to the casket and stood there quietly for a moment. When I glanced at the priest, he had his head down. I couldn't tell whether he was deep in prayer or trying to avoid watching someone else conduct a funeral service in his church.

Across my mind flashed the scripture that declares: "I do not want you to be ignorant, brethren, concerning those who have fallen asleep, lest you sorrow as others who have no hope" (1 Thess. 4:13).

In front of a shocked audience I began to pound the casket with my fist. Then I grabbed the coffin with both hands and literally shook it. "He's not in there!" I announced. "My daddy is not in there."

As I pounded that coffin I caught a glimpse of the priest. His eyes were now open wide. He was on the edge of his chair, transfixed. The entire audience came alive as I continued, "He's not in there! My father was born again and the Bible says to be absent from the body is to be present with the Lord."

I began to preach the gospel. Instead of talking about my father I talked about the Lord Jesus—how He came, how He died and rose from the dead, and how those who believe on Him will live with Him forever through the power of the Holy Spirit. Paul says, "If *the Spirit of Him who raised Jesus from the dead* dwells in you, He who raised Christ from the dead will also give life to your mortal bodies through His Spirit who dwells in you" (Rom. 8:11, emphasis added).

When I finished the thirty minute message I called my mother and my brothers and sisters to join me at the casket. All of them had found Christ as their Savior and three of my brothers were in the ministry. My wife, Suzanne, joined us as we made a circle around the casket and began to sing:

> *He is Lord, He is Lord,*
> *He is risen from the dead and He is Lord.*
> *Every knee shall bow, every tongue confess.*
> *That Jesus Christ is Lord.*

We raised our hands to heaven and repeated the chorus. Then with great joy we united in praise: "Then sings my soul, my Savior God to Thee. How great Thou art, How great Thou art."

I wish you could have been there. There were no musicians. The only sound in the building was from one solitary family who knew the Lord Jesus. We stood there with our eyes closed, worshiping the Lord.

A few moments later, as we continued to sing, I looked out at the audience and noticed that several people were wiping tears from their eyes. Immediately, I gave an invitation for people to accept Christ as their Savior.

The first person to step forward was one of my cousins. He took my hand and said, "I want the same thing you have." As a result of that service souls were born into the Kingdom of God.

It was just impossible for me to look at that casket and say, "My father is in there." It was not true. There was only a body—only a shell.

It was as if a hand had been removed from a glove. We can't say, "Look what the glove can do." It is lifeless. It is dead. My father was not in that casket. But one day God through the power of the Holy Spirit is going to resurrect that shell. The dead in Christ will rise. Mortals will put on immortality.

Your Closest Friend

The resurrection of Christ and the promise of the resurrection of the dead is the foundation of Christian living. Without it, our faith is futile, our forgiveness from sin is an illusion, and our hope of being reunited with "the dead in Christ" is a fantasy. In short, we are to be "pitied more than all men" (1 Cor. 15:12–19 NIV). But because of the sure and certain hope each believer has of the resurrection, our faith is secure, our forgiveness is certain, and our hope of being reunited with those who have gone before us will not fail.

The certainty of our resurrection is based on the certainty of the resurrection of the Lord Jesus: "But each one in his own order: Christ the firstfruits, afterward those who are Christ's at His coming" (1 Cor. 15:23). And how do these resurrections take place? Paul says, "If *the Spirit of Him who raised Jesus from the dead* dwells in you, He who raised Christ from the dead will also give life to your mortal bodies through His Spirit who dwells in you" (Rom. 8:11, emphasis added).

The Holy Spirit, then, is the key to conquering that implacable foe of humankind, namely death. But is the Spirit of the Lord a *force* or a *Friend?* Is the Holy Spirit a *power* or a *Person?* The answer to this question makes all the difference in the world.

The Holy Spirit is so much more than a force or a power. Early in my Christian walk, I didn't think much about the Holy Spirit one way or the other. It wasn't until that marvelous morning in Pittsburgh when Kathryn Kuhlman looked out over those seated in the audience for her healing service and said of the Holy Spirit, "He's more real to me than you are."

Kathryn's statement stopped me in my tracks. She wasn't referring to some remote, impersonal force floating on some mystical cloud which she wanted to bend to do her bidding, she was referring to a *Person,* and *Friend* whom she knew in a deeply personal way. And when I grasped the personhood of the Holy Spirit I told Him that I wanted to know Him as Friend too. It was this breakthrough that led not only to power in ministry, but also to a growing friendship with the sweetest and most wonderful Person I know on earth: the Holy Spirit. Make no mistake about it, there's glory in grasping the personhood of the Holy Spirit!

I can tell you from personal experience that when you stop learning *about* the Holy Spirit and begin to *know Him* as a person, your life will never be the same. Instead of trying to add His power to your life, you will surrender to Him, His love, His will, and His direction.

Yonggi Cho, pastor of the world's largest church in Seoul, Korea, writes of this same experience in his book *Successful Home Cell Groups* where he says: "When I start to preach, I say in my heart, 'Dear Holy Spirit, now I'm starting, Let's go! Supply all the knowledge and wisdom and discernment, and I'm going to give it out to the people.'" Then he adds, "After finishing the sermon, I will sit down and say, 'Dear Holy Spirit, we did a wonderful job together, didn't we? Praise God!'"[1]

So you see, the difference between the Holy Spirit being a power or a Person couldn't be more profound:

- If the Holy Spirit is a *power,* we'll want to get hold of it. If the Holy Spirit is a Divine *Person,* we'll want Him to get hold of us.
- If the Holy Spirit is a *power,* we'll want it to accomplish our will and whim. If the Holy Spirit is a Divine *Person,* we'll want to surrender more to Him in awe and wonder.
- If the Holy Spirit is a *power,* we'll be proud we have it and feel superior to those who do not. If

the Holy Spirit is a Divine *Person,* we'll be humbled that in His great love the very Third Person of the Trinity has chosen to dwell within us.[2] Unfortunately, millions of people nevertheless view the Holy Spirit merely as a heavenly power or influence. They hold Him in the utmost regard and speak of Him with great reverence, but they don't know His communion and fellowship. This is doubly sad because *first,* it's absolutely futile to attempt to understand the work of the Holy Spirit without first knowing Him as a person; and *second,* they fail to take advantage of the marvelous fellowship of the Holy Spirit.

Like Christ, the *Person* of the Holy Spirit is eternal and living. Now when I say that the Holy Spirit is a person, I *don't* mean that He has a body as you and I know it. Yet, He is not without form. And in one sense, you might even say that we become His body when He lives within us.

Like you and me and every other person, He has an intellect, a will, and emotions. My friend Rodman Williams sums up the theology so well, "That the Holy Spirit is the one God, that He is a person, and that His person is a distinct reality—all of this transcending intellectual comprehension—is the universal affirmation of those who have experienced the mystery of His sending and coming. We know that He is wholly God and that He is profoundly personal. He is not the Father or the Son but is deeply experienced through their activity. He is, to be sure, the Spirit of both (such has been confirmed again and again); however, He is identical with neither. Thus the Christian faith can rejoice in singing the Doxology, 'Praise Father, Son, and Holy Ghost!'"[3]

How We Know the Spirit Is a Person

The Lord Jesus Himself put an exclamation point on the personhood of the Holy Spirit when He refused to speak of the Comforter (the blessed Holy Spirit) as an "it." The word for "spirit" in Greek *(pneuma)* would normally take the pronoun "it"—but Jesus showed the personhood of the Holy Spirit by speaking of "He" instead: "When *He,* the Spirit of truth, has come, *He* will guide you into all truth" (John 16:13, emphasis added).

Just as you have a unique personality, so does the Holy Spirit. In fact, there are characteristics ascribed to Him that only a person (that is, a being with intellect, emotion, and will) can possess. Not only does He have the ability to think, to communicate, and to express His love; He is also easily wounded by our careless words and actions.

Here are some of the specific ways we know the Holy Spirit is a person.

1. He has an intellect.

Can the Holy Spirit think? Can He reason and remember? According to God's Word, He has those abilities, for as a Person He has an intellect.

Only someone with an intellect has the ability to explore, examine, and search. But that is what the Spirit of the Lord can do. For example, we cannot fathom the things that God has prepared for our future, "But God has revealed them to us through His Spirit. For *the Spirit searches* all things, yes, the deep things of God" (1 Cor. 2:10, emphasis added).

God's Spirit has all knowledge, but even so He searches the depth and magnitude of the Father's plans.

And He shares that knowledge with us. "For what man knows the things of a man except the spirit of the man which is in him? Even so no one knows the things of God except the Spirit of God" (v. 11). It's clear from this passage He is not merely a Revealer of truth, but also a being who Himself *knows* the truth.

The Scripture itself declares that the Holy Spirit has a mind: "Likewise the Spirit also helps in our weaknesses. For we do not know what we should pray for as we ought, but the Spirit Himself makes intercession for us with groanings which cannot be uttered. Now He who searches the hearts knows what *the mind of the Spirit* is, because He makes intercession for the saints according to the will of God" (Rom. 8:26, 27, emphasis added).

Now notice three things in this passage: *First,* the Holy Spirit *prays* for us. *Second,* He *searches* the hearts. *Third,* He has a mind ("mind of the Spirit"). The word "mind" here is a comprehensive word which encompasses "the ideas of thought, feeling, and purpose."[4]

The Holy Spirit works on our behalf. The Lord Jesus made that clear when He promised that the Holy Spirit would "*teach* you all things, and *bring to your remembrance* all things that I said to you" (John 14:26, emphasis added). The Holy Spirit did this for the nation of Israel as well: "You also gave your good Spirit to *instruct* them, and did not withhold Your manna from their mouth, and gave them water for their thirst" (Neh. 9:20). These verses highlight the Holy Spirit's active teaching role, an action only possible for a being with intellect.

In John 15:26, we learn that He not only *teaches,* He also *testifies:* "But when the Helper comes, whom I shall send to you from the Father, the Spirit of truth who proceeds from the Father, He will *testify* of me" (emphasis added). He doesn't just help us to testify, He Himself testifies, an action which requires intellect.

In John 16:12–15, the Savior refers to the Holy Spirit as our *guide*. How does He guide? "He will take of Mine and declare it to you" (v. 15). This is not some mystical imparting of knowledge; this is "hearing" the things of God and "speaking" them to believers (v. 13). This action of hearing and repeating clearly requires an intellect.

2. He has a will.

When Christ returned to heaven, He placed the Holy Spirit in charge of the Church. He has a will of His own and has decision-making responsibilities on earth.

The variety of spiritual gifts available to believers is not given at random. Paul said, "The same Spirit works all these things, distributing to each one individually *as He wills*" (1 Cor. 12:11, emphasis added).

And those working in the Kingdom of God are subject to the direction of the Spirit of the Lord as well. Paul told the elders of the church at Ephesus: "The Holy Spirit has *made* you overseers" (Acts 20:28, emphasis added).

Even Christ after admonishing the seven churches in Revelation said, "He who has an ear, let him hear what *the Spirit says* to the churches" (Rev. 2:7, emphasis added).

It is vital that we stay in tune with the direction of the Holy Spirit.

3. He has emotions.

The Holy Spirit is not some unemotional entity, incapable of compassion or concern. He is a person with feelings and heart. Here are two ways His emotions are expressed.

First, the Holy Spirit can love.

Love is more than a characteristic of the Holy Spirit, it *is* His character.

One of my favorite scriptures was written by the apostle Paul: "Now I beseech you, brethren, for the Lord Jesus Christ's sake, and for the love of the Spirit, that ye strive together with me in your prayers to God for me" (Rom. 15:30 KJV).

That verse is so special to me because I have personally known the love of the Holy Spirit. He has cared for me in such a special way.

Let me tell you the greatest love story I know. *God so loved me* that He sent His Son. *His Son so loved me* that He died for me. And *the Holy Spirit so loved me* that He came and revealed the Lord Jesus to me. And the same Holy Spirit continues to love me and help me become more and more like the Lord Jesus.

Second, the Holy Spirit can be grieved.

God's Spirit is so gentle and loving that He has been likened to a dove. He is easily wounded. Just as the Lord Jesus was *"grieved* by the hardness of their hearts" (Mark 3:5, emphasis added), the Holy Spirit can also be grieved by our actions and our wrong attitudes.

Paul was not speaking to the world, but to the Church, when he gave this stern warning: "Do not grieve the Holy Spirit of God, by whom you were sealed for the day of redemption" (Eph. 4:30).

The word "grieve" means "torment, cause sorrow, vex, offend, insult, or cause pain." The Holy Spirit has a tender heart that will easily weep for you and me. We cause Him pain and even reproach when we fail to live the Christian life as we should.

Just prior to the warning that we should not grieve the Holy Spirit we are told:

- Don't give place to the devil. (Eph. 4:27).
- Don't take what is not yours (v. 28).
- Don't engage in corrupt communication (v. 29).

Then Paul goes on to tell us how to *please* Him rather than grieve Him. "Let all bitterness, wrath, anger, clamor, and evil speaking be put away from you, with all malice. And be kind to one another, tenderhearted, forgiving one another, as God in Christ ever forgave you" (Eph. 4:31, 32).

The Spirit of the Lord knows our hearts, and as we keep them pure and just we will not grieve Him.

4. He can speak.

Shortly after I began to know the Holy Spirit I read the Scripture that declares "Because you are sons, God sent the Spirit of his Son into our hearts, the Spirit who *calls out*, "Abba, Father." (Gal. 4:6 NIV, emphasis added).

When I realized that the Holy Spirit fills us and enables us to speak with intimacy to the Father, I cried out, "Lord, fill me and enable me to speak to the Father—enable me to pray in the way that pleases Him." And suddenly from the very depths of my soul, my whole being was crying out, "Father, Father."

While the believers at Antioch were worshiping the Lord, "*the Holy Spirit said, 'Now separate to Me Barnabas and Saul for the work to which I have called them'*" (Acts 13:2, emphasis added). It is worship that invites His presence, worship that sets the stage for Him to speak *to* us and *through* us.

Timothy wrote: "*The Spirit expressly says* that in latter

times some will depart from the faith" (1 Tim. 4:1, emphasis added).

The Holy Spirit not only speaks directly, He also chooses to speak *through* His people. David stated, *"The Spirit of the LORD spoke by me,* and His word was on my tongue" (2 Sam. 23:2, emphasis added).

And remember the voice of the Holy Spirit is not limited to special individuals or special occasions. He longs to speak to you today and every day. And my prayer for you is that you will always hear His voice.

5. *He can be insulted.*

The writer of the book of Hebrews discussed the dangers of sinning after receiving the knowledge of the truth. He recalled the fact that anyone who rejected the Law of Moses died *without mercy* on the testimony of two or three witnesses.

Then he asked, "Of how much worse punishment, do you suppose, will he be thought worthy who has trampled the Son of God underfoot, counted the blood of the covenant by which he was sanctified a common thing, and *insulted the Spirit of grace?*" (Heb. 10:29, emphasis added). Now the word "insult" here carries with it the idea of "treating with utter contempt or arrogantly insulting."

When we fail to appreciate the significance of Christ's death on the cross for us, we *insult* the Holy Spirit.

I was appalled when a clergyman recently announced, "We are not going to sing any hymns about the blood. It upsets too many people."

What an insult to the Holy Spirit!

It is dangerous to remove the blood or to decrease the importance of Christ's sacrifice for us and in our place. When that happens, you have closed the door to the Holy Spirit and have made room for satan. Remember, the Holy Spirit would have never been sent to the world on the day of Pentecost if Christ had not shed His blood and returned to the Father.

I find it astonishing that there are churches where the message of repentance and salvation is never presented. Christ is spoken of as a good moral person, but people are never invited to come to His cross to be cleansed of sin.

Why is insulting the Holy Spirit such a serious matter? It will result in losing His presence—something I never want to experience.

The removal of the Holy Spirit's anointing and divine fellowship would be worse than any punishment I can imagine.

6. He can be lied to.

One of the Commandments God gave Moses to give to Israel was "Do not lie" (Lev. 19:11). The decree was not only to guide our dealings with man, but also with God's Spirit.

The apostle Peter had a growing relationship with the Holy Spirit following his remarkable Upper Room experience. He knew the Holy Spirit's gentle and sensitive nature, and how easily He can be grieved. Peter's fierce love for the gentle Holy Spirit was such that it is recorded in the book of Acts that he raged with holy anger when he discovered the conspiracy of Ananias and Sapphira to lie to the Holy Spirit. You probably know the story, but perhaps you've wondered why their punishment was so severe.

The couple had sold a piece of property and pretended that they gave the entire amount to the Lord when in fact they had only given part. Peter said, "Ananias, why has Satan filled your heart *to lie to the Holy Spirit* and keep back part of the price of the land for yourself?" (Acts 5:3, emphasis added). He said, "Why have you conceived this thing in your heart? *You have not lied to men but to God*" (v. 4, emphasis added). First Ananias and then Sapphira were struck dead after sinning against God by lying to the Holy Spirit (vv. 5, 9, 10).

Since the Spirit of the Lord is a person, He can be lied to. And we believers must be so careful and must never forget that He is *God Almighty!*

7. He can be blasphemed.

There has been much discussion concerning the "unpardonable sin"—blaspheming the Holy Spirit. The Lord Jesus addressed the matter when He said, "Every sin and blasphemy will be forgiven men, but the *blasphemy against the Spirit* will not be forgiven men . . . either in this age or in the age to come" (Matt. 12:31, 32, emphasis added).

Now it is very important to understand the context of these verses. Jesus had just cast demons out of a demon-possessed man, and in the process healed him of the blindness and muteness that afflicted him (Matt. 12:22). The reaction of the crowd that witnessed these miracles was amazement, saying: "Could this be the Son of David?" (v. 23).

The Pharisees, however, had a different reaction altogether. Seeing what the Lord Jesus did, they intoned, "This fellow does not cast out demons except by Beelzebub, the ruler of the demons" (v. 24). Please understand how *deliberate* their action was. They were students of the law, rulers of the people, and *eyewitnesses* to the miracles of the Lord Jesus. In their anger, spite, and pettiness, *knowing exactly what they were doing,* they attributed the miracles of Christ to the working of satan. They attributed the power of the Holy Spirit at work in the life of the Lord Jesus to the infilling of the evil one.

This dread act is blasphemy against the Holy Spirit, and as the Lord solemnly explains in the account written by Mark. "He who blasphemes against the Holy Spirit *never* has forgiveness, but is subject to eternal condemnation" (Mark 3:29).

In both Matthew and Mark, the "unpardonable" sin was *willfully* attributing to Satan the miracles performed by Christ through the power of the Holy Spirit,[5]

I would not want to be in the shoes of someone who willfully points his finger at the work of God saying, "That's of the devil."

If you are worried about committing the unpardonable sin it is unlikely you ever will. Blasphemy is a *willful* act and not an *accidental* mistake.

Paul's rejection of Christ and his persecution of the Church, for instance, was *accidental* as opposed to *willful.* He said, "Although I was *formerly* a *blasphemer,* a persecutor, and an insolent man; but I obtained mercy because I did it *ignorantly* in unbelief" (1 Tim. 1:13, emphasis added). He experienced full forgiveness for his unintentional sin and became one of the greatest apostles in the history of the church.

8. He can be resisted.

Can you imagine resisting the loveliest Person on earth? It is the constant practice of those who do not know Him.

Stephen, filled with the Holy Spirit, stood before the Sanhedrin—the high court of the Jews—and said, "You stiff-necked and uncircumcised in heart and ears! *You always resist the Holy Spirit;* as your fathers did, so do you" (Acts 7:51).

He was not talking to saints of God, but unbelievers— those who appeared *religious* but were actually *rebellious*.

Although these religious men were physically circumcised, they were behaving like the pagans in the uncircumcised nations that surrounded Israel. When Christ was on earth they hated Him and fought everything He stood for.

Now Stephen, defending his faith in the face of death, looked his accusers in the eyes and said, "You always resisted the Spirit."

Rejecting God was nothing new for these outwardly religious people. Do you remember what the Children of Israel were doing while Moses was on Mount Sinai receiving the Law? They were making a golden calf, rejecting God and His spokesman. They said to Aaron, "Come, make us gods that shall go before us" (Ex. 32:1).

And continual resistance of the Holy Spirit will silence the voice of God as Zechariah declares in chapter 7, verses 11–13, "But they refused to pay attention; stubbornly they turned their backs and stopped up their ears. They made their hearts as hard as flint and would not listen to the law or to *the words that the LORD Almighty had sent by his Spirit* through the earlier prophets. So the LORD Almighty was very angry [and said], When I called, they did not listen; so *when they called, I would not listen,'* says the LORD Almighty" (NIV, emphasis added). Instead of heeding the words of the Holy Spirit, Israel deliberately ignored them. It is *very* dangerous to refuse to hearken to the words of the Holy Spirit, for there can come a point when He will ignore our words if we ignore His.

Throughout my ministry I have encountered people who resisted the moving of the Holy Spirit—not once, but dozens of times. In so doing they have quieted His Spirit. Those who resist the Holy Spirit must realize that God has given this sobering warning: "My Spirit shall not strive with man forever" (Gen. 6:3). Scripture declares God is long-suffering but there is a limit to His dealings with man. Proverbs 29:1 says "A man who remains stiff-necked after many rebukes will suddenly be destroyed—without remedy" (emphasis added).

9. He can be quenched.

The *world resists* the Holy Spirit, but *believers can actually quench* Him. Paul's admonition, "Do not quench the Spirit," is a clear order (1 Thess. 5:19). The imagery used is that of putting out a fire.

The apostle was not talking to sinners, but to the "brethren" (v. 12).

How important is this directive? It follows a list of commands that include:

- recognize those in ministry (v. 12).
- live at peace with each other (v. 13).
- warn the idle,
- encourage the timid,
- help the weak,
- be patient with everybody (v. 14).
- don't return cvil with evil (v. 15)
- pursue what is good—for you and everyone else (v. 15).
- rejoice always.
- pray without ceasing.
- give thanks for everything (vv. 16–18).

After presenting this marvelous list as being "in God's will for you," Paul states: *"Quench not the Spirit"* (v. 19, emphasis added).

There is a great difference between *resisting* and *quenching*. An unbeliever *resists* Him by rejecting the message of the gospel and refusing to allow the Holy Spirit to work in his life. The child of God, however, *quenches* a flame that has already started to burn.

I have met people who pray for *some* of the gifts of the Holy Spirit—but not all of them. Oh, they love the gift of faith and the gift of teaching, or the gift of giving, but when it comes to the supernatural power of God and the gifts of healing, then they pull out their spiritual fire extinguisher and douse the flame.

Always remember that when we *quench* Him we deny Him the opportunity to bless and touch our lives, and to touch the lives of others through us.

The Circle of Love It seems that all of heaven is joined together in their loyalty and unwavering love for the Holy Spirit. *In the Old Testament,* we see the Holy Spirit so loved by the *Father* that the Father defended Him from any attack. While wandering through the desert, the children of Israel "rebelled and grieved His Holy Spirit; so He turned Himself against them as an enemy, and He fought against them" (Isa. 63:10).

In the Gospels, we see the Holy Spirit so loved by the *Son* that He solemnly warns the Pharisees who were insolent enough to attribute the works of the Holy Spirit to satan, "Do not speak against the Holy Spirit" (Matt. 12:32).

In the *book of Acts,* we see the Holy Spirit so loved by *Peter,* that with great boldness he rose to the defense of the Holy Spirit in the face of those who sought to lie to Him, saying in essence, "Don't ever lie to Him" (Acts 5:3).

In the *book of Ephesians,* we see the Holy Spirit so loved by *Paul* that he warns the Ephesian church, "Don't grieve the Holy Spirit" (Eph. 4:30).

In all this I see the Father, the Son, and the Church continually on guard for the One they love.

It is only natural to defend those for whom we have deep feelings. In the Godhead, the Holy Spirit is the One we are warned not to wound and offend.

Thus the Lord Jesus said, "You can speak about me and I will pardon you. But if you speak about Him, I won't forgive."

The Father did not say, "You have grieved *Me.*" He declared, "You have grieved *my Spirit*" (Isa. 63:10)

I have asked several theologians and diligently searched the Scripture, but nowhere can I find the Word commanding, "Grieve not the Father," or "Grieve not the Son." But we *do* read: "Grieve not the Spirit."

A New Mantle   I wish there were words to describe my year-long introduction to the person of the Holy Spirit. During the entire year of 1974 God Almighty allowed me to come into His innermost sanctuary.

The ministry the Lord has entrusted to me was not born in weakness, but in a life-transforming visitation of the Holy Spirit. I did not receive an anointing or a "mantle" from Kathryn Kuhlman or anyone else. What the Spirit of the Lord gave me was fresh and new and it continues to this day.

Night after night I would lock myself in my bedroom—sometimes until two or three o'clock in the morning, talking and fellowshiping with the Holy Spirit.

The moment I said "Holy Spirit," He would come. My room would fill up with an atmosphere so electric and so beautiful that my entire body would begin to tingle. And as that presence would intensify, a numbness would come on me. At times it was so great that I would feel weak and could not move.

I could not understand why I had such a feeling. If I was standing, I would collapse to the floor. If I was on my bed, I would have to bend my legs underneath me and lean against the wall.

During those moments, as I would begin conversing with the Holy Spirit, every word that came out of my mouth seemed to be heavy, so rich with meaning and emotion. I lost all sense of time, aware only of the richness of the fellowship we were sharing. Many times during these wonderful seasons of fellowship, I would hear myself speaking words of love and poetry to the Lord Jesus, and literally listen to the inner recesses of myself uttering the most incredible things to the Lord. Oh, the sweetness of those moments of addressing the Lord Jesus with the most beautiful, heavenly names.

I came to know the Holy Spirit intimately and understand His great love for the Lord Jesus. I began to understand what the Scriptures meant when they declared that the Savior is "the fairest of 10,000" (Song 5:10), and why the Holy Spirit used so many wonderful titles to describe Jesus Christ, the altogether lovely One. And in my heart, a great crescendo of love for the Lord Jesus began to build. I truly entered into the experience of the songwriter, lost in praise and exaltation, who adoringly declared:

Beautiful Savior!
Lord of the Nations!
Son of God and Son of Man!
Glory and honor,
Praise, adoration
Now and forevermore be Thine![6]

The Change in Claudio

It is impossible to predict what will happen when God's Spirit becomes real in your life. Several months after *Good Morning, Holy Spirit* was translated into the Spanish language, a minister from Buenos Aires, Argentina, flew to Orlando to spend time with me. His name is Claudio Freidzon.[7] Claudio is the founding pastor of a church in Buenos Aires that had grown to 3,000 people in just four years. Claudio read *Good Morning, Holy Spirit* and was convinced that God was leading him to come to Orlando so I could pray with him. Although many of his friends tried to talk him out of it, he obeyed the Holy Spirit.

During the Sunday evening service, I laid my hands on him and prayed that God would do a great work in Argentina. What I didn't realize was that the message of that book had totally transformed his life. The Holy Spirit had become powerfully real to him and was about to become powerfully real to multitudes of Argentineans.

When Claudio returned to Argentina, we began to hear some *amazing* reports. He began preaching the message of the reality of the Holy Spirit and revival swept the country. As Claudio led people into an experience of worship and praise, missionaries reported that the Shekinah glory of the Lord seemed to descend on the meetings. The Assemblies of God magazine, *Mountain*

Movers, reports that "In December 1992, Claudio rented a 12,000 seat auditorium, Buenos Aires' largest, for a service. When the building was filled and police closed the doors, 25,000 people were still waiting in line, closing off 2 major avenues. They waited 3 hours for a second service."[8] What began with Claudio's willingness to follow the Holy Spirit has now spread to hundreds of pastors and churches.

More than 2,000 ministers have flown from Argentina to our crusades in the United States to witness the power of God in action, and returned to their country with the power of God for their life and ministry.

And recently when we conducted a crusade in Buenos Aires, more than 100,000 attended the first service alone. But it all began with Claudio Freidzon coming to Orlando.

If you are ready to experience the work of the Holy Spirit, let me invite you to first know Him as a person. As R. A. Torrey said, "Before one can correctly understand the work of the Holy Spirit, he must first of all know the Spirit Himself. A frequent source of error and fanaticism about the work of the Holy Spirit is the attempt to study and understand His work without first coming to know Him as a person."[9]

The Holy Spirit Is Divine

He is a Person, yes, but you must also understand that He is a *divine* Person. Just as the Father (John 6:27; Eph. 4:6) and the Son (Heb. 1:8) are divine, so is the Holy Spirit (Acts 5:3, 4).

The Lord Jesus fully communicated the Spirit's deity when He said: "Go therefore and make disciples of all the nations, baptizing them in the name

of the Father and of the Son and of the Holy Spirit"
(Matt. 28:19). If the Holy Spirit were not divine, we
would not find Him linked equally with the Father and
the Son in the Scripture.

Peter refers to the Holy Spirit in Acts 5:4 as "God."
When Ananias and Sapphira held back some of the proceeds from the sale of their property and pretended that
they gave the full amount, Peter asked, "Ananias, why
has Satan filled your heart *to lie to the Holy Spirit* and keep
back part of the price of the land for yourself?" (Acts
5:3, emphasis added). Then he said, "You have not *lied*
to men but *to God*" (v. 4, emphasis added).

There is no difference between lying to the Holy
Spirit or to God for the Holy Spirit is divine, that is,
fully possessing all the attributes of deity.

Not only is the Holy Spirit God, He is also Lord.
The Bible declares, "Now the *Lord is the Spirit;* and where
the Spirit of the Lord is, there is liberty" (2 Cor. 3:17,
emphasis added). And furthermore, "We . . . are being
transformed into his likeness with ever-increasing glory,
which comes from *the Lord, who is the Spirit*" (v. 18 NIV,
emphasis added).

Psalm 95 is a wonderful declaration of praise to the
Lord. Verse one calls us to sing "unto the Lord," and
then goes on to praise who He is and what He has done.
We find this same Scripture quoted in Hebrews 3:7–11,
but where the Psalmist uses *Lord,* the author of Hebrews
attributes the same words to *the Holy Spirit:* "Therefore,
as the Holy Spirit says: 'Today, if you will hear His voice,
do not harden your hearts as in the rebellion, in the day
of trial in the wilderness. . .'" (Heb. 3:7, 8).

Who is speaking? The "Holy Spirit" who spoke in
Hebrews 3 is the same "Lord" who spoke in Psalm 95.

The Holy Spirit is just as much God as the Father and the Son. They are Three in One. He is the God of Abraham, Isaac, and Jacob. Always remember that both the Old and New Testaments recognize the Holy Spirit as God and Lord.

My friend, you can never begin to give the Holy Spirit the place that belongs to Him until you see who He is. But once you see *who He is,* you can begin to appreciate *what He does.*

To fully comprehend the work of the Holy Spirit, we need to realize that He is not merely an ambassador of the Almighty—He is a divine member of the Godhead. As Billy Graham said, "There is nothing that God is that the Holy Spirit is not. All of the essential aspects of deity belong to the Holy Spirit."[10]

As a young Christian, before my life-changing encounter with the Holy Spirit, I did not really know about or fellowship with Him. He was an inscrutable, distant entity whom I reverenced and feared more than loved. He had not been revealed in the light I see Him today. Now I know Him as God Almighty, equal to the Father and the Son in glory, majesty, honor, and beauty and have experienced His tender love. And like the other members of the Trinity, the Holy Spirit has three distinctive characteristics.

The Holy Spirit Is Omnipresent

The Holy Spirit is omnipresent—present everywhere. Often when I'm away from my family on a Crusade or a speaking engagement, I'll hear something funny and want to share it with my wife, but I won't be able to because she's back in Orlando. Or I'll see a child do something that will remind me of one of my precious children, and in that instant I'll miss them terribly.

For all the theological ramifications of omnipresence, the thing about omnipresence that means the most to me is that the most wonderful and gracious Person in existence is with me *wherever* I go. I never have to miss Him, never have to wish He was with me, never have to travel to a place and leave Him behind.

Wherever I go, He's there. I love what the psalmist wrote:

> *Where can I go from Your Spirit?*
> *Or where can I flee from Your presence?*
> *If I ascend into heaven, You are there;*
> *If I make my bed in hell, behold, You are there.*
> *If I take the wings of the morning,*
> *And dwell in the uttermost parts of the sea,*
> *Even there Your hand shall lead me,*
> *And Your right hand shall hold me* (Ps. 139:7–10).

The Holy Spirit Is Omniscient

The Third Person of the Trinity is all-knowing. A host of verses make this clear. For instance, Isaiah asked: "*Who has directed the Spirit of the LORD,* or as His counselor has taught Him? With whom did He take counsel, and who instructed Him, and taught Him in the path of justice? Who taught Him knowledge, and showed Him the way of understanding?*" (Isa. 40:13–14, emphasis added). Paul adds, "*The Spirit searcheth all things,* yea, the deep things of God. For what man knoweth the things of a man, save the spirit of man which is in him? Even so the things of God knoweth no man, but the Spirit of God" (1 Cor. 2:10,

11 KJV). Lewis Sperry Chafer says it well: ". . . none can deny that, if the knowledge which the Spirit possesses reaches to the deep things of God, *all else would likewise be comprehended by Him.*[11]

Not only does God's Spirit know about the things of God, *He knows all about you; in fact—He knows you better than you know yourself.* The words of the psalmist about God relate completely to the Holy Spirit: "O LORD, you have searched me and you know me. You know when I sit and when I rise; you perceive my thoughts from afar. You discern my going out and my lying down; you are familiar with all my ways. Before a word is on my tongue you know it completely, O LORD. You hem me in— behind and before" (Ps. 139:1–4a NIV).

The Holy Spirit makes this knowledge available to His servants through the "word of knowledge," which is an insight into the condition of a person's life. In my case, not only does He reveal to me certain sicknesses, He also tells me what to do and sometimes reveals to me *what He's doing* in the service. That's how I know whom He's healing and from what, what choruses He wants me to sing and what to do next. I obey the Holy Spirit's leading because of His omniscience. I trust Him completely.

The Holy Spirit Is Omnipotent

The *omnipotence* of the Holy Spirit is demonstrated conclusively by three powerful acts:

- *Creation,* bringing the universe from nothingness
- *Animation,* bringing life from non-life
- *Resurrection,* bringing life from death

The Holy Spirit was actively involved in the *creation* of the universe, "hovering over the face of the waters" (Gen. 1:2). Commenting on this verse, Allen Ross so correctly observes: "It was by the Spirit that the Lord God sovereignly created everything that exists (v. 2b)."[12]

The Holy Spirit was also actively involved in the work of *animation,* that is, giving life. "The Spirit of God hath made me, and the breath of the Almighty hath given me life" (Job 33:4 KJV).

We reach a crescendo with the Holy Spirit's power in the *resurrection of the Lord Jesus.* For the Bible says, "For Christ also suffered once for sins, the just for the unjust, that He might bring us to God, *being put to death in the flesh but made alive by the Spirit*" (1 Peter 3:18, emphasis added). For all of the power that we humans have by virtue of our ingenuity and science, no human has yet been able to bring the dead back to life. But the Holy Spirit has, and the Holy Spirit will! And while we look for that resurrection day, don't forget that this mighty resurrection *power* is available to you *right now.*

> I pray also that the eyes of your heart may be enlightened in order that you may know the hope to which he has called you, the riches of his glorious inheritance in the saints, and *his incomparably great power for us who believe.* That power is like the working of his mighty strength, which he exerted in Christ when he raised him from the dead and seated him at his right hand in the heavenly realms, far above all rule and authority, power and dominion, and every title that can be given, not only in the present age but also in the one to come. And God placed all things under his feet and appointed him to be head over

everything for the church, which is his body, the
fullness of him who fills everything in every way
(Eph. 1:18–23 NIV).

It's time to live, work, and minister to others, not in our
own strength, but in the mighty resurrection power of
the Holy Spirit!

Every time I look at an electric light I realize that
the source of that light is hidden from view. Somewhere
there is a generator producing power. We don't always
appreciate this, let alone understand it—but we enjoy
the benefits. The Holy Spirit is our generator for abundant life—hidden from view. He is the source of the
abundant life we enjoy.

Yes, when you get to know the Holy Spirit, you will
find that He is the "power of the Highest," you'll learn
that nothing happens in your life without His power,
and you'll become more and more dependent on Him
for your daily Christian walk, glorifying the Lord Jesus
daily. You'll learn that He's not only mighty and strong,
but He is also gentle, sensitive, and kind. And He *will*
brighten your path.

The Holy Spirit Is Eternal   The writer of Hebrews declares "How
much more shall the blood of Christ, who
through *the eternal Spirit* offered himself
without spot to God, cleanse your conscience from dead works to serve the living
God?" (Heb. 9:14, emphasis added).

He *is* eternal, He has always been, He is, and always
will be. He is without beginning or end. The Holy Spirit
did not suddenly and abruptly come onto the scene when
He was sent to earth to empower believers after the

ascension of Christ. Reliable, consistent, loving—He's always the same and He will always be the same, and the eternal Holy Spirit will never let you down. He's the same, yesterday, today, and forever!

After I came to know the Holy Spirit, I found Him reliable, consistent, and very loving. He *never* changes, *never* lets you down, and is *always* understanding and so very patient. Truthfully, I've just begun to know Him—and there's so much more to discover about Him still. I'm so glad I'll have eternity to get to know Him!

"Suddenly from Heaven"

Uncle Michael   I can still remember the wonderful leathery smell of my Uncle Michael's Ford Model T. To the casual observer it looked like a vintage car, but to me it was a time machine, a vehicle that transported me to the places I had read about in the Bible. As a young boy growing up in Israel in the early sixties, exploring the West Bank and the Old City of Jerusalem with Uncle Michael in his Model T was absolutely the greatest adventure I had ever known.

"Are those *really* skulls?" I asked, my eyes wide as saucers. Before me were row upon row of little skulls. The Greek Orthodox monastery that was the repository of these skulls maintained that they were the skulls of the precious infants killed by Herod in his mad attempt to snuff out He who was born King of the Jews. "Oh yes," Uncle Michael replied, and then went on to tell me the terrible story of that dark night of slaughter, of the mournful cries of desolate women who would have gladly exchanged their lives for the lives of their sons. I could picture myself as one of those children, my sobbing mother hurled out of the way by the centurions as they came toward me with swords drawn. "Never forget from this, Benny," my Uncle Michael said, "that though man do his worst, God's purposes will not fail."

I only got to see Uncle Michael and the rest of my mother's family a few days each year. You see, we lived in Israel while Uncle Michael and the rest of my mother's family lived in the West Bank city of Ramalah, a city under Jordanian rule before 1967. My family lived in Israel, and while we were just a few miles away from each other, we only got to see each other once a year for a few days at Christmas when travel to the West Bank was permitted. Depending on the day of the week that Christmas fell on, we had anywhere from two to four days.

The Armenians, Catholics, and Orthodox communities often celebrated Christmas on different dates. I'm a little embarrassed to tell you this, but depending on whichever date gave us the most time in Ramalah, my father (unsaved at the time) told the border guards we were either Armenian, Catholic, or Orthodox! And I must confess that I'm glad the border guards looked the other way at this.

I can't tell you how much I enjoyed the times with Uncle Michael. I used to dream about it months in advance. Even today I can describe his car far better than his house because our trips to Uncle Michael's were one constant road trip.

In the early sixties when the television show "Mission Impossible" was popular in America, Uncle Michael had his own real-life "mission impossible": cram as many relatives into the Model-T as possible (and then some) and visit as many sites in the West Bank as possible in the few days we had together.

Uncle Michael took both parts of his mission very seriously. As a result, into the Model T went Uncle Michael, my mother, my brothers Chris and Willy, my sister Rose, my three cousins—and me. Seatbeltless, airbagless, "crumple-zone-less," careening off together through the Judean hills, an accident waiting to happen. We sang together, gossiped (in several languages at once), fought for space, grabbed for food, and yelled instructions to Uncle Michael—all at the same time. It was marvelous.

And the places we went! You see, Uncle Michael didn't consult a travel guide to pick the places we went; he consulted the Bible. We went to Jericho, Absalom's tomb, the Church of the Holy Sepulcher, Golgotha (both traditional sites), the old city of Jerusalem, and the markets. Truthfully, we explored every nook and cranny of that great and historic city. We visited Bethlehem, and not just the manger—out-of-the-way places that few people get to see. We went to all these places and more in record time, and with so much warmth and love. These memories are sacred to me.

And at every spot, Uncle Michael told us the stories in the Bible that related to the place we were visiting. Oh, it added so much depth and richness to the stories. My sense of the context for the stories of the Bible came not from a book, a map, or a chart—it came from places I had actually seen and experienced.

Through Uncle Michael, the field trips we took in school, and just living in the land of Bible, I was able to gain at a very young age an understanding of the places where the events recorded in the Bible actually happened which remains imprinted in my memory even today.

The Collège de Frère

From the moment my father put me in preschool, the nuns and monks taught me the catechism lessons of the Catholic Church from the New Testament in French. In my middle school years we studied the Law and the Prophets of the Old Testament in Hebrew at the Collège de Frère in my hometown of Jaffa, Israel. Living in Israel, we were taught the Old Testament much the same way American history might be taught to our children. The Old Testament contained the history of our nation. This training gave me the framework on which to hang the great unfolding drama of redemption.

The School of the Spirit

After over a decade of Bible instruction, a lifetime of living in the Holy Land, and my marvelous journeys with Uncle Michael, I had assimilated more knowledge of God's Word than I realized. You could say I had mastered the Bible—but the Bible hadn't mastered me. It was not until I was born again in Toronto that everything I had learned began to take on new meaning and significance.

Then, when the Holy Spirit burst upon the scene, the Word became like a fire that burned within me. The Bible suddenly abounded with clarity and conviction, wonder and power. I hungered to learn more than the history and geography of the prophets—I yearned to know what was in the prophets' hearts. I could finally identify with the prophet Isaiah when he cried, "With my soul I have desired You in the night, yes, by my spirit within me I will seek You early" (Isa. 26:9).

As the Lord began to reveal His Word to me, I discovered that just as the coming of the Lord Jesus to earth had been predicted by the prophets, so was the coming of the Holy Spirit.

Preparing the Way In the Old Testament God's Spirit rested on specific individuals who were appointed to carry out the Lord's special mission. Some were common ordinary people and others were kings and priests. Moses knew what it was to feel God's presence and he prayed, "Oh, that all the Lord's people were prophets and that the LORD would put His Spirit upon them!" (Num. 11:29).

The cry of his heart would one day be answered when God would send His Holy Spirit upon His people, which took place on the day of Pentecost. God began to speak in Old Testament times through His servants the prophets about this great visitation that would surely come. The Lord promised, "And it shall come to pass afterward that *I will pour out My Spirit* on all flesh; your sons and your daughters shall prophesy, your old men shall dream dreams, your young men shall see visions" (Joel 2:28, emphasis added). Then He told Isaiah, "I will pour water on him who is thirsty, and floods on the dry ground; *I will pour My Spirit* on your descendants, and My blessing on your offspring" (Isa. 44:3, emphasis added).

And through the prophet Ezekiel, who ministered later, God said: "*I will put My Spirit within you* and cause you to walk in My statutes, and you will keep My judgments and do them" (Ezek. 36:27, emphasis added).

Ezekiel described an unusual vision. He saw a valley that was filled with dry bones. The Lord asked him to "Prophesy to these bones, and say to them, 'O dry bones, hear the word of the LORD!'" (Ezek. 37:4).

Here is what God promised. He said that He would put breath into the bones and they would once again come alive. It happened. While Ezekiel was prophesying there was a noise—a rattling sound. The bones came together. Tendons and flesh appeared and they were covered with skin. And "breath came into them, and they lived, and stood upon their feet, an exceedingly great army" (v. 10).

Ezekiel's vision portrayed a future event. God said, "*I will put My Spirit in you, and you shall live*" (Ezek. 37:14, emphasis added).

This great event of prophecy was promised by the Lord in Proverbs 1:23: "Behold, *I will pour out my spirit unto you,* I will make known my words unto you" (Prov. 1:23 KJV, emphasis added). Note that the Hebrew word for "spirit" here, "ruach" *can* and in my opinion *should* be translated as "Spirit."

The mighty visitation that transformed my life was also spoken of long ago by God's Old Testament servants including Isaiah, Ezekiel and Joel. And He told Zechariah, "Not by might nor by power, but by My Spirit,' says the LORD of hosts" (Zech. 4:6).

How would God's word to the prophets be fulfilled? When would He send His Spirit to the world?

Jesus Made a Promise

Regarding the coming of the Holy Spirit, the Lord Jesus at several key times in His ministry told His disciples to get ready for an outpouring from above.

First, He told the disciples that His return to heaven was in their best interest. "Nevertheless I tell you the truth. It is to your advantage that I go away; for if I do not go away, the Helper will not come to you; but if I depart, I will send Him to you" (John 16:7).

There is a great reason the Lord left the earth when He did. As long as Jesus Christ, the Second Person of the Trinity, was here in the flesh, He was limited in this way: only a few could know Him, hear Him, and have fellowship with Him. There were twelve apostles, but only three of them developed a close personal relationship with the Lord Jesus—Peter, James, and John. The Lord Jesus was limited by His earthly body.

The Savior also said, "There is so much that I want to tell you and show you, but I can't." Further, He had so much to teach them, but apart from the work of the Holy Spirit to help them understand and apply what the Lord Jesus taught, they could only learn so much.

They couldn't bear all he could have taught them while on earth (John 16:12). He gently declared, "However, when He, the Spirit of truth, has come, He will guide you into all truth; for He will not speak on His own authority, but whatever He hears He will speak; and He will tell you things to come. He will glorify Me, for He will take of what is Mine and declare it to you. All things that the Father has are Mine. Therefore I said that He will take of Mine and declare it to you" (John 16:13–15).

Nothing could replace the wonderful times the disciples had with the Lord—witnessing the miracles and listening to the Master's voice. Yet He said, "It is better for you that I go away." Then He made this promise: "And I will pray the Father, and He will give you another Helper (a Comforter), that He may abide with you forever" (John 14:16).

There was so much the Lord wanted to impart, but

they were not ready to receive it yet, for He said, "I still have many things to say to you, but you cannot bear them now" (John 16:12).

I'm glad the Lord added the word, "now." Nested in this is the tremendous promise that there would come a time when they would be able to understand the transforming truths He wanted to impart to them, which took place after the Holy Spirit came on the Day of Pentecost.

Speaking to the "Inner Man"

When the Lord Jesus was on earth, so much of what He taught wasn't fully grasped by His followers. There were times when He had to rebuke His listeners and say, "Why are you of such little faith? Can't you see it? Can't you understand it?"

The natural mind has great difficulty truly receiving the things of God. That is one of the reasons why the Lord Jesus often spoke in parables.

The Lord Jesus knew that when the Holy Spirit made His entrance, the disciples would discover more about the Master than when He walked with them on earth. The Holy Spirit would reveal the Lord Jesus to their hearts. And as a result of this, they at last would be able to receive truth, retain it, and live with the abundance of life that the Savior had for them.

Jesus our Lord made this promise: "When He, the Spirit of truth, has come, He will guide you into all truth; for He will not speak on His own authority, but whatever He hears He will speak; and He will tell you things to come" (John 16:13).

Now that the Holy Spirit has come, you and I can receive truth that many diligently sought in ancient times yet could not attain. But because of the coming of the Holy Spirit, God's truth is available to every hungry and seeking believer, truth that will fill our hearts, not just our minds.

You've Been Adopted!   When I became a Christian, my earthly father and I became estranged. At that time, he could not even comprehend—let alone condone—my faith.

During those years of conflict in our home, I had only one place to turn. Through the marvelous work of the Holy Spirit my heavenly Father became real to me, abundantly providing the warmth and intimacy so lacking at home. Many times, the moment I would say the word "Father," I would begin to weep. Through the Holy Spirit I had a growing fellowship with Him, and oh the comfort this brought me!

Even more important, I was *adopted* into the family of God. I began to understand what the Lord Jesus meant when He said, "I will not leave you orphans; I will come to you" (John 14:18).

It is the Holy Spirit who changes our status from orphans to children of God with all of its rights and privileges. When He comes we begin to understand the Father's love and His grace. Paul said, "For you did not receive the spirit of bondage again to fear, but you received the Spirit of adoption by whom we cry out, "Abba, Father" (Rom. 8:15).

Our adoption begins at salvation. "But as many as received Him, to them He gave the right to become children of God, to those who believe in His name" (John 1:12). And as a child of God I rejoice every day that I have been forgiven, reconciled, and made one of His own, for the Bible says, "*he predestined us to be adopted as his sons* through Jesus Christ, in accordance with his pleasure and will" (Eph. 1:5 NIV, emphasis added).

And remember, it is the Holy Spirit who makes it possible for every believer to be welcomed into the family of God.

"I Want It!" It is impossible to glorify the Lord Jesus Christ unless the Holy Spirit imparts truth. The Scripture says, "He will bring glory to me by taking from what is mine and making it known to you" (John 16:14 NIV). Lifting up the name of the Lord Jesus is not just saying, "I am glorifying You," or, "I am praising You." It is more than that. It happens with our actions—with every word and every deed as we live the rest of our lives in the power of the Holy Spirit, living in His truth daily. When that occurs, the world is then reproved of sin, and people come under the convicting power of the Holy Spirit because of the way they live.

The Lord Jesus also said that when the Holy Spirit comes "He will convict the world of sin, and of righteousness, and of judgment" (John 16:8).

My friend Jim Poynter used to tell me about the great evangelists of earlier years, John Wesley, Charles Finney, and Dwight L. Moody. They carried the presence of the Lord with them in such a way that it is reported that on many occasions these men would simply walk to the platform and people in the audience would sense the piercing power of the Holy Spirit.

When Jonathan Edwards delivered his famous sermon, "Sinners in the Hands of an Angry God," those listening would cry aloud, "Oh, God, deliver me!" They would literally fall to their knees begging for mercy.[1]

A Burning Flame

You may feel like an insignificant candle in a giant world. But the darker the world, the brighter your light will seem, piercing the night with the truth of God's Spirit. John 1:5 says: "And the light shines in the darkness, and the darkness did not *comprehend* it," (emphasis added). Now the word "comprehend" in Greek means "to seize, to grasp, to overcome, to grasp with the mind, to understand." The idea here is darkness can neither *understand* the light, nor *quench* it.[2] The people around you in darkness will not understand you, but their darkness can *never* quench your light. The light has power—and you have the light.

Take heart and be very courageous: if you are the only light, people will follow you and beg, "Show me the way out." You can lead them with authority by saying, "His name is Jesus."

Remember, you are not *carrying* a candle. You *are* the candle. The Lord Jesus is living *in* you, and through the Holy Spirit there's a brightness shining *out* of you.

According to my light meter, the world is becoming darker and we are getting brighter, and the Holy Spirit is the power that keeps our flame ablaze.

Someone may come to you and say, "You've got something I don't have. And whatever it is, I want it!"

Rejoice—the truth is, you have *Someone,* not *something!* That's the power of the Holy Spirit at work.

Everything the Father has, He has given to the Lord Jesus, and everything the Lord Jesus has, He wants you to have. And the only way you'll receive it is through the Holy Spirit. The Lord Jesus said, "All things that the Father has are Mine. Therefore I said that He will take of Mine and declare it to you" (John 16:14).

The Lord Jesus in this verse was telling us that we could receive nothing from Him without the Holy Spirit enabling us.

And it is because of the Third Person of the Trinity we are able to pray, "Holy Spirit, tell me more about the Lord Jesus. Show me more. Impart things I don't yet know."

People often wonder, "What makes the Christian life so exciting?" I believe it is because the Holy Spirit is always revealing something unique and original. It is certainly never dull or monotonous.

When the Lord Jesus was about to return to the Father, He told the disciples not to be sorrowful because of the wonderful benefits of the Spirit-filled life they were about to receive. "But because I have said these things unto you, sorrow hath filled your heart. Nevertheless I tell you the truth; It is expedient for you that I go away: for if I go not away, the Comforter will not come unto you; but if I depart, I will send him unto you" (John 16:6, 7 KJV).

The Day the Spirit Came

After the dramatic ascension of the Lord Jesus into heaven, 120 of his followers gathered together in the Upper Room (Acts 1:15). They were obeying the words of the Lord Jesus when He commanded them "not to depart from Jerusalem, but to wait for the Promise of the Father" (Acts 1:4).

Who were these believers? The Bible lists some of their names in Acts 1:14.

- Mary, the mother of the Lord Jesus was there. She had sensed the power of God come upon her when Jesus was conceived, but she was about to experience the Holy Spirit in a different way now.

- The Lord Jesus' brothers, who now believed on Him, were also there.
- Simon Peter, who had denied the Lord three times, was there, and he was about to receive the Promise of the Father.
- John, the son of thunder, the beloved apostle was there.
- Matthew, the tax collector who left his work to follow the Lord Jesus, was also there.

Who were the others in that fervent group of 120? The Bible doesn't tell us, but I believe certain people may very well have been there.

- How could Jairus stay away? His little girl had been raised from the dead (Luke 8:41–56).
- How about Zacchaeus, the publican with whom the Lord Jesus lodged in Jericho (Luke 19:1–10)?
- And Mary Magdalene who had been delivered from demonic power (Luke 8:1–3).
- And Bartimaeus, whose blind eyes were opened. How could he have stayed away?
- And so many others whom the Master had touched and healed. How could they stay away?

For ten days they waited and prayed for the promise.

Then, while they were in one place in one accord, the Holy Spirit made His entrance. It was mighty and powerful. "And suddenly there came a sound from heaven, as of a rushing mighty wind, and it filled the whole house where they were sitting" (Acts 2:2). Oh what a moment that must have been.

Wind and Fire Immediately there appeared what seemed to be tongues of fire that separated and sat upon each of them (Acts 2:3). "And they were all filled with the Holy Spirit and began to speak with other tongues, as the Spirit gave them utterance" (v. 4).

The Spirit of the Lord was poured out in full measure that day. He swept in the midst of that room like a heavenly tornado—not to destroy but to build. And the "fire" that began to descend out of that circle of wind fell upon the heads of each person and they were filled with the Holy Spirit.

God joined wind and fire—the invisible and the visible—just as was promised. The Lord described the Holy Spirit as being like the wind (John 3:8) and said that the One coming after Him will "baptize you with the Holy Spirit and fire" (Matt. 3:11).

Oh how I wish I could have been there to see the expressions on the faces of James, Andrew, Philip, and Thomas when that powerful wind began to blow and the fire rested over their heads. I can only imagine how they must have felt as their lives were transformed by a visitation of the Holy Spirit that day as they were gathered together.

When I reflect on the first time I was touched by the glorious presence and power of the Holy Spirit, I'm filled with such emotion for in those precious hours my destiny was changed! What an incredible experience it must have been to be gathered in the Upper Room with the 120 when the wind of the Holy Spirit began to blow and they were baptized with the Holy Spirit and with fire.

Author John Rea states: "Pentecost marked a new

beginning of the work of the Spirit in two ways: His coming was universal, and it was permanent."³ The power of the resurrection began to flow out of their innermost being like a river. They lifted their hands and voices to God and began to praise Him with other tongues. So great and mighty was the sound of that wind and the praise that followed it that all Jerusalem heard (Acts 2:5, 6).

What is Happening?   Pentecost happened during the Feast of Weeks—the fourth of four great festivals held annually in Jerusalem (after Passover, Unleavened Bread, and Firstfruits). Historians tell us that these important events often attracted over 150,000 people from throughout the known world. They were there "from every nation under heaven," united by their faith in the God of Abraham, Isaac, and Jacob (Acts 2:5).⁴

It is thought that as many as 120,000 were pilgrims who spoke another language as their native tongue.⁵ "What is happening?" the people wondered as they came running toward the sound. They were amazed when they heard Spirit-filled believers "speak in [their] own language[s]" (v. 6).

Those from Parthia said, "They're speaking Parthian." Those from Pamphylia said, "They're speaking Pamphylian." And those from Rome said, "They're speaking Latin."

Until this glorious moment, many of Christ's followers had paid a horrible price for their commitment. Their Leader was crucified and they were held in disdain by both the Roman civil government and the Jewish religious government. They had been thrown out of synagogues, disavowed by family members, and filled with constant fear and anxiety. But when they walked out of the Upper Room they were transformed. They began to declare the gospel with power—world-shaking power.

Peter raised his voice and addressed the crowd. "For these are not drunk, as you suppose, since it is only the third hour of the day. But this is what was spoken by the prophet Joel" (Acts 2:15–16).

He quoted the Old Testament prophet: "'And it shall come to pass in the last days,' says God, 'That I will pour out of My Spirit on all flesh; your sons and your daughters shall prophesy, your young men shall see visions, your old men shall dream dreams. And on My menservants and on My maidservants I will pour out My Spirit in those days; and they shall prophesy'" (Acts 2:17–18).

Pentecost not only came after the Ascension, it was *dependent* on it for the Holy Spirit could not come until the Lord Jesus had ascended to the right hand of the Father in heaven!

Without question, the followers of Christ greatly missed Him after His Ascension, but the Holy Spirit was everything the Lord Jesus had promised He would be. As the noted Christian leader A. J. Gordon said: "All the recognition and honor that the disciples paid to their Lord they now pay to the Holy Spirit, His true representative, His invisible Self present in the body of believers."[6]

Greater Works?

One of the promises made by the Lord was most remarkable. He said one day, "Verily, verily, I say unto you, He that believeth on me, the work that I do shall he do also;

and greater works than these shall he do; because I go unto my Father" (John 14:12 KJV).

When the Lord says, "Verily, verily" we know He means, "Pay special attention. This is of utmost importance."

The *first* thing that is of utmost importance is that the ministry of believers was to look like the ministry of the Lord Jesus. He said: "the work that I do shall he [the believer] do also." The Lord Jesus was a man of action. He *did* things as He taught about them. The Word records "all that Jesus began both to *do* and *teach*" (Acts 1:1).

The Lord Jesus taught the people and then demonstrated His authority as a teacher by the miracles He performed. It is remarkable to me that the religious leaders of Jesus' day accepted His ability to heal but rejected His ability to forgive sin. Today it's just the opposite: many believers who have no problem believing that Jesus forgives sin are absolutely resistant to the idea that He wants to heal His people. Yet the Bible declares that the Lord Jesus Christ is "the same, yesterday, today, and forever" (Heb. 13:8). And because He never changes, He is still saving, healing, and delivering His people today. For He *is* the God of miracles—not *was* the God of miracles, He still *is,* and because He *is,* miracles still happen.

The *second* thing that is of utmost importance is that as a result of the Lord Jesus going to the Father and sending the Holy Spirit, believers would be able to do *greater* works: "greater works than these shall he do; because I go unto my Father" (John 14:12 KJV).

When some people read "greater works will you do" they have the mistaken notion that God is transferring

His spiritual power to them. But we do not have the ability to save, heal, or deliver. Instead, we are instruments in the hands of the Almighty and He performs the miracles.

Can I tell you something that offends and wounds me deeply? I greatly dislike it when people call me a "faith healer" or a "healer." I want to be very clear on this point. There is only *one* healer, and His name *isn't* Benny Hinn—it's the Lord Jesus. Regardless of whether it's in a crusade, a service, on television, in a hospital, or even while reading this book, don't focus on me. *The Lord Jesus is the One who heals!*

What "works" were done by Jesus Christ that would be superseded by His followers? Certainly it can't be saving, healing, delivering, and setting the captives free. How could these things be done to a greater extent than the Lord Jesus did?

So since the Lord Jesus raised the dead, cast out demons, and caused a storm to cease, what is one thing Jesus Christ could not do that we can? He could not stand before a crowd and say, "Once I was lost and now I am found. Once I was blind and now I can see."

Something He Can't Do

Do you know what is greater than the healing of cancer? Or greater than commanding leprosy to be cleansed? Or greater than commanding the wind to be calm? The most pivotal miracle in God's kingdom is the miracle of salvation. You can tell the world, "My sins are under the blood. I have been delivered." When Peter preached this message on the day of Pentecost, "about three thousand souls" were added to the church (Acts 2:41).

The Lord Jesus could not testify of His own salvation, for He did not get saved—He *is* the Savior. But you can testify about your salvation. You can stand and say, "Once I belonged to satan but now I belong to God the Father and His Son Jesus Christ.

- The Lord Jesus was not lost—He was the Way.
- He was not blind—He was the light.
- He was not bound—He set the captives free.
- He did not belong to satan—He vanquished satan, for the Scripture declares, "The reason the Son of God appeared was to destroy the devil's work" (1 John 3:8 NIV).[7]

And He has not chosen angels to declare the gospel; he has chosen you. Because of His sovereign choice to work through believers, God *will not* do it without us, and we *cannot* do it without Him.

The Announcement

From the account of Pentecost we know that when the Holy Spirit arrives He announces His entry. But remember this: *The Holy Spirit never announces His departure.*

- Samson had great strength when he was anointed. But he disobeyed and "did not know that the LORD had departed from him" (Judg. 16:20). He lost God's power.
- When the Lord rejected Saul as king, "the Spirit of the LORD departed from Saul" and was replaced by an unclean spirit (1 Sam. 16:14).
- David sinned with Bathsheba and he knew the consequences. That's why he prayed, "Do not cast me away from Your presence, And do not take Your Holy Spirit from me" (Ps. 51:11).

The Scripture declares it is not God's desire to take His Holy Spirit from us. His will is that His Spirit becomes a permanent part of our lives, and just as He transformed 120 believers in Jerusalem, He is ready to do a great work in you.

4

Part 1

The Names and Titles of the Holy Spirit

What's in a Name?

A few days after I was born, according to custom, my parents took me to the Greek Orthodox Church to be christened. Because of my father's prominent position, both in the political life of Israel and in the Greek Orthodox community, the Greek Orthodox Patriarch of Jerusalem himself was present to christen me.

Of course, I don't remember anything about the ceremony, and though all that remains are some faded photographs, my parents told me many times what that day was like. I have also had the opportunity to see the place where I was christened and attend the christenings of other family members while I was growing up.

They said the church was beautiful in the classic Greek Orthodox way: ornately carved wood, majestic stone, muted lighting, icons everywhere with their arresting, other-worldly look. The suggestion of mildew and the pungent aroma of incense pervaded the air. My parents, as fitting the occasion of the christening of the first-born son, were in their best clothes.

They told me then how the Patriarch appeared with his attendants: you could hear the rustle of their vestments even before you could see them. The Patriarch himself was a magnificent sight, resplendent in a long flowing robe encrusted with semi-precious stone;, on his head was a miter, which lent a certain gracefulness and majesty to him. His face was adorned by a majestic white beard—and eyes that could look right through you.

My parents told me that as the Patriarch presided in this ancient ceremony, there came a time where he was actually to christen me, giving me my "Christian" name. Of course, my parents had no idea what name he would choose, and no there was barely-concealed excitement as we came to the place in the ceremony when the Patriarch would declare my name. Looking at me with great care, and somewhat wistfully, he gave me the name Benedictus—his very own name.

The word "Benedictus" comes from two Latin words, "Bene," which means "good"; and "dictus," which means, "speak." This then was my birthright, my commission.

In the Middle East the naming of a child has always been significant. In fact, it was so important that many Jewish people believed that before they could truly know a person they must first know the meaning of their name. Names described what people were—or what they hoped to be.

Parents often hoped that the meaning behind a child's name would be a self-fulfilling prophecy. The name Gideon, for example, means "great warrior"—and that's what he became. The name "John" is derived from and means, "Yahweh is gracious," and of course,

John's ministry was to prepare the way for the Lord Jesus, the ultimate expression of the graciousness of Yahweh.

Scripture also gives examples of names that were changed by God to fit their new circumstances. Abram "the father is exalted" became Abraham "father of multitudes." God told Abraham, "I will make you a great nation; I will bless you and make your name great; and you shall be a blessing" (Gen. 12:2). The apostle "Paul" *(little)* was originally known as "Saul" *(asked of God)*. Saul is called Paul in Acts due to the fact that he is now entering the Gentile phase of his ministry.[1]

In some cases, people used a new name to reflect the circumstances of their life. In the Book of Ruth, for instance, Naomi said, "Do not call me Naomi *(pleasant)*; call me Mara *(bitter)*, for the Almighty has dealt very bitterly with me" (Ruth 1:20).

The Lord Jesus changed Simon's name to Peter— meaning *rock*. He said, "Blessed are you, Simon Bar-Jonah, for flesh and blood has not revealed this to you, but My Father who is in heaven. And I also say to you that you are Peter, and on this rock I will build My church, and the gates of Hades shall not prevail against it" (Matt. 16:18).

Benedictus?

In my case, the name "Benedictus" was cruelly ironic—until the Holy Spirit came into my life. You see, instead of being a "good speaker" (Benedictus), I was a pathetic stutterer. It created a barrier between me and other people, as much from my own shame as from their mocks and taunts.

But then the Holy Spirit saved me and transformed me. The transformation started with dreams and visions in which I was preaching. At one level it seemed like a complete fantasy—yet on another level I simply could not dismiss them. When I was invited to preach for the first time, I knew I had to accept, and I knew that God was going to do something wonderful, in spite of my weakness.

If you've read my book *Good Morning, Holy Spirit,* or for that matter ever heard me preach, you know the miracle the Holy Spirit did. The moment I opened my mouth to preach that evening, the Holy Spirit completely and totally healed my stutter.

Name above All Names

In the next two chapters we're going to be looking at the names and titles of the Holy Spirit, and what we can learn about *Him* from those names. In this chapter we'll look at the names and titles that relate Him to other members of the Trinity. In the next chapter we'll look at the names and titles of the Holy Spirit that give us insight into His character and work.

A great variety of names are attributed to the Father, Son, and Holy Spirit. They are not meant to cause confusion—just the opposite. Rightly understood, they add immensely to our understanding of the nature and character of our Triune God.

God, the great "I AM" (Ex. 3:14), is given dozens of names from "The Most High" (Ps. 91:9) to "The Lord of Hosts" (Isa. 54:5).

The name of the Lord *Jesus* is the Greek form of the Hebrew name "Joshua," which means "Yahweh saves," and this is exactly what Yahweh did—through the blood of Jesus Christ. Throughout the pages of Scripture, we see many other titles and names used for the Lord

Jesus—from "Prince of Peace" (Isa. 9:6) to "The Good Shepherd" (John 10:11).

The names of the Holy Spirit given in Scripture aren't meaningless synonyms for the Third Person of the Trinity. Rightly understood, these names provide tremendous insight into the will, ways, and work of the Holy Spirit.

The Holy Spirit   The "Holy Spirit" is both the predominant name we use for the Third Person of the Trinity and a power-packed summary of what He is. He is Spirit—as opposed to flesh, not having a body; and He is Holy—as opposed to common or defiled.

It is difficult for me to describe my feelings when I am in the presence of the Holy Spirit. He can turn an ordinary hotel room into a sacred cathedral. He can take an arena or stadium designed for sporting events and transform it into the very Holy of Holies.

When the Spirit of the Lord descends in my private devotion or public ministry, I am reminded of Moses when he looked at the burning bush. He took off his shoes because God said, "the place where you stand is holy ground" (Ex. 3:5). The Holy Spirit is termed *Holy* because He "is holy in himself, quite apart from all evil."[2]

Throughout Scripture, the Third Person of the Trinity is referred to as *the Holy Spirit:*

- The Psalmist prayed, "Do not take Your *Holy Spirit* from me" (Ps. 51:11).
- Mary became pregnant with the "child of the *Holy Spirit*" (Matt. 1:18).
- The Lord Jesus declared, "If you then, being

evil, know how to give good gifts to your children, how much more will your heavenly Father give the *Holy Spirit* to those who ask Him!" (Luke 11:13, emphasis added).

- John said, "He will baptize you with the *Holy Spirit* and fire" (Matt. 3:11, emphasis added).
- The apostles wrote: "It seemed good to the *Holy Spirit,* and to us" (Acts 15:28, emphasis added).

Romans 1:4 also declares Him to be "the Spirit of holiness," in a passage referring to the Holy Spirit's role in the resurrection of the Savior.

Titles That Relate the Holy Spirit to the Father

There are at least sixteen titles for the Holy Spirit that shed light on His relationship with the other Persons of the Trinity. Eleven of the sixteen relate specifically to the Father. "While there is some distinction in meaning in the various titles, the chief significance is to bring out the relationship of the Holy Spirit as the Third Person of the Trinity, all affirming His deity and procession."[3]

The Spirit of God

The Spirit of God is the name of the Holy Spirit associated with *power, prophecy,* and *guidance.*

At creation, it was "the Spirit of God" who was hovering over the face of the waters" (Gen. 1:2).

Later, the same "Spirit of God" came upon Saul and caused him to prophesy (1 Sam. 10:10). He came upon Zechariah and enabled him to proclaim the Word of the Lord (2 Chron. 24:20). And Ezekiel's vision of the restoration of Israel was given "by the Spirit of God"

(Ezek. 11:24). But not only is the Spirit of God associated with *prophecy,* He's also associated with *power.*

There is a remarkable story in the New Testament
of what occurred when the Lord Jesus healed a demon-
possessed man who was blind and deaf. The Pharisees
accused Him of using the power of Satan to perform
such a miracle.

The Lord Jesus, who knew their thoughts, declared
that He "cast out demons by *the Spirit of God*" (Matt.
12:28, emphasis added).

The Spirit of God is the Spirit of *prophecy,* He's the
Spirit of *power,* and He is also the Spirit of *guidance,* for
the Scripture declares: "As many as are led by *the Spirit
of God,* these are sons of God" (Rom. 8:14, emphasis
added).

Just think of the implications of the fact that the
Holy Spirit that created the universe, the Holy Spirit
that inspired prophecy, and the Holy Spirit that cast out
demons is dwelling inside of you, making resurrection
power available moment by moment. Hallelujah for the
Spirit of God, and hallelujah that "the Spirit of God
dwells in you" (1 Cor. 3:16, emphasis added).

The Spirit of the Lord

We need to recognize that the Holy Spirit is more than
a representative of the Supreme Being, He is the Spirit
of the Yahweh we worship. The Spirit of the "I AM."
This title for the Holy Spirit is used repeatedly in both
the Old and New Testaments.

I love the story of Gideon. After years of oppression
by the Midianites, Gideon answered God's call on behalf of the Israelites. Scripture tells us that "the Spirit
of the LORD came upon Gideon," and he called his

armies together (Judg. 6:34). Thirty-two thousand men were present. God told him that the army was too large and that might allow Israel to boast in the future, "My own hand has saved me" (Judg. 7:2).

So God had him reduce the army to 300 men whose only weapons were a lamp and a trumpet. When they surrounded the vast armies of Midian and blew their trumpets, the enemy fled. It was "the Spirit of the Lord" that led Gideon to such a glorious victory.

Isaiah said, "When the enemy comes in like a flood, *the Spirit of the LORD* will lift up a standard against him" (Is. 59:19, emphasis added).

When the Lord Jesus began His ministry, He stood in the synagogue and quoted Isaiah, saying, "*The Spirit of the LORD* is upon Me" (Luke 4:18, emphasis added).

Paul used the same title to explain the workings of the mighty, victorious Spirit of the Lord, who uses His power to free us: "The Lord is the Spirit; and where *the Spirit of the Lord* is, there is liberty" (2 Cor. 3:17, emphasis added).

My Spirit

When God addresses the Holy Spirit, He does it in a very personal way. He refers to Him as "My Spirit," clearly demonstrating the mystery of the Trinity. They are One, yet They are Three.

- God declared through Joel that in the last days, "I will pour out *My Spirit* on all flesh" (Joel 2:28, emphasis added).
- God also warned humankind in Genesis 6:3 to heed the Holy Spirit, saying, "*My Spirit* shall not always strive with man" (KJV, emphasis added).

- Zechariah reminded us that it is not by might or power, but "by My Spirit," says the Lord of Hosts (Zech. 4:6).

The Spirit of the Living God

I love the work of the Holy Spirit. He makes God's Word so real to *us* and *in* us. The Scriptures use the title "Spirit of the Living God" in association with the work of the Holy Spirit in making His Word live and His children "living epistles" (2 Cor. 3:3).

Instead of concentrating on "living epistles" and giving the glory to the Lord, it is unfortunately true that sometimes some ministers can try to establish their importance by talking about the number of people in their church, the size of their campus, the number and size of their crusades, how many potential viewers there are for their broadcasts, how much people give, etc. But for me there is only one test, and it's very simple: "Are lives changed?" And how are lives changed? By the *Spirit of the living God.*

What matters are not ledger sheets and membership rolls, but are people set free and living the abundant life by the Spirit of the *living* God? A person miraculously transformed by the Spirit of the living God is a living epistle, a walking and breathing testimonial to the power of the living God in the world today.

Paul was so clear on this when some at the church of Corinth questioned his credentials. His reply was simple: all of them in the church at Corinth were his credentials *because of the Spirit of the living God.*

Are we beginning to commend ourselves again? Or do we need, like some people, letters of recommendation to you or from you? You yourselves are our letter, written on our hearts, known and read by everybody. You show that you are a letter from Christ, the result of our ministry, written not with ink but *with the Spirit of the living God,* not on tablets of stone but on tablets of human hearts. Such confidence as this is ours through Christ before God. Not that we are competent in ourselves to claim anything for ourselves, but our competence comes from God. He has made us competent as ministers of a new covenant—not of the letter but of the Spirit; for the letter kills, but the Spirit gives life (2 Corinthians 3:1-6 NIV, emphasis added).

Oh, and I know today that your longing is for a fresh anointing of the Spirit that will affect your life and others through your walk with God. And believe me there is nothing I long for more than to be used of God and to know His presence in a greater dimension than ever before. That's why I love to sing from the depths of my heart:

> *Spirit of the Living God,*
> *Fall fresh on me.*
> *Melt me, mold me*
> *Fill me, use me!*
> *Spirit of the Living God,*
> *Fall fresh on me.*

The Power of the Highest

When I get to heaven, there are many things I want to do, and many people I want to meet. Mary, the mother of Jesus is one of those people. Her encounter with "the power of the Highest" has never been experienced before or since.

I want to know what it was like to experience God's power in the way she did. Oh how I wish even now to sit with the great prophets of the Old Testament and discover things I am so hungry for. How I wish I could sit with Peter and ask him about the experience He had when his very shadow healed the sick, or with Paul who God's presence descended so strongly upon, he was caught up to the third heaven. But Mary's experience with the Holy Spirit stands out as one of the greatest in Scripture.

As you know, one of the great central teachings and prophecies of Scripture is that the Messiah would be born of a virgin: "Therefore the Lord Himself will give you a sign: Behold, the virgin shall conceive and bear a Son, and shall call His name Immanuel" (Isa. 7:14).

When Mary learned from the angel Gabriel that she would bear the Messiah, she asked the natural question: "How can this be, since I do not know a man?" (Luke 1:34)

Scripture records Gabriel's powerful reply, "The Holy Spirit will come upon you, and the *power of the Highest* will overshadow you; therefore, also, that Holy One who is to be born will be called the Son of God" (Luke 1:35).

And of course that's *exactly* what happened. The impossible becomes possible when "the power of the Highest" comes. Have you heard the story about the little boy who was trying to move a huge rock? He pulled and pushed, straining with all his might against this great rock. He even tried to move it with leverage from a board, all to no avail. His dad asked him, "Son, have you used all your resources?" The son answered, "Yes, Dad. I've tried everything and I can't make it move." His father replied, "No, you haven't. You haven't asked me to help you yet."[4]

Oh I know that like me you are hungry to see God's power transform your life, your relationships, and your work. Surrender anew to the Holy Spirit and let the full measure of the power of the Highest be unleashed in your life!

Titles That Relate the Holy Spirit to Jesus Christ the Son

The Spirit of Christ

"What do those black diamonds stand for?" I asked my friend as we were about to get on a ski lift in Aspen, Colorado, for my first and absolutely last attempt at skiing. Now I don't like the cold, and I don't like the snow, but somehow I got talked into going skiing. When you watch people skiing, it looks so effortless, so easy.

But I think there must be a *conspiracy* to lure unsuspecting people like me to the slopes and there to break every bone in their bodies.

My idea was to begin on a gentle bunny slope manned by a kind, reassuring instructor and punctuated by rest and hot chocolate at the ski lodge. My friend was thinking more along the lines of slaloming down Mount Everest in the Winter Olympics!

If you know anything about skiing, you know that a "black diamond" run is the most dangerous, to be attempted by experts only. Because I knew very little about skiing, I was not aware of this when I got on the ski lift.

We were heading toward the biggest mountain I had ever seen in my life, what Saddam Hussein might have called, "the mother of all mountains." "Relax, Benny, it'll be all right," my friend said. I wondered how many people now in cemeteries could testify that the last words they heard were, "Relax, it will be all right."

The best part of the whole experience was the lift ride to the top—the beautiful snow-covered slopes below looked so peaceful and inviting. They gave no indication of the misery in store for me when I actually tried to ski down the summit, much like the last meal of a condemned man provides no inkling of the execution that follows. I did make it down the slope in one piece, out of control and sitting on my skis until a woman was kind enough to stop my descent by colliding with me. I took my skis off and walked down the rest of the way.

But as the lift carried us higher and higher before that fateful event, it became clear that what looked like a single mountain was actually a series of peaks, separated by valleys. Only when we got closer to the peaks did this become clear.

Similarly, long before the Lord Jesus Christ came, the prophets foretold the majestic mountain top of salvation He would bring. They saw the two great peaks of Bible prophecy: the first coming of Christ as the *suffering* Messiah, and the second coming of Christ as the *conquering* Messiah. But as far away as they were, the peaks appeared as one mountain to the prophets of old. They didn't see two comings of the Savior. Instead they saw His two great missions, suffering for the sins of mankind and conquering this fallen world as occurring at the same time. It wasn't until the times of the New Testament that it became clear that the missions of the Savior would occur, one during His first coming, and the other during His second coming.

I think this is what Peter wrote about when he declared, "Of this salvation the prophets have inquired and searched carefully, who prophesied of the grace that would come to you, searching what, or in what manner of time, *the Spirit of Christ* who was in them was indicating when He testified beforehand of the sufferings of Christ and the glories that would follow" (1 Peter 1:10–11, emphasis added). The title is so interesting here in this prophetic passage because it is a reminder of several things.

First, that the Spirit of the Lord inspired the human authors of Scriptures: "for prophecy never came by the will of man, but holy men of God spoke as they were moved by the Holy Spirit (2 Peter 1:21). Related to this is the clear testimony of the Word that the work of the Holy Spirit is to lift up the Lord Jesus Christ. The Lord Jesus said "He will testify of Me" (John 15:26).

Second, that the Scriptures focus on Jesus Christ. "The testimony of Jesus is the spirit of prophecy" (Revelation 19:10). Prophecy is all about the Lord Jesus, so when the Spirit of the Lord is involved with prophecies and prophets, He is working to get the message out about the Lord Jesus.

The Spirit of Jesus Christ

Philippians is such a marvelous book! Written from a dank Roman prison cell, Paul teaches us how we can have joy in spite of the *place* we're in, the *people* we're with, and *person* we are. That's pretty remarkable when you think about it. Just about every challenge we face comes from one of these areas. How could Paul be so confident of joyful living? After all, he was in prison, shackled to a Roman centurion twenty-four hours a day, and in the midst of this his reputation was being attacked by fellow believers. He himself gives us the answer: "I know that this will turn out for my deliverance through your prayer and the supply of *the Spirit of Jesus Christ*" (Phil. 1:19, emphasis added).

Part of the great comforting work of the Holy Spirit is to give us peace and even joy in situations like these. In the context of this book about joy, it makes sense that Paul would identify the connecting link to joy as *the Spirit of Jesus Christ*, for after all, the Lord Jesus wanted our joy to be complete (John 16:24) and prayed for the Father to send *another* Helper to abide with us and make our joy complete. The Holy Spirit that the Lord Jesus prayed for brings the joy that the Savior wanted each of us to have.

So you see, joy comes through the Spirit of Jesus Christ *regardless* of our condition. The joy that you want, the joy that you are so diligently searching for, the joy that your spirit is crying out for can only truly come from one Person: *the Spirit of Jesus Christ*.

The Spirit of His Son

"And because you are sons, *God has sent forth the Spirit of His Son* into your hearts, crying out, 'Abba, Father!' Therefore you are no longer a slave but a son, and if a son, then an heir of God through Christ" (Gal. 4:6, 7, emphasis added).

If you've read any of my previous books or been present in any of my services, you've probably heard me talk about my *father*. The best way I know of to describe the way our father ran our family is to picture the movie, *The Sound of Music*. Except for the location and the singing, that's how our house functioned. Strict discipline; well-understood, comprehensive rules; everything neat and tidy; and plenty of work to do. Swift, sure punishment when we failed to live up to the rules. Our home was run with military-like discipline. My brothers and sisters and I were even dressed in matching uniforms.

A former boxer, my father was a 6'2", 260-pound powerhouse. But even that doesn't begin to describe him. By virtue of his commanding personality he was larger than life, really—and there was no doubt who was in control.

In his own stern way, he loved us, even though I never heard him say, "I love you" until the very end of his life. For almost the first thirty years of my life, my human father was detached, distant, and emotionally cold to me, not intentionally, but by his very makeup he was undemonstrative. As I child I lived with him, ate bread from his table, and was physically provided for in every way by him, but I didn't really commune with him. It wasn't until he was born again that I experienced the relationship with him that I desired for so long.

So can you imagine the joy I felt when I met the Lord and instantly felt a tremendous intimacy and affection with my heavenly Father. What took me thirty years to experience with my earthly father took me less than thirty seconds to experience with my heavenly Father.

I will never, ever lose my appreciation for the relationship the Holy Spirit gives me with the Father because of the sacrifice of the Lord Jesus. I'm no longer a slave to sin and alienated from the Father. I'm not in the

Father's family as a step-child, emotionally distant and never really accepted. I've been adopted as a full-fledged son and joint-heir, and so I can cry out, "Abba, Father!" (Gal. 4:6). Now "Abba" is the term in Aramaic that small children would use in addressing their father, like "Daddy," or "Papa."[5] The term is polite, intimate, even tender. And how can it be that we can have this kind of relationship with the Father? "God has sent forth *the Spirit of His Son* into [our] hearts, crying out, 'Abba, Father!'" (Gal. 4:6, emphasis added).

Part 2

The Names and Titles of the Holy Spirit

"IN YOUR NAME . . ."

Check the chapel first; she's probably in there praying." That's what coach Denny Duron would say whenever anyone at Evangel College in Springfield, Missouri, was looking for Suzanne Harthern (now my wife, Suzanne Hinn) for Suzanne is a woman of prayer.

Suzanne's mother and father, Pauline and Roy, are great ministers of the Gospel, and in fact both of her grandfathers were healing evangelists in England. Suzanne's parents even tell me that in my preaching and ministering style, I'm very much like her grandfather Charles. Suzanne's grandfathers were tremendously influenced by the renowned English healing evangelist, Smith-Wigglesworth. It is reported that 19 people were raised from the dead through his ministry. Suzanne's family was profoundly impacted by this great man of God, and they imparted this influence to her.

As a traveling evangelist in 1978, I had been praying for three years for a woman like Suzanne. I asked the Lord to send me a wife so that I wouldn't have to search for one. And that's exactly what He did. In fact,

I was asking God for twenty-one things in a wife, and Suzanne was every one of those twenty-one things and more. For one, I wanted a wife who was a prayer warrior, and Suzanne has been that ever since I've known her. Now the other twenty things are between Suzanne and me, but let me tell you more about how the Lord brought us together.

I was ministering in Vallejo, California, in July 1978 for Ronn Haus (now my associate evangelist) when he introduced me to Roy Harthern, Suzanne's father and the pastor of Calvary Assembly at that time, a large church in Orlando, Florida. He invited me to speak in his church a few weeks later, and we had some tremendous meetings. Our time together was the beginning of a great friendship. But I didn't meet Suzanne then. She was away for the weekend.

A couple of months later, Ronn Haus invited me to Singapore to attend a conference called "John 17:21" led by David Duplisse. When I arrived in San Francisco, I learned that my flight had been canceled, and that the only way to get to Singapore was on a flight that would go through Thailand and Hong Kong before arriving at Singapore. That meant leaving on Monday and not arriving until Thursday. But I had to be home on Saturday. Now normally I don't fly 9,300 miles to sit in the audience for one night of an event, but this time I felt the Holy Spirit compelling me to go, so off I went.

I arrived in time for the Thursday night meeting, but frankly I was too tired to get much out of it. When I returned to the hotel, who should I see in the lobby but Roy Harthern. And as the Lord would have it, we sat next to each other during the flight back to the U.S. The Lord used this to really cement our friendship. It was during that trip that Roy first told me about Suzanne, and during that same trip the Lord told Roy that I was the one who would marry Suzanne.

When Roy returned home, he told Suzanne that he had met the man she was going to marry. When he told her that his name was "Benny Hinn," she asked, "Who is Benny Hinn?"

Quite apart from all of this, at about this time Suzanne's grandmother, Lil Skin, received a word from the Lord that Suzanne was to marry someone named "Benny Hinn." By now Suzanne was really wondering what was going on, and again she asked, *"Who is this Benny Hinn?"* Lil didn't know.

I didn't know about any of this, but when Roy invited me to preach at his church again during Christmas in 1978, I again felt compelled to go. It was then that Suzanne and I met for the first time. The minute I saw her, the Lord told me, "That's your wife." And a few months later she was.

And what a precious gift from God she has been to me. She is a spur to my faith, an encourager of my soul, and a fellow minister with me of the Gospel. Because of the reality of the Holy Spirit in her life, she does everything "heartily, as unto the Lord."

For example, when we had our children, Suzanne put a great deal of time and effort into researching and selecting the names of each of our children. We have *three* books of names at our house which she used to research the names. We wanted them to have names that they would not only like, but that they would feel proud of, names that would affect their personalities and influence their destinies.

You see, we tell each of our children what their names mean, and inevitably they begin to identify personally, not just with the name, but with the *meaning* of the name. Suzanne and I also think that it is true that people's names affects how they feel about themselves. So our children know that we chose their names with great care because we wanted them to know how dear they were to us.

Recently I was having devotions with my four-year-old son, Joshua. I asked him if he knew what his name meant. Of course he did not. So I read to him from the Bible about Joshua, the great leader who possessed the land for Israel. Looking at me with eyes full of wonder and innocence, he asked, "Is that why you named me after Joshua—because He was a great man of God?" "Oh yes, Joshie," I answered. He said to me with the conviction and finality that only four-year-olds can muster, "I want to be like that." Oh the joy that welled up inside of me. It was a holy moment.

- My firstborn is Jessica Cheri. Her first name, means "wealthy," while her middle name means "dear one." And how wealthy Jessie has made us feel! I don't believe that anyone realizes the place that children hold in your heart until you have one. And as our firstborn, she became so dear to us so quickly—and is even more dear today.

- My second child is Natasha Pauline. "Natasha" means "God's gift of joy," while "Pauline" means "gentle spirit." Suzanne's pregnancy with our second child was a difficult one. In the natural, there was a possibility that there could be problems with the birth—but when Natasha was born she was absolutely perfect. And true to her name, what a gentle gift of joy she has been to us since those difficult months. She is easy-going, a natural entertainer, and she always knows how to make us laugh. And because we have explained the meaning and heritage of her name, she works hard to be a joy giver to those around her.

- My third child and only son is Joshua Benjamin. "Joshua" means "Yahweh is salvation," while "Benjamin" means "son of my right hand." My wife had a leading from the Holy Spirit years before Joshua was born that if she should have a son, his name was to be "Joshua." Then a couple of years before Joshua was born, we were having dinner with our very dear friend Reinhart Bonnke and his wife after a Sunday evening service. Reinhart is one of the greatest evangelists in the world today. A native of Germany, he has been mightily used of God, especially in Africa. We were having delightful fellowship when all of the sudden he got very quiet and serious. Then he uttered the words that Suzanne and I have never forgotten: "God is telling me to tell you that your Joshua is on the way." If there was any doubt about what we would name our son, it ended right there. His middle name is "Benjamin," and my prayer is that when he is of age he will assist me and become "the son of my right hand." I tell him this even today, and he will tell you the same.

- My fourth child is Eleasa. The name "Eleasa" has a double meaning for us. On the one hand, the name means "God is his salvation." On the other hand, the name hearkens back to Elisha and his boldness to seek a double portion of the Holy Spirit's anointing. Even before precious Eleasa was born, the Lord Jesus revealed to me that she would be a great prayer warrior and that God was going to pour a double portion of His anointing on her life. As she begins to understand, Suzanne and I will explain the meaning of her name to her, and the promise behind it. I am confident that she will begin to look expectantly for that double portion of God's presence in her life.

So you see, like so many parents, the names of our children were not chosen at random, they were chosen with a purpose, they were chosen in hope. Even so the names and titles of the Holy Spirit are rich with significance, revealing the eternal nature and immutable character of our sovereign God. And just like you now have more insight into our family because of what I've shared with you about the names of my children, you will gain a dynamic insight into the person and work of the Holy Spirit as you study *His* names and titles. In fact, understanding these names and the passages in which they occur will allow you to *appreciate* and *appropriate* His work in new and more powerful ways.

In the last chapter we explored those names and titles for the Holy Spirit that related to His interaction with the Father and the Son. In this chapter we'll explore some of the names and titles of the Holy Spirit that relate to His work in our lives.

Titles That Relate to the Holy Spirit's Work in Our Lives

The Spirit of Adoption

Something wonderful transpires the moment we believe on Christ as our Savior. We are adopted into God's family. Instantly, we are given power to become "children of God" (John 1:12). It is a fulfillment of the Father's great plan. He called us to "adoption as sons by Jesus Christ to Himself, according to the good pleasure of His will" (Eph. 1:5).

Who arranges for our adoption? It is the Holy Spirit. Paul writes, "For as many as are led by the Spirit of God, these are sons of God. For you did not receive the spirit of bondage again to fear, but you received *the Spirit of adoption*" (Rom. 8:14–15, emphasis added).

Now the concept of adoption points to two great truths, both conveyed through the Holy Spirit. The first one is mentioned above: the great *fact* of our adoption into God's family with all the rights, privileges, and responsibilities that go with being a member of the family.

The second one is the great *fulfillment* of adoption, the transformation of our bodies at the Rapture when we *receive* the promised inheritance: "Not only that, but we also who have the firstfruits of the Spirit, even we ourselves groan within ourselves, *eagerly waiting for the adoption, the redemption of our body*" (Rom. 8:23, emphasis added).

The most wonderful miracle now won't compare to that great miracle of the Rapture when we'll exchange our mortal bodies for immortal bodies—bodies that will never be subject to sickness, disease, or death. Don't get me wrong, until that Day everyone should absolutely

seek their miracle from the Lord. Now what's the foretaste or firstfruits of this great miracle to come? *The
Spirit of Adoption!* When will our adoption be culminated?
When our bodies are redeemed at the Rapture. Even
so, come quickly Lord Jesus!

The Spirit of Glory

It seems to me more and more evident that Christians
are coming under attack in North America. And that
these attacks are increasing in intensity as well. We can't
sit idly by and let this happen. That's why I believe in
what I call "violent" faith, faith that isn't passive, that
doesn't pussyfoot around, that isn't afraid of what people think or the consequences.

Peter wrote in his epistle to believers in Asia Minor
who were experiencing the sting of persecution. He
strongly and boldly declared, "If you are reproached for
the name of Christ, blessed are you, *for the Spirit of glory and
of God* rests upon you." (1 Peter 4:14, emphasis added).

The Holy Spirit speaking through Peter gave these
courageous believers two great assurances as they were
going through persecution: *first,* He assured them that
they hadn't done anything wrong or believed anything
wrong. Instead their persecution showed that the very
Spirit of the Lord rested upon them.

Second, He promised these brave believers that His
glory would rest on them, the magnificent glory of
God—the same glory that the nation of Israel experienced in the wilderness and appeared as a cloud by day
and the pillar of fire by night, the same glory that the
high priest experienced in the Holy of Holies, the same
glory that appeared to the shepherds keeping watch the
night the Lord Jesus was born. The same glory that

came upon the Apostles in the Upper Room—is the same glory that will be ours forever when we allow that glory to strengthen us.

Now believe me, I'm no stranger to persecution. When I trusted Christ, my whole family turned against me and ostracized me. But as I held firm, the Holy Spirit came upon me with His glory, energizing my spirit and giving me the strength to go on. And soon my entire family came to know Christ as Savior. Now for all of you hanging tough in the midst of opposition, take heart—the Holy Spirit of glory has promised to rest on *you* and He *will* keep His promise!

The Spirit of Grace

Have you taken time lately to reflect on the wonder of salvation? Without salvation we would still be "without Christ, being aliens from the commonwealth of Israel and strangers from the covenants of promise, *having no hope and without God in the world*" (Eph. 2:12, emphasis added). It is God's grace, His kindness and undeserved favor that reached to us, even when we were His enemies He saved us. It is His grace that covered our guilt with His righteousness. It is His grace that keeps us, for we were *saved by grace* through faith and *kept by grace* through faith. It is His grace which brings us to the foot of the cross, unable to brag, able simply to say that our best was as filthy rags in His sight. It is His grace that not only covers our failures—it transforms them into distinctive points of power and ministry.[1] It is because of His grace that He gifts us, enabling us to experience the joy of service, the delight of laboring with the Savior as He builds His Church. It is because of His grace that He puts resurrection power at our disposal, allowing us to persevere and prevail. It is because of His grace that He rewards us, even in our unworthiness. It is because of His grace that He indwells us, allowing us to experience the richness of moment-by-moment fellowship with the Spirit of the Lord. It is because of His grace that He is returning for us, to transform us and allow us to experience the wonder of all He has prepared for us.

As Paul reflected on God's grace in salvation, he couldn't help but break out in a hymn of praise for the grace of God in executing His plan of redemption: "Oh, the depth of the riches both of the wisdom and knowledge of God! How unsearchable are His judgments and His ways past finding out! 'For who has known the mind of the Lord? Or who has become His counselor?' 'Or who has first given to Him and it shall be repaid to him?' For of Him and through Him and to Him are all things, to whom be glory forever. Amen" (Rom. 11:33–36).

How marvelous is the grace of God. And Who do you suppose conveys this grace to us? *The Holy Spirit.* He ministers grace to us moment by moment.

Yet incredibly some people feel the temptation to abandon the cause of Christ, to forsake the streams of living water for cisterns which hold no water. One of the reasons the book of Hebrews was written was to convince these kinds of people not to do it. The Scripture declares: "Anyone who has rejected Moses' law dies without mercy on the testimony of two or three witnesses. *Of how much worse punishment,* do you suppose, will he be thought worthy who has trampled the Son of God underfoot, counted the blood of the covenant by which he was sanctified a common thing, and insulted the Spirit of grace?" (Heb. 10:28–29, emphasis added).

If rejecting God's Law brought swift judgment in

Old Testament days, then to directly hold in contempt the *Son of God* and His sacrifice and the *Spirit of God* and His grace is too fearful to imagine. The Father *will not* take lightly the despising of the Son and the Spirit, "It is a fearful thing to fall into the hands of the living God" (Heb. 10:31).

The Spirit of Grace and of Supplication

There are some people who minimize the importance of Bible prophecy, and even some who make fun of it. Mark Twain said, "If the world comes to an end, I want to be in Cincinnati—things always come twenty years later in Cincinnati." But it's important to realize that 25 percent of the Bible is prophetic in nature, an amount equal in size to the entire New Testament. Do you think God would devote 25 percent of His Word to an *unimportant* subject? I certainly do not.

I am waiting and watching for the Rapture, the inauguration of so many of the great prophetic events of Scripture. Martin Luther, the father of the Protestant Reformation, said he only had two days on his calendar—today and "that day!" That's the way I want to be too! I want to live today for "that day."[2]

One of the great prophetic passages of Scripture is Zechariah 12. It describes the reconciliation of the Jewish people with the Savior they rejected. This great event occurs at the Second Coming of Christ. Try to imagine the emotion of this moment.

On the one hand is the Lord Jesus, the rejected King, now returned as Conqueror. The One who said with such emotion, "O Jerusalem, Jerusalem, the one who kills prophets and stones those who are sent to her! How often I wanted to gather your children together, as a hen gathers her chicks under her wings, *but you were not willing!*" (Matt. 23:37, emphasis added).

On the other hand is the Jewish nation. They have lived through the horrors of the Tribulation. They have seen the awesome power of the glorified Savior returning to earth with His armies to destroy His enemies. And now in a moment of time they realize that the One they had so steadfastly rejected is the precious Son of God and they turn to Him in faith. Who prepared the way for this reconciliation? *The Holy Spirit!*

More than five hundred years before Christ, the prophet Zechariah had the scene described to him by the Lord: "I will pour on the house of David and on the inhabitants of Jerusalem the Spirit of grace and supplication; then [or, "so that" in NASB] they will look on Me whom they have pierced. Yes, they will mourn for Him as one mourns for his only son, and grieve for Him as one grieves for a firstborn" (Zech. 12:10).

When the Lord poured out His Spirit upon His battered and bedraggled people, He broke through their resistance so they could experience God's *favor* (grace), and that freed their hearts to call out to Him in *repentance*.

"Supplication" as used here to describe the Holy Spirit refers "less [to a] formal entreaty . . . than the outpourings of a troubled soul."[3] Whereas before they hid in caves and cried out to the rocks, "Fall on us and hide us from the face of Him who sits on the throne and from the wrath of the Lamb!" (Rev. 6:16), now they went to the Lord in brokenness and love. That's what the Holy Spirit does, no matter what we've done, He helps us come to the Father in freedom and find forgiveness and mercy so abundantly available to all.

The Spirit of Wisdom and Understanding

Isaiah 11 is one of those mountain-top passages of Scripture: so powerful and moving. As Isaiah describes the coming of the Messiah, He uses a series of three couplets to describe the work of the Holy Spirit in the life and ministry of Christ Jesus:

- The Spirit of wisdom and understanding
- The Spirit of counsel and might
- The Spirit of knowledge and of the fear of the Lord (v. 2)

As part of the God-head, one of the attributes of the Holy Spirit is that He is unchanging. Because of this, we can expect that the Holy Spirit will make manifest these same qualities in *us* as we allow Him to work.

The first couplet describes Him as, "The Spirit of wisdom and understanding" (Isa. 11:2).

Wisdom is nothing more than living with skill—it is the ability to apply the knowledge of God's Word in our daily life—and nothing less. It involves using knowledge in the right way to select the proper ends and to achieve those ends in a proper fashion. It involves the application of God's truth to human experience. Properly mastered, it can lead to a happy and successful life.

This skillful living manifested itself in the life of the Lord Jesus even from His childhood: As a child, Jesus was "filled with wisdom" *and* "increased in wisdom" (Luke 2:40, 52).

It was also evident in His preaching: "And when the Sabbath had come, He began to teach in the synagogue. And many hearing Him were astonished, saying, 'Where did this man get these things? And what wisdom is this which is given to Him, such that mighty works are performed by His hands!' " (Mark 6:2). They marveled at the wisdom of His words, the practical skill that His words imparted. And did you notice the connection they made between the wisdom of His teaching and His mighty works: "wisdom . . . that such mighty works are performed by His hands!"? Wisdom is about actions as well as words.

And because wisdom is so rare, the wisdom of the Lord Jesus' actions routinely baffled and angered those without this wisdom: The Lord Jesus recounted the words of His critics: "The Son of Man came eating and drinking, and they say, 'Here is a glutton and a drunkard, a friend of tax collectors and "sinners."' But wisdom is proved right by her actions" (Matt. 11:19 NIV). And the mighty, Spirit-led growth of the Church, growing in every continent and country, every village and hamlet, every community and county bears ample testimony to the wisdom of the Master's strategy. "Wisdom *is* justified by all her children" (Luke 7:35, emphasis added).

"Understanding" is about discernment in wisdom, not the accumulation of facts. The idea here is that a person with "understanding" has the insight to choose with skill between the options that come his way. "*bin* [the Hebrew word for "understanding" in Isaiah 11] is the power of judgment and perceptive insight and is demonstrated in the use of knowledge."[4]

This kind of perception comes from the Holy Spirit, and yet must be diligently sought for by us: "My son, if you receive my words, and treasure my commands within you, so that you incline your ear to wisdom, and apply your heart to understanding; yes, if you cry out for discernment, and lift up your voice for understanding, if you seek her as silver, and search for her as for hidden treasures; *then you will understand the fear of the* LORD, *and find the knowledge of God.* For the Lord gives wisdom; from His mouth come knowledge and understanding" (Prov. 2:1–6, emphasis added).

Since this understanding comes from God alone, the wicked are infamous for their lack of ability to perceive the wisdom of the Lord: "The righteous considers the cause of the poor, but the wicked does not understand such knowledge" (Prov. 29:7).

What an incredible comfort these words are! There are many choices, alternatives, and options in the world. It is so difficult sometimes to choose between them. Thanks be to God that through the Holy Spirit we can have the *skill* in living life, and the *discernment* to choose between the alternatives we face.

The Spirit of Counsel and Might

In the second of three couplets, Isaiah describes the Holy Spirit as "the Spirit of counsel and might" (Isa. 11:2).

With the counsel and might of the Holy Spirit controlling us, our perspective is insightful and fresh, our outlook optimistic. But without it, this present existence is at best dark, dreary, and depressing. Bertrand Russell, one of the foremost atheists of our time described his perspective like this: "The life of man is a long march through night surrounded by invisible foes, tortured by weariness and pain, toward a goal that few can hope to reach and where none can tarry long. One by one as they march, our comrades vanish from our sight, seized by the silent orders of omnipotent death. Brief and powerless is man's life. On him and all his race the slow sure doom falls, pitiless and dark. Blind to good and evil, reckless of destruction, omnipotent matter rolls on its relentless way. For man, condemned today to lose his dearest, tomorrow himself to pass through the gates of darkness, it remains only to cherish, ere the blow falls, the lofty thoughts that ennoble his little day."[5]

I'm so glad the Holy Spirit as our counselor gives us meaning and fulfillment in life which this ungodly man so obviously needed. But there is no doubt that this shows how the ungodly view life. To us it is sorely bankrupt for there is no meaning to their life.

As the prophet Isaiah emphasized, the Holy Spirit was "the Spirit of counsel and might." In chapter 11 and verse 2, Isaiah is prophesying again about the coming of the Lord Jesus. It is the counsel and might of the Holy Spirit in the mystery of the Trinity that allows the Lord Jesus to be called "wonderful counselor" and "mighty God" (Isa. 9:6). "The attributes of the Holy Spirit would characterize the Messiah. Because of His wisdom, understanding, counsel, and knowledge He is the Wonderful Counselor" (Isa. 9:6).[6]

The Holy Spirit also delights to counsel us. Quit trying to figure it out all by yourself, let the Holy Spirit counsel you. Quit trying to muster the power to gut your way through. With the Holy Spirit, your motto can be, "Not somehow, but *triumphantly!*"

The great-grandparents of a friend of mine went from a hardscrabble existence in Kentucky to Oklahoma because they heard that it was the land of opportunity. The land they farmed on wasn't very productive and consequently they never had much to live on. They eked out an existence. Eventually they sold the land and moved to another state.

The person who bought the land from them discovered oil and became wealthy. The reason the land wasn't very good for farming was because it was so saturated with petroleum nothing would grow. Think of it! For years these dear people lived near poverty when at their very feet was all they needed, not only to survive—but to thrive! If they had dug a little deeper in the ground a gusher would have come up!

In the same way we have the great resources of the Holy Spirit at our disposal, and yet some of us live our lives in spiritual poverty and frustration, not using the riches that are at our *immediate* beck and call.

Not only does He give us guidance, but He imparts the strength and energy to carry out His plans. Remember, the Lord Jesus said, "You shall receive power when the Holy Spirit has come upon you" (Acts 1:8).

The Spirit of Knowledge and the Fear of the Lord

The third couplet in Isaiah 11 describes the Holy Spirit as imparting "The Spirit of knowledge and of the fear of the Lord."

Now "knowledge" here refers to the knowledge we gain through our senses, both about how the world works and about God's moral law. Thus the Holy Spirit gives us the ability to look at the world and perceive His handiwork and purposes in it. The Bible declares that "since the creation of the world His invisible attributes are clearly seen, being understood by the things that are made, even His eternal power and Godhead" (Rom. 1:20). When we are in tune with the leading of the Holy Spirit, we gain a fuller understanding of the world around us, and every day can be a day of awe and wonder.

But not only does He bring knowledge, the Holy Spirit also brings the "fear of the Lord." This is so important to understand. Solomon under the inspiration of the Holy Spirit said, "The fear of the Lord is the beginning of knowledge, but fools despise wisdom and instruction" (Prov. 1:7).

Now I want to say something, and I don't want you to misunderstand me. I'm grateful for all the emphasis these days on spiritual warfare. I believe it has made us more sensitive to the spiritual struggles going on around us. But I fear that an unintended result of all this teaching is that men and women now fear the devil more than they fear God. *Fear God, and you will not need to fear the devil.* You'll be aware of his power and act accordingly as the archangel Michael did (Jude 8, 9), but you will not fear Him, for "He who is in you is greater than he who is in the world" (1 John 4:4).

By the way, there's a difference between fearing the Lord and being afraid. Exodus 20 brings this out so beautifully. The nation of Israel is gathered at Mt. Sinai to enter into a covenant relationship with Yahweh and receive the ten commandments from Him. Mt. Sinai was ablaze with "thunderings and lightnings, and a thick cloud [was] on the mountain; and the sound of the trumpet was very loud, so that all the people who were in the camp trembled" (v. 16).

In fact, the nation of Israel said to Moses, "You speak with us, and we will hear; but let not God speak with us, lest we die" (v. 19).

Then Moses utters these remarkable words: "*Do not be afraid.* God has come to test you, *so that the fear of God will be with you* to keep you from sinning" (v. 20 NIV, emphasis added). He said, don't be *afraid,* but *fear*! See the difference? They were trembling at God's power. But what the Father wanted was for them to have a healthy respect for His power that would lead to a sense of awe which would in turn keep them from sinning. Thus the "fear of the Lord" doesn't mean being *afraid,* it means *understanding* Him and *respecting* Him such that we live a life of loving obedience.

And who brings this ability to fear the Lord? *The Holy Spirit!*

The Spirit of Life

I love the words of the Lord Jesus, "I have come that they may have life, and that they may have it more abundantly" (John 10:10). Abundant life—there is something so compelling about that. Something that says within us, "Yes, I *must* have this." And who ministers this abundant life to us? *The Holy Spirit.* The Lord Jesus said, "It is the Spirit who gives life; the flesh profits nothing. The words that I speak to you are spirit, and they are life" (John 6:63). Now the life that's being referred to is salvation, but it is also true that "what God promises for eternity, He begins to do in this lifetime."[7]

Oh my dear friend, when the Spirit of the Lord comes, He brings *life,* breaking the power of canceled sin and death as the hymn says. And not just *endless* life, but *better* life *right now.* Paul says, "the law of the Spirit of life in Christ Jesus has made me free from the law of sin and death" (Rom. 8:2).

Are you experiencing all the life the Holy Spirit has for you? Someone gave me this quote, and I think it sums up the issue so magnificently: "I believe that only one person in a thousand knows the trick of really living in the present. Most of us spend fifty-eight minutes each hour either living in the past, regretting for lost joys, or feeling shame for things badly done (both utterly useless and weakening); or living in the future which we either long for or dread. The only way to live is to accept each minute as an unrepeatable miracle, which is exactly what it is—a miracle that will not be repeated."[8] The Spirit of the Lord is waiting just now to *heal* your past, *guarantee* your future, and *liberate* you to experience abundant life *right now.*

The Holy Spirit of Promise

Paul declared that those who trusted Christ as their savior are "sealed with the Holy Spirit of promise, who is the guarantee of our inheritance" (Eph. 1:13, 14). Now I'm going to talk much more about this passage in chapter nine, but for now I want you to notice two things.

First, He is the "Holy Spirit *of promise.*" That is, "the promised Spirit."[9] The Lord Jesus *promised* in the Upper Room Discourse that He would send the Holy Spirit, but the Lord Jesus made the promise *in conjunction* with the Father ("whom the Father will send in my name" John 14:26; "I will send to you from the Father . . . who goes out from the Father" John 15:26, 27 NIV). Thus the Holy Spirit was promised by the Father as well, and is termed in Acts 1:4, "the Promise of the Father." Because of their faith in the words of the Father and the Son, that early band in Jerusalem took God at His word and waited for the Holy Spirit, and God did not disappoint them.

Don't ever forget that "God is not a man, that He should lie, nor a son of man, that He should repent. Has He said, and will He not do? Or has He spoken, and will He not make it good?" (Num. 23:19). Some would have you believe that God's Word, the Bible isn't true, or isn't completely true. Regardless of how they articulate their words, what they're doing is calling each member of the Godhead a liar. It's an old saying but a true one, "God said it. I believe it. That settles it." And might I add, "I'm going to live like it." Just like the expectant followers in the Upper Room, take Him at His word in *everything* He says.

Second, the indwelling of the Holy Spirit within us is a promise that one day we will receive all that has been promised and prepared for us: a *new* body, a *new* nature, and a *new* home. The Holy Spirit living within us is demonstrating moment-by-moment that God will one day present us with the full measure of our inheritance.

The Spirit of Truth

One of the great titles ascribed to the Promise of the Father is "The Spirit of Truth." The Holy Spirit has a specific assignment from God to communicate and impart what is true and valid. The Lord Jesus described Him as "the Spirit of truth, whom the world cannot receive, because it neither sees Him nor knows Him; but you know Him, for He dwells with you and will be in you" (John 14:17).

Not only does He teach truth, He *is* truth.

- He will teach you the truth about *Jesus* (the direct meaning of John 14:17).[10]
- He will teach you the truth about the Bible. The Lord Jesus declared, "When He, the Spirit of truth, has come, He will guide you into all truth" (John 16:13; 1 Cor. 2:10, 11).
- He will teach you the truth about *yourself.* David was so refreshingly honest when He asked the Lord, "Who can discern his errors? Forgive my hidden faults" (Ps. 19:12 NIV). No one can fully

discern their own errors, but as we listen to the voice of the Holy Spirit and follow His prompting, the areas in our lives that are invisible to us will be refined and sublimated by the Holy Spirit. "And we, who with unveiled faces all reflect the Lord's glory, are being transformed into his likeness with ever-increasing glory, which comes from the Lord, who is the Spirit" (2 Cor. 3:18 NIV).

The Comforter

I'm going to really go into depth on this in chapter nine, but the meaning of this word is so strong that I want to introduce you to it now. If any of you have had to appear to defend yourself in court or before the government, you know what a harrowing experience it can be. Although our system of justice dictates that a person is innocent until proven guilty, that's rarely how you actually *feel*. What you feel is powerless, alone, and hurting. Oh for someone to help you bear the burden.

And this is *exactly* what the Holy Spirit does. The Lord said, "I will pray the Father, and He shall give you another Comforter, that he may abide with you forever" (John 14:16 KJV). The word "comforter" in the Greek language is *Paraclete*—meaning "one called alongside to help." A defense attorney, and an advocate, a helper who will fight your battles, a helper who is so good at what He does that He calms your restless fears.

Mere words are insufficient to express the affection I feel toward the Holy Spirit for the many ways and the many times He has helped me. He truly has been my constant Helper. And when I stand before the people to preach the gospel, He is there helping me. As Paul said,

"My speech and my preaching were not with persuasive words of human wisdom, but in demonstration of the Spirit and of power" (1 Cor. 2:4).

Praise God for our *Comforter.*

The Eternal Spirit

As a Member of the Godhead, the Holy Spirit was present before time, and will remain after "time shall be no more."

The writer of the book of Hebrews recognized His eternal nature when he wrote that if the blood of bulls and goats was once used as a sacrifice, "how much more shall the blood of Christ, who through *the eternal Spirit* offered Himself without spot to God, purge your conscience from dead works to serve the living God?" (Heb. 9:14 KJV, emphasis added).

Just as the Melchizedekian priesthood of Christ is superior to the priesthood of the Old Testament law, so the redemption effected through the eternal Spirit is superior to the temporary remedies of the law—remedies designed not so much to redeem man as to point out man's *need* for redemption through faith in Christ.

That He is an "eternal Spirit" is as much as saying He is a "divine Spirit." "The term *eternal,* which with all propriety can also be assigned to God the Father or God the Son, is here assigned to the Holy Spirit. Since of God alone this attribute may be predicated, the Spirit is understood as God."[11]

The Spirit

The Word of God gives many wonderful names to the Holy Spirit, but perhaps the most unadorned name is the most profound. He is often referred to in the Scripture simply as "the Spirit."

That was the term John the Baptist used when he described what happened at the baptism of the Lord Jesus. He said, "I saw *the Spirit* descending from heaven like a dove, and He remained upon Him" (John 1:32). You might even say, *the* Spirit, the unique Spirit, the *one and only* Spirit, for after all, in person, in work, and in our personal experience of His indwelling, there is none like Him.

The Lord Jesus also used the same words. He declared to Nicodemus, "Unless one is born of water and *the Spirit,* he cannot enter the kingdom of God" (John 3:5, emphasis added).

Again and again we are encouraged to "be filled with *the Spirit*" (Acts 9:17; Eph. 5:18, emphasis added).

The names given to the Holy Spirit are significant and glorious. But they are not given simply that we may know *about* Him. They are names we can use every day to welcome Him into the very recesses of our lives.

Yes, He is the Spirit of the Father and the Son. But He is ready to be your Paraclete—your Counselor, your Helper, your Teacher and Guide.

The Wind of the Spirit

The Holy Spirit is telling me that you must start a church in Orlando, and that if you don't, someone else will. God has a plan for your life." I couldn't have been more shocked when my good friend, Kenny Foreman, said this to me quite out of the blue in 1982 at lunch after I had preached that morning at his church in San Jose, California.

Really, I was both shocked and *skeptical*. You see, although I already knew that God wanted me to start a church, I also felt I knew exactly where it was supposed to be: Phoenix, Arizona. I was an evangelist in those days, and my home base was Orlando. In fact we rented office space at the large church in Orlando that my father-in-law pastored.

I knew that the Lord was calling me to start a church, and I knew the one place it *wasn't* to be: Orlando, Florida. It's true that I loved the people in Orlando, but not much else. I didn't like the climate (and I still don't most of the year). I hated the humidity, the rain, and the bugs, and the bugs, and the bugs. . . . But Phoenix on the other hand—wonderful Phoenix—was warm, sunny, dry, and (by comparison) bug-free. The climate reminded me so much of my beloved hometown of Jaffa.

Also, and more painfully, it had become difficult for my wife and me to remain in Orlando. My father-in-law had to resign his church, and we were soon told that we would have to find another place to rent office space. The emotions associated with my father-in-law's resignation were extremely painful for my wife. Every time we drove by the church she would start to cry. Suzanne had absolutely no interest in staying in Orlando, and that confirmed it for me. I began taking more frequent trips to Phoenix, gaining a feel for the city and scouting out possible locations.

Then came the fateful trip to San Jose and the faithful words of my friend, Kenny Foreman. Actually, the whole trip was very unusual. The first leg of the trip routed me through Dallas, and the Holy Spirit arranged for me to sit by an Episcopal layman who was an executive with the Orlando airport authority. I have long since forgotten his name, but I'll never forget his demeanor or his words. He was brilliant, eloquent, and dignified. The kind of man who leaves a lasting impression everywhere he goes.

We struck up a conversation on the plane, and it wasn't long before he asked me what I did. I told him about the ministry and showed him a copy of our newsletter, which in those days was called, "Day Spring."

He immediately noticed my travel schedule, which was listed on the back of the newsletter. He looked at the schedule and at me with a knowing look, the kind of look one veteran traveler gives to another, the look of someone who knows from personal experience how grueling a travel schedule like the one listed on the newsletter can be. His look was really more of a question, "Are you really traveling this often?"

Although by nature I'm a very private person, and sharing with a stranger on a plane is about the last thing I want to do, somehow the Holy Spirit led me to open up my heart to this man. "Yes, I do travel quite a lot, and recently I've been giving a lot of thought to moving out of Orlando."

You'd have thought I just told this man that the left engine was on fire! All of the sudden he came absolutely alive. He leaned into me like a sailor would lean into a fierce north wind, and with great interest he asked me, "Why in the world would you want to leave Orlando?" I told him a few things about my father-in-law's resignation, and I was surprised to learn that this Episcopal layman knew all about it.

Looking me square in the eye, and with a tone of absolute and unshakable confidence, he said, "If I were you I wouldn't move. The day is coming when Orlando will be like Atlanta or Dallas—the entire world will be coming to Orlando." Then he got quiet and even more serious, "You travel around the world, but if you wait long enough, *the world will come to you.*"

I was impressed by his words, but more impressed by the weather in Phoenix. So in spite of this gentleman and the word of knowledge of Kenny Foreman, I was an arrow pointed straight for Phoenix.

Two months later, I was preaching in Tampa for a man I didn't know particularly well, and what do you think happened? The service was winding down, and all of the sudden this man began to prophesy over me. Can you guess the words? "The Holy Spirit is telling me that you must start a church in Orlando, and that if you don't, someone else will. God has a plan for your life." Well, by now the Holy Spirit definitely had my attention! I was still an arrow pointed toward Phoenix, but I was slowing down rapidly.

Shortly thereafter I preached for Tommy Reid, who pastors a large church in Buffalo, New York. Now Tommy is one of my dearest friends in the world—the man I regard as *my* pastor.

I hadn't shared a word with Tommy about the prophetic words uttered over me, but sure enough after the service Tommy sat me down and said, "The Holy Spirit is telling me that you must start a church in Orlando, and that if you don't, someone else will. God has a plan for your life." Tommy went on to say, "The Holy Spirit wants you to start a church because there are people drowning and if you start a church it will be a lifeboat that God will anoint to rescue people."

By now I knew the Holy Spirit was moving, and I was truly open to follow His leading, even if it meant staying in Orlando. I began visiting San Jose once a month. On one of the return trips from San Jose, the Holy Spirit spoke the same words to my heart that He had first spoken months earlier through the others, "Benny, you must start a church in Orlando, and if you don't, someone else will. I have a plan for your life."

I was ready to follow the Holy Spirit's guidance, but there was anguish in my soul over the words. My wife had sacrificed so much for the sake of my ministry, and she was so unhappy in Orlando. How could I ask her to stay? So I told the Holy Spirit as I was agonizing over the direction He was leading me, "Lord, if it's you, you'll have to tell my wife because she wants to leave Orlando."

When I arrived back in Orlando, the car ride from the airport to my house seemed like the longest one I had ever taken. Imaginary conversations between Suzanne and me swirled through my mind, and questions seized my heart, one after the other: *What if she's not willing to stay in Orlando? How will she respond when I tell her what the Lord has said to me?* Oh, how I prayed on the way home that God would speak to her, for I knew Suzanne would hear His voice.

Suzanne met me at the door. She was absolutely radiant. "Honey, there's something that I *must* tell you!"

"Great, Suzanne, but first I've got something to tell you."

"No, what I've got is so great yours will have to wait."

"Well, Suzanne, mine's great too, but go ahead."

"Benny, the Holy Spirit told me that you are supposed to start a church here in Orlando, and I believe you should too."

I wanted to fall to my knees right there in thankfulness to the Lord. It is no cliché to say that "Where God guides, He provides!"

What a glorious experience I had that day as I entered the Lord's presence and began to thank Him for the guidance and direction of the Holy Spirit. As I continued to commune with Him in prayer, the reality of what might be ahead for Suzanne and me became more apparent. "Orlando? Lord, are You sure? We've never had very large crowds when we've ministered in Orlando." I was confident that I had heard from the Lord and that the Holy Spirit was leading me. However, as I continued in prayer I said, "Lord Jesus, if you really want me to start a church in Orlando, confirm it to me once again. Let me rent the Tupperware auditorium (one of the largest in Orlando at the time) and *let it be full.*" I wanted to be certain and I knew that my answer could only come by supernatural means.

The Lord was so gracious and understanding, so quick to respond, so wise to build my faith. We reserved the auditorium, and waited for the day. Word began to spread about the meeting. I was confident, and excited at the same time to see how the Holy Spirit was going to glorify the Lord Jesus in this meeting.

Finally, the day arrived, the day the Holy Spirit had been leading up to through all of these confirming words and signs. As I walked out onto the platform, my heart swelled with praise to God as every seat in that 2,200 seat auditorium was full. The Holy Spirit did not disappoint me, He did "*exceedingly abundantly beyond all I could ask or think!*" (Eph. 3:20, emphasis added) And so, in March of 1983 we began Orlando Christian Center, a church that over 7,000 people call home. *To God be the glory!*

I'm so grateful that the wonderful Spirit of the Lord, "the breath of God" guides us today. Without the guidance of the Holy Spirit I'd be writing this to you from Phoenix, and I'd have missed the joy of pastoring the great congregation of Orlando Christian Center, and the thrill of seeing the Holy Spirit raise up a "lifeboat" that has rescued and redeemed so many precious people.

Yes, the blessed Holy Spirit plays a vital, indispensable role, not only in guiding us, but in so many other areas as well, and from the very beginning of all things. In this chapter we'll begin to explore the incomparable work of the Holy Spirit, both in history and today. But prepare yourself, for once you begin to *appreciate* and *appropriate* the work of the Holy Spirit, you will never be the same!

You see, the breath of the Almighty, the Holy Spirit, is:

- the "wind" of *creation,* fashioning the universe from chaos
- the "wind" of *animation,* giving Adam his physical and spiritual life.
- the "wind" of *perception,* allowing us to hear the gentle breezes of God's voice.
- the "wind" of *direction,* gently guiding in the paths we should go.
- the "wind" of *revitalization,* quickening and renewing us every day, giving us strength for the journey.

Millions of people can quote the first verse of the Bible from memory: "In the beginning God created the heaven and the earth" (Gen. 1:1). The very next verse introduces us to the power behind creation—God's Holy Spirit. We are told that the earth was without form, and void; and darkness was on the face of the deep, "And the Spirit of God was hovering over the face of the waters" (v. 2).

Into a universe of absolute formlessness something began to move. Suddenly there was a spark of life. Just above a void, barren planet, something was "hovering" over the surface of the earth.

Do you recall what happened on the first day of creation? *God spoke.* Scripture tells us, "Then God said, 'Let there be light'; and there was light" (v. 3).

It is thrilling to know that God spoke the world into existence. By His Word He brought light and order in the very midst of darkness and chaos. But many fail to realize that before God spoke (v. 2) the Holy Spirit moved (v. 2). That's the way it was at creation and it's still that way today: *Before God speaks, the Spirit always moves.* The pattern has never changed.

When people ask, "Benny, how can I hear God's voice?" (by the way, that's a great question to ask), I always tell them, "Let the Spirit of the Lord move first."

Igniting the Word

The Father, the Son, and the Holy Spirit were all present at creation. They are equal—Three in One. The Father is the Source (John 5:26), the Son is the Channel of that Source (Acts 2:22) and the Holy Spirit is the Power that flows through that Channel (Acts 1:8; 2:33). He releases the Source and touches our life.

From day one the Spirit of the Lord was at work. He ignited God's spoken word to produce light in the midst of darkness.

When Isaiah thought about the marvels of creation, he asked, "Who has directed the Spirit of the LORD, or as His counselor has taught Him? With whom did He take counsel, and who instructed Him, and taught Him in the path of justice?" (Isa. 40:13, 14).

Our God is one God. The Holy Spirit is one of the three Persons of the Godhead, fully sharing all the attributes of Deity.

I often find myself singing the words of a song I have known for years: "It took a miracle to put the stars in place. It took a miracle to hang the world in space."

The source of that miracle is the Holy Spirit. Job wrote, "By His Spirit He adorned the heavens; His hand pierced the fleeing serpent. Indeed these are the mere edges of His ways, and how small a whisper we hear of Him! But the thunder of His power who can understand?" (Job 26:13–14).

The strong, yet quiet Spirit of God was totally involved in everything the Father designed—from a twinkling star to a thundering storm. What we know, however, is only a fraction of His creative work.

Just a word from the Creator and mighty things began to happen.

- He spoke and dry ground was separated from the waters (Gen. 1:9).
- He spoke and grass began to grow (v. 11).
- He spoke and there was daylight and darkness (v. 14).
- He spoke and fish began to swim and birds began to fly (v. 20).
- He spoke and animals appeared (v. 24).

Oh, the power of His voice. The psalmist declared:

"By the word of the LORD the heavens were made,
And all the host of them by the breath of His mouth"
(Ps. 33:6).

"For He spoke, and it was done; He commanded, and it stood fast" (v. 9).

That word contained the authority of the entire Godhead.

Was the Father there? Yes. Was the Holy Spirit there? Absolutely. And the Son of God was there too, for John said, "In the beginning was the Word, and the Word was with God, and the Word was God. He was in the beginning with God. All things were made through Him, and without Him nothing was made that was made" (John 1:1-3).

The writer of Hebrews makes it clear that God spoke to the world "by His Son, whom He has appointed heir

of all things, through whom also He made the worlds"
(Heb. 1:2).

The Breath of Life

The fact that the Father spoke reveals an important truth. Just as your breath carries your voice, so the Holy Spirit carries the voice of the Father. You might even say that the Holy Spirit is the *"outbreathing"* of the Father. That is why I am so dependent on the Holy Spirit. Without Him I would never be able to hear the voice of God (1 Cor. 2:6–16).

The *"inbreathing"* of the Holy Spirit became the focal point for what happened on the sixth day. "Then God said, 'Let Us make man in Our image, according to Our likeness; let them have dominion over the fish of the sea, over the birds of the air, and over the cattle, over all the earth and over every creeping thing that creeps on the earth'" (Gen. 1:26).

Observe closely how it happened. The Lord formed man from the dust of the ground "and breathed into his nostrils the breath of life; and man became a living being" (Gen. 2:7).

Noted Bible scholar J. Rodman Williams says, "The Breath that God breathes into man's nostrils is more than physical breath (though it is that, too). It is also spiritual breath because God is spirit."[1] Note also the association between the Spirit of God and the breath of God in Job 33:4: "The Spirit of God has made me, and the breath of the Almighty gives me life"; and again in John 20:22: "And when He had said this, He breathed on them, and said to them, 'Receive the Holy Spirit.'"

Can you imagine what took place when Adam was created? When he opened his eyes, the first thing he became aware of was the breath of God, the Holy Spirit still moving through him, in him, and around him.

I like to think of Adam as the first person to ever be introduced to the Holy Spirit. Adam was created as the result of a "word" spoken by God. But that word was animated by the Spirit. As a result, you might even say that Adam experienced the Holy Spirit *before* he met the Father—he could still feel the Holy Spirit on him.

That's what also happens to you at salvation. The first person you become aware of is the Holy Spirit. He is the one convicting and drawing you to a place of surrender. You may not know His name or who He is, but you are keenly aware of a presence drawing you toward the Savior. You feel it. You sense it.

As a teenager in Toronto, it was the Holy Spirit who introduced me to the Lord Jesus, and I began to become acquainted with Him. Then I got to know the Father. But my first contact was with the Holy Spirit.

The Lord gives us both our breath (life) and our spirit. It was the Almighty, "Who created the heavens and stretched them out, Who spread forth the earth and that which comes from it, Who gives breath to the people on it, and spirit to those who walk on it" (Isa. 42:5). He is also the one who "forms the spirit of man within him" (Zech. 12:1).

Not only was the Spirit of the Lord present and vitally involved with the creation of life, He also has two other important functions.

1. The Holy Spirit sustains life.

The Spirit of God is the planet's lifeline for survival. Here is how the psalmist describes the dependency of all life on the Holy Spirit: "You hide Your face, they are troubled; You take away their breath, they die and return to their dust. You send forth Your Spirit, they are created; And You renew the face of the earth" (Ps. 104:29–30). Without Him we'd be like a deep-sea diver whose oxygen was suddenly cut off. The Holy Spirit has been given an awesome task: to *create, maintain, and renew*—in both our physical body and the material world.

The writer of Hebrews tells us that the Son's task also includes "upholding all things by the word of His power" (Heb. 1:3).

When the Holy Spirit arrives, things are restored and refreshed. The Psalmist says, "You send forth Your Spirit, they are created; And You renew the face of the earth (Ps. 104:30).

Because of God's mighty sustaining power, fear and dismay can be vanquished, replaced by refreshing and strengthening, as the Lord says in Isaiah: "Fear not, for I am with you; Be not dismayed, for I am your God. I will strengthen you, yes, I will help you, I will uphold you with My righteous right hand" (Isa. 41:10).

Why am I breathing? Why am I alive? The Scripture declares that it is because the Spirit of God has placed breath in my nostrils (Job 27:3). He's enabling me to live. Not only spiritually, but He is the source of my physical being. God's Word declares that the same Spirit that raised the Lord Jesus from the dead dwells in you as a believer and He will quicken your mortal body.

Life without the Holy Spirit is really no life at all. Romans chapter 8 is the great triumphal testimony of this. I could quote the whole chapter, but look at these precious jewels: "For to be carnally minded is death, but to be spiritually minded is life and peace. For if you

live according to the flesh you will die; but if by the
Spirit you put to death the deeds of the body, you will
live. For as many as are led by the Spirit of God, these
are the sons of God" (Rom. 8:6, 13, 14).

I thank God every day for sending the Holy Spirit
to feed, nourish, and preserve my life. Like Job, I know
that "The Spirit of God has made me, and the breath
of the Almighty gives me life" (Job 33:4). Notice the
tense here: "*gives* me life"—that is, moment-by-
moment, day-by-day He sustains and gives life. That's
one of the reasons it's so important to have a vital relationship with the Holy Spirit.

2. The Holy Spirit imparts order.

A friend who is an architect once told me, "My greatest
thrill is to design a spectacular building and watch every
step of the construction process."

That's how God must have felt from the moment
His power began to move upon the waters. Every day
there was a new act of creation and the Spirit of God
was more fully revealed.

Remember this: Sin had not entered the world during God's six day construction project. And because of
this it was not a time of conflict or turmoil. After each
phase of creation He paused to say, "It was good." (Gen.
1:10, 12, 18, 21, 25). Then after the Holy Spirit
breathed life into Adam and Eve, He looked at everything He had made and "indeed it was *very* good."
(v. 31). What started as good, continued to become
better.

Perhaps I am a product of my childhood because I
am a perfectionist. From my clothes to my office, I want
everything neat and tidy. There's a picture at my house

of me as a little boy. It's obvious from the picture that
even then, everything had to be just right—from my
hair to my clothes to my shoes—everything had to be
just right.

Often when I see that picture, I reflect on memories
of that time in my life. I remember so vividly the school
I attended in Jaffa. It was operated by Catholic nuns, and
they were very exacting and strict. Every morning we
started the day with a rigorous inspection. Our clothes,
our nails, our hair, and even our ears were checked.

A nun came by with a stick in her hand. If my
nails were dirty or anything was out of place—Wham!
I would receive a slap from her stick.

I did not leave my perfectionism in Israel. After we
moved from Jaffa to Toronto my father told the older
children that we had to work after school. This was
totally foreign to me. I got a job at a gas station, but,
unfortunately, it didn't last long. You see, every time I
finished pumping gasoline into a car, I headed for the
rest room to wash my hands. (Force of habit from my
childhood.) It was a busy station and the cars just kept
lining up waiting for me to return.

I was fired the same day.

In the Old Testament we find that Moses led the
Children of Israel by an orderly plan. The manner in
which Israel placed their tents around the tabernacle
was organized. Their journey toward the Promised Land
was precise and specific.

In our crusades I operate with that same sense of
order. I insist that the sound, the lights, the platform
arrangements, and even the air temperature are perfect.
And I am troubled when things do not go smoothly and
when things do not operate according to plan.

I just believe God honors people when they are organized. Even in my personal devotions and Bible reading
I use seven different colored pencils to highlight scriptures in specific categories.

In our ministry, organization has enabled us to
reach vast numbers of people for the Lord Jesus. And
good financial planning is one of the reasons our ministry is fiscally sound. The Holy Spirit has honored that.

But let me add this word of caution. Even though
we make our plans, we must never attempt to organize
the Holy Spirit. He cannot be put in a box, and He will
not. He must be allowed to do His perfect will. *Always
flow with His plans and never expect Him to flow with yours.*

Years ago God told me, "If you organize a service
I will honor it. But never allow your organization to
become bondage." I never step onto a platform unprepared, but I do not allow my preparation to come before
His plans.

In 1 Corinthians 12 He is the Spirit of power. In
chapter 13 He is the Spirit of love. In chapter 14 He is
the Spirit of order. These three *always* work together. You
will never find order without love and power. Nor will
you find love without power and order.

**Here Comes
the Wind**

Some ask if you can actually physically feel
the wind of the Spirit, or His movement
today. If you're looking for a negative answer, I am the wrong person to ask. I have
shared the story of my first encounter with the Holy
Spirit so many times. As you may recall, it was at a
meeting conducted by Kathryn Kuhlman in Pittsburgh.
For several minutes, an unusual breeze—more like a
wave—was moving over me.

Experiencing a tangible Spirit-produced wind has not been an ordinary occurrence in my life, but in several crusade services, I, along with hundreds of people, have experienced the manifestation of the breath of the Holy Spirit. It came in the form of an unexplained wind sweeping over us. Specifically, it has happened in Atlanta, Georgia; Pretoria, South Africa; Baltimore, Maryland; and Worcester, Massachusetts.

Throughout the Bible, the wind has been a spiritual symbol. What did the Lord Jesus tell Nicodemus, a member of the Jewish ruling council, when he asked about being born again? The Lord said, "The wind blows where it wishes, and you hear the sound of it, but cannot tell where it comes from and where it goes. So is everyone who is born of the Spirit" (John 3:8).

Those who receive salvation are vessels in the hands of God, bringing His life-giving Holy Spirit to others. Like the wind, you begin to be moved by the Spirit of the Lord.

After Christ ascended to heaven, the promised Holy Spirit descended in the Upper Room on the Day of Pentecost. This time it was more than the sound of a breeze. "And suddenly there came a sound from heaven, as of a rushing mighty wind, and it filled the whole house where they were sitting" (Acts 2:2). They heard the noise of a mighty torrent of wind, violently rushing by.

What's the Forecast?

I was recently asked by a sincere Bible school student, "Benny, what is it like to understand the Holy Spirit so well that you know what He is going to do next in a service?"

"Young man," I responded, "where did you ever get such an idea. I *never* know what the Holy Spirit will do next in a service."

Scripture informs us: "As you do not know what is the way of the wind, or how the bones grow in the womb of her who is with child, so you do not know the works of God who makes all things" (Eccl. 11:5).

Have you ever watched a weather forecaster on television, surrounded by his charts and high-tech computers, predict rain, and yet, the next day not a cloud can be seen in the sky? I have. The weatherman prepares as thoroughly as he can and uses every resource at his disposal, but in the back of his mind (and ours) he knows that the weather could change on him in a minute. And that's what I've learned about the Holy Spirit. Try as we might, we can't always (or even often) predict what He's going to do.

How does this affect me? Let me explain it this way. I've already stated that the Holy Spirit is unpredictable. Consequently, when you follow the Holy Spirit, as I strive to do as best I can, at times you can also appear unpredictable. Now balance this with what I've said about order: there is a difference between order and predictability—always orderly, not always predictable.

There is a great difference between being led by the Holy Spirit and being guided by a printed "Order of Service" or a prayer book. When a servant of the Lord begins to flow in the power of the Holy Spirit the entire church feels the "wind" of change. There is an obvious difference in a service when the Holy Spirit is present and in control.

When I stand before thousands of people in a miracle crusade, I never know what is going to happen.

You ask, "Benny, are you telling me you don't plan everything about the service?"

Yes, that's correct, for when you are led by the Holy Spirit, only His plans matter. Now don't misunderstand; I *never* go into a service unprepared. I pay close attention to every detail: the temperature of the auditorium, the sound and lighting, even the seating on the platform. I know who is going to lead the choir and even what they are going to sing. I know who is going to play the piano and the organ and what the musicians will be singing in the service. I carefully review a list of song titles and point out the ones I consider to be the most appropriate. Basically, I know every detail about what is going to happen *before* I walk out on the platform. But from the moment I take that first step onto the platform, I never know what will take place because at that point my plans yield to His purposes.

In some cases I don't even know the next word I will speak. But when the Holy Spirit is in charge, everything flows together in perfect harmony and with great ease. Nothing distracts or takes attention away from worshipping the Lord, for the Holy Spirit always points to the Lord Jesus.

I am not opposed to agendas, plans, and preparation, for I believe that the Lord deserves our best. Proper planning is good stewardship of time and talent. But when the Holy Spirit is orchestrating the service, your preparation becomes a point of departure rather than a destination.

Countless times musicians have not sung the songs which they have rehearsed. Many times I have not preached the message for which I have spent days in preparation. Why? Because the Holy Spirit leads with perfection, and when His presence graces a service, agendas fall away in the light of His glorious presence. The thirsty drink from a well that never runs dry and the hungry are fed. Suddenly, nothing matters. You just want to glory in His marvelous presence.

Let the Wind Take You

Have you ever watched as a glider caught a warm breeze and lazily drifted higher and higher? You know—a lightweight plane that has no engine and sails effortlessly on an ocean of air. It's fascinating to watch the peaceful flight, willingly captured by a draft of air.

Although I have never flown a glider, I think I understand what it must be like. For in a spiritual sense I think I have had similar experiences. I can recall many times that I have stood on a platform worshiping the Lord with thousands, singing songs of praise and worship to Him during a service. We may begin by singing a simple chorus or familiar song. If the Spirit of God is on the song, I can sense it, and we'll sing it again. As we repeat it a second time, I can feel that we are climbing. We'll sing it again and soar higher still. The breath of the Spirit begins to lift our hearts and voices higher and higher, just like the wind carries a glider, until we are transported into the very presence of the Lord.

What happens if a song does not carry that anointing? I change the song immediately. If a chorus does not continue to lift us into His presence, I won't sing it more than once. If the next song leads into worship and carries the anointing, I will sing it until God has touched every heart in the building. I put no boundaries on the way the Spirit moves. Experiencing that precious touch of His presence is the goal, and I will change the song as many times as necessary until we are lifted into the heavenlies.

You may ask, "Benny, what do you do if the Holy Spirit does not anoint the music or worship?"

I begin to preach.

And as I preach I use the same principles. Remember this, if you ever stand before an audience to proclaim God's Word, do not simply memorize your message and absolutely do not *over*-prepare. Study to the best of your ability and organize your thoughts, but be totally aware of the Holy Spirit at work.

If the Lord touches a statement you make—make it again. It will lift the service higher. At some point in the message you may feel led to stop preaching and begin to minister just as I often do. I'm sure you know the difference. Preaching proclaims the Gospel. Ministering is meeting the spiritual needs of the listeners as you flow in God's Spirit.

The musicians who are part of our team are so sensitive to the anointing that all I have to do is make the slightest motion of my finger and they know I have "tasted" the anointing of the Lord. Immediately they begin to softly play worship music as the wind of the Spirit begins to carry us higher.

What happens next? I allow the Holy Spirit to carry the service and I *follow* wherever He leads.

If there is one thing I have learned in more than two decades of ministry, it is this: the Holy Spirit responds to hunger. The longing and desire of His people for Him draws Him closer.

When I was a boy we used to have fun taking a can of gasoline or oil and transferring the liquid to another can with just a little rubber hose. It was called a siphon.

Sometimes we would need to suck on the hose to get the liquid flowing, but once it began, the flow of that fuel wouldn't stop until it reached the other container.

That is how it is with the Holy Spirit. In a service, I am like a hose (and nothing more!) that the Holy Spirit uses to flow through and fill someone who is empty.

During a service I constantly search for those whose faces are aglow with God's anointing. It could be a minister seated behind me, a teenager in the front row, or a grandfather half-way across the auditorium. When the Spirit of the Lord directs me to begin to minister, I may walk over to that person and lay hands on him. It's like inserting a power cord into a "live" outlet instead of a dead one.

When just one person receives an anointing it produces an electricity that spreads quickly to others. It continues to multiply until people across the auditorium are touched by the Holy Spirit.

What happens to Benny Hinn in such a situation? The anointing on me intensifies; it doubles and triples.

Why do I pray with people who are ready to receive something from God? It builds the atmosphere of the anointing to the place that even those who were *not* hungry develop a sense of expectancy and are suddenly drawn to the Lord.

Please allow me to share something with you about the Holy Spirit from my own experience. As He is using you, a mighty "knowing" sweeps over your being. He tells you what to do—even though you don't know why.

- Moses did not know exactly what was going to happen when he started for the Promised Land.

- The river didn't separate for the Children of Israel until the priests who carried the Ark of the Covenant put their feet in the water (Josh. 3:13–17).
- The missionary journeys of the apostle Paul were constantly redirected by the Holy Spirit's plans.

Any sea captain will tell you that it is impossible to maneuver a giant ship until it is in motion. The Great Commission doesn't say, "When your plans are complete, you may begin." It says "Go."

You may wonder, "What if I don't know what to say when I witness?" Don't worry about it! Get moving. Share the Gospel and depend on the Holy Spirit, for God declares in the Psalms, "Open your mouth . . . and I will fill it" (Ps. 81:10).

Make no mistake: the Holy Spirit is *already* moving—and you had better get in motion too. You are no longer in a classroom waiting for the buzzer or bell to signal your next move of the day. This is real life and the Spirit of the Lord wants to do a great work through you. Start moving.

I have always said, "If the Holy Spirit can turn mud into a man, what will happen when 'the breath of the Almighty' touches you again?"

The Lord Jesus said, "It is the Spirit who gives life; the flesh profits nothing. The words that I speak to you are spirit, and they are life" (John 6:63).

Who is the One who quickens you? It is the Holy Spirit. "But if the Spirit of Him who raised up Jesus from the dead dwell in you, He that raised up Christ from the dead shall also quicken your mortal bodies by His Spirit that dwelleth in you" (Rom. 8:11 KJV).

Such a task is impossible for the flesh. When men allow the anointing of the Holy Spirit to touch and transform them, His word will impart life, not death. The apostle Paul tells us that we are "ministers of the new covenant, not of the letter but of the Spirit; for the letter kills, but the Spirit gives life" (2 Cor. 3:6).

The Holy Spirit has the power to transform death into life. God told Ezekiel to "Prophesy to the breath, prophesy, son of man, and say to the breath, 'Thus says the Lord GOD: "Come from the four winds, O breath, and breathe on these slain, that they may live"'" (Ezek. 37:9). The Hebrew word for "breath" here, "ruach" is translated as "Spirit" in verse 14, and may very well be the best translation for the word.[2]

The prophet Isaiah heard a voice that said, "Cry out!" and he said, "What shall I cry?" "All flesh is grass, and all its loveliness is like the flower of the field. The grass withers, the flower fades, because the breath of the LORD blows upon it; surely the people are grass. The grass withers, the flower fades, but the word of our God stands forever" (Isa. 40:6-8).

Here is the prophet's warning. All men are like grass and their glory is like a flower. And the same Holy Spirit that imparts life can bring judgment and even death (Acts 5:1-11). Never forget that if the Spirit is sinned against, the person who sins against Him is in danger of losing Him forever. The wicked do not know His awesome power to bring judgment and even remove life.

The breath of the Almighty on a believer will quicken. But when He blows on a sinner, it can bring death. That's why He must be feared.

The Lord wants us to be

Like a tree planted by the rivers of water,
That brings forth its fruit in its season,
Whose leaf also shall not wither;
And whatever he does shall prosper.
The ungodly are not so,
But are like the chaff which the wind drives away
(Ps. 1:3,4).

The wind of God's Spirit removes chaff—symbolic of wickedness. Those who resist the Holy Spirit are driven away, but those who yield to Him are brought into His presence.

Those who think they can hide from the "Wind" need to re-read the headlines of Hurricane Andrew or Hurricane Hugo. If natural wind can lift buildings from their foundations, imagine what the Breath (or Wind) of the Almighty can do in the life of the child of God.

You see, with the wind of the Holy Spirit under your wings, you will be able to soar to heights in your Christian life that you never thought possible. As Dwight L. Moody said, "If you have been born of the Holy Spirit, you will not *have* to serve God—it will be the natural thing to do."[3] Get the picture: the *supernatural* makes the *impossible* seem *natural!*

How could something "without form and void" become a world of beauty? How could God even think about entrusting His message of healing and deliverance to a self-conscious, stuttering child like myself? It is only because of the power of the Breath of God.

Are you ready for the "wind of the Spirit" to blow upon you?

The Work of the Spirit in the Life of Christ

Have you ever begun in prayer and found that as you spoke from your heart, it was as though your prayers went to the wall and bounced right back at you? When this happened to me shortly after I was saved, I didn't understand it. There was no life, no power, no intensity connected to my prayer life. But the day I really met the Holy Spirit, everything changed.

When Kathryn Kuhlman introduced me to the Holy Spirit I immediately wanted to know more about Him. But when I met the Holy Spirit, the thing that most amazed me was that my hunger for the Lord Jesus so intensified that I wanted to know more and more about the Lord.

Suddenly there was an eruption within me wanting to know the Lord Jesus in a way I had never experienced. I began to understand that I had been trying to know the Lord Jesus by myself. But when the Holy Spirit fully came into my Christian experience, I began to understand His role and His purpose. I discovered that knowing the Holy Spirit is simply the means by which we can know Christ in a deeper way.

When I attempted to know the Lord Jesus on my own, it was a struggle. I would pray like any Christian would pray, but nothing was happening. I was struggling; my prayers went to the wall and came right back at me. There was no life, no intensity, no hunger. I was trying to create hunger without the Holy Spirit doing it and it wasn't happening. I was trying to make myself hungry. It was all mental, all flesh. But when the Holy Spirit came, a God-given hunger began to burn in my soul and I was changed.

Paul's Declaration

When the Holy Spirit came, a prayer was born because of His presence that still burns within me with great love and longing. With Paul I say, "Oh, that I may know Him and the power of His resurrection, and the fellowship of His sufferings, being conformed to His death, if, by any means, I may attain to the resurrection from the dead" (Phil. 3:8–11).

You see, the Holy Spirit did not come to promote His own agenda. The Lord Jesus Himself declared the mission of the Holy Spirit when He said, "He will glorify Me, for He will take of what is mine and declare it to you" (John 16:14).

Jesus Christ is the central figure in world history, and it is the Holy Spirit who reveals Him to human hearts.

Child of the Spirit

Few people have stopped to consider the powerful role of the Holy Spirit in the birth of the Lord Jesus. Mary was a virgin from Nazareth who was pledged to be married to a man named Joseph. She was surprised when the angel Gabriel appeared to her and said, "Behold, you will conceive in your womb and bring forth a Son, and shall call His name JESUS" (Luke 1:31).

Gabriel's words troubled her greatly. "'How will this be,' Mary asked the angel, 'since I am a virgin?'" (v. 34 NIV). The angel answered, "The Holy Spirit will come upon you, and the power of the Highest will overshadow you; therefore, also, that Holy One who is to be born will be called the Son of God" (Luke 1:35).

It was customary for parents to arrange for the marriage of their children in those days. An actual marriage contract would be negotiated between the parents of a man and a woman, followed by a one-year waiting period. Although both the man and woman continued to live with their own parents, they were considered married and were referred to as husband and wife. The waiting period was intended to demonstrate the bride's faithfulness and purity as a virgin. If she was not found to be with child during the course of the year, she was considered pure and the contract was binding, and the husband and wife began their life together. If not, however, the marriage was annulled and the bride might even be stoned.[1]

When Joseph heard the story that his fiancee was "found with child," he was determined to quietly divorce her to avoid public humiliation and disgrace (Matt. 1:18, 19). Then, in a dream, an angel of the Lord told him not to be afraid to take Mary as his wife, "for that which is conceived in her is of the Holy Spirit" (v. 20).

What a divine miracle! In order for God to send His Son, the Holy Spirit came upon Mary and conceived within her the very Son of the Living God. He who is One with the Eternal God was made flesh and entered the world as a tiny baby. The Word of God became a seed within her womb. "And the Word became flesh and dwelt among us" (John 1:14). When I think about God becoming flesh, I see Him stamping our flesh forever with dignity.

It was nothing less than the power of the Holy Spirit that brought forth the Son of God in the form of a man. Continually I thank God that He who is limitless, whom the heavens cannot contain, came to earth in the form of flesh in order to save you and me.

The Confirmation Eight days after the birth of the Lord Jesus, God's Spirit was at work again. There was a "just and devout" man in Jerusalem named Simeon who was "waiting for the Consolation of Israel, and the Holy Spirit was upon him. And it had been revealed to him by the Holy Spirit that he would not see death before he had seen the Lord's Christ" (Luke 2:25, 26).

"Moved by the Spirit" (v. 27 NIV), Simeon hurried to the temple courts where the Lord Jesus was to be consecrated. It must have been a touching scene as Simeon "took he him up in his arms, and blessed God, and said, Lord, now lettest thou thy servant depart in peace, according to thy word: For mine eyes have seen thy salvation." (Luke 2:28, 29, 30 KJV).

By the way, Simeon stands as an example of the wonderful things that happen when a person is in fellowship with the Holy Spirit. Notice: the Holy Spirit was "upon him" (v. 25); the Holy Spirit revealed truth to him (v. 26); and the Holy Spirit guided his steps (v. 27).

From the very earliest days of the incarnation, Jesus Christ experienced the operation and instruction of the Holy Spirit even as Isaiah has foretold (Isa. 11:2).

The Lord did not speak on His own authority, but said, "the Father who sent Me gave Me a command, what I should say and what I should speak" (John 12:49).

The Lord Jesus was fully aware that the words He spoke were not those of His own choosing, but that He was a messenger of the Father, even as John the Baptist wrote of Him, "For the one whom God has sent speaks the words of God, for God gives the Spirit without limit" (John 3:34 NIV).

And just as Christ promised that the Holy Spirit "will teach you all things" (John 14:26), God allowed Him to experience that same instruction. The Lord Jesus relied on the guidance and direction of the Holy Spirit to fulfill what the Father called Him to do, for in the Old Covenant we find the Scriptures saying that it is the Holy Spirit who instructs, "You also gave Your good Spirit to instruct them" (Neh. 9:20a).

God and Man

When the Lord Jesus was on earth He was fully God and fully Man. The apostle Paul called Him "the Man Christ Jesus" (1 Tim. 2:5).

We need to remember that while Jesus Christ was on earth He was fully God and completely human. He was the God-man. And as a total man:

He knew what it was to be hungry. "And when he had fasted forty days and forty nights, he was afterward an hungered" (Matt. 4:2 KJV).

He experienced thirst. "After this, Jesus knowing that all things were now accomplished, that the scripture might be fulfilled, saith, I thirst" (John 19:28 KJV).

He became tired when He traveled. " Now Jacob's well was there. Jesus therefore, being wearied with his journey, sat thus on the well: and it was about the sixth hour" (John 4:6 KJV).

He grieved with people. "And when he had looked round about on them with anger, being grieved for the hardness of their hearts, he saith unto the man, 'Stretch forth thine hand.' And he stretched it out: and his hand was restored whole as the other" (Mark 3:5 KJV).

He experienced joy. "In that hour Jesus rejoiced in spirit, and said, I thank thee, O Father, Lord of heaven and earth, that thou hast hid these things from the wise and prudent, and hast revealed them unto babes: even so, Father; for so it seemed good in thy sight" (Luke 10:21 KJV).

He had compassion for people for He knew what they went through. "But when he saw the multitudes, he was moved with compassion on them, because they fainted, and were scattered abroad, as sheep having no shepherd" (Matt. 9:36 KJV) "So Jesus had compassion on them, and touched their eyes: and immediately their eyes received sight, and they followed him" (Matt. 20:34 KJV).

And as a man, Jesus relied on the vital guidance of the Holy Spirit. The same Holy Spirit that was working in the life of Christ is the same Holy Spirit Who wants to work in your life today.

"Heaven Opened"

John the Baptist, the cousin of the Lord Jesus, was perhaps the most sought-after preacher in Israel. He preached repentance and was sent by God "to make ready a people prepared for the Lord" (Luke 1:17).

People from "Jerusalem, all Judea, and all the region around the Jordan" came to him "and were bap-

tized by him in the Jordan, confessing their sins" (Matt.
3:5, 6).

John said, "I indeed baptize you with water unto
repentance, but He who is coming after me is mightier
than I, whose sandals I am not worthy to carry. He will
baptize you with the Holy Spirit and fire" (Matt. 3:11).
Some time after this, the Lord Jesus presented Himself to John, having traveled from Galilee to the Jordan
River to be baptized. Can you imagine how John felt?
Of course, John tried to discourage Him, saying, "I
need to be baptized by You, and are You coming to
me?" (Matt. 3:14). But the Lord persuaded him that
"it is fitting for us to fulfill all righteousness" (v. 15).

John agreed and "when all the people were baptized, it came to pass that Jesus also was baptized"
(Luke 3:21).

All three persons of the Trinity were manifest that
day. Oh, how I wish I could have been there when the
Lord Jesus came up out of the water. The Bible declares
that "the heaven was opened. And the Holy Spirit descended in bodily form like a dove upon Him, and a
voice came from heaven which said, 'You are My beloved Son; in You I am well pleased'" (Luke 3:21–22).

It is extremely significant that the Holy Spirit appeared in visible form then because six important things
happened at the baptism of the Lord Jesus:

1. **It marked the beginning of Christ's Messianic
   ministry.** R. A. Torrey says that "it was at the
   Jordan in connection with His baptism that Jesus
   was anointed with the Holy Spirit and Power, and
   He did not begin His public ministry until He
   was baptized with the Holy Spirit."[2]

2. **It showed humankind the importance of the baptism of the Holy Spirit to ministry.** The Lord Jesus would not embark on His public ministry without the special power of the Holy Spirit in His life. What an example this is to us. What a spur to seek greater fellowship with the Holy Spirit before attempting greater things for the Holy Spirit. R. A. Torrey again puts it so well, "If such a One, leaving us an example that we should follow His steps, did not venture upon His ministry, for which the Father had sent Him until thus definitely baptized by the Holy Spirit, what is it for us to dare to do it? . . . It is evident that the baptism with the Holy Spirit is an absolutely necessary preparation for effective work for Christ along every line of service."[3]

3. **It "fulfill[ed] all righteousness"** (Matt. 3:15). And the presence of the Holy Spirit whose very name is Holy was a manifest confirmation of the righteousness of Christ. His very presence was declaring that Jesus Christ was all righteousness as He identified with sinners in His baptism.[4]

4. **It demonstrated that the Lord Jesus belonged to God and was officially approved by Him.** For the Father declared, "You are *My* beloved Son; in You I am *well pleased.*"

5. **It showed God's approval of His Son's identification with humanity through His baptism.** As Louis Barbieri said, "If Messiah were to provide righteousness for sinners, He must be identified with sinners. It was therefore the will of God for Him to be baptized by John in order to be identified . . . with sinners."[5]

6. **It showed humankind the importance of water baptism, not for *salvation,* but for *identification* with the Savior in His death, burial, and resurrection** (Acts 2:38; 10:48; Matt. 28:19).

Immediately after His baptism, "Jesus, being filled with the Holy Spirit, returned from the Jordan and was led by the Spirit into the wilderness" (Luke 4:1).

Led into Temptation

Many people are surprised to read that after the Lord Jesus was so mightily filled with the Holy Spirit, He was immediately led by that same Holy Spirit into the greatest temptation of His life. Mark even says the Holy Spirit *drove* Him into the wilderness (Mark 1:12). What a remarkable word! John Grassmick says it so well, "the word [drove] is from a strong verb *(ekballo)* meaning "drive out, expel, send away . . . The thought is that of strong moral compulsion by which the Spirit led Jesus to take the offensive against temptation instead of avoiding them."[6] Get the picture? Christ came to break the power of sin, and instead of waiting for satan to come, the Holy Spirit led Christ to a "face-to-face" confrontation right away. The power of the strong man was to be broken by the God-man—right now!

For the next forty days the Lord Jesus went without food and was tempted by satan. First, the devil said, "If You are the Son of God, command this stone to become bread" (Luke 4:3).

The Lord Jesus answered with the Word. He said, "It is written, 'Man shall not live by bread alone, but by every word of God'" (v. 4).

Next, satan led the Lord Jesus up to a high place

and showed Him the kingdoms of the world. The devil said "This has been delivered to me, and I give it to whomever I wish. Therefore, if You will worship before me, all will be Yours" (vv. 6, 7).

Again, the Lord answered with the Word. He declared, "Get behind Me, satan! For it is written, 'You shall worship the LORD your God, and Him only you shall serve'" (v. 8).

Finally, the devil took the Lord Jesus to Jerusalem and had Him stand on the highest pinnacle of the temple, and said "If You are the Son of God, throw Yourself down from here" (v. 9). Satan even quoted Psalms 91:11, "For He shall give His angels charge over you, To keep you in all your ways" (v. 10).

How did the Lord Jesus respond? You guessed it. He used the Word of God and declared: "It has been said, 'You shall not tempt the LORD your God'" (v. 12).

And the same Word that Christ Jesus used then is available to you and me today. The message is clear. The only way we can cope with the onslaught of the evil one is through a Spirit-filled, Word-centered life. And the Word of God promises that you *can* conquer through Christ (Jude 9; Rom. 8:31–37).

Do you think I am somehow shielded from the attacks of satan? Absolutely not! But do I have the power through the Holy Spirit to be victorious? Absolutely yes! Night after night as the Spirit of the Lord is about to do a mighty work in our crusades, satan tries every trick imaginable to distract me. He has attempted everything from a power failure to causing a commotion in the audience. Even worse, he will try to whisper in my ear, "Benny, the Lord isn't here tonight. No one will be saved. No one will be healed. There will be no anointing." That's when I call upon the Holy Spirit to come and assist me.

Now the Lord returned to Galilee, "in the power of the Spirit" and the news about Him spread throughout the region (v. 14). He had fought satan and won. Remember, if you rely on the power of the Holy Spirit as Christ did *in the midst* of temptation, you'll come through in His power, seasoned and effective for life and ministry.

It was with that power that the Lord began His public ministry in the synagogue of Nazareth—the town where He had been raised. On the Sabbath, as was the custom, people would stand and read from a scroll that was handed to them. That day, the Lord Jesus was given the writings of Isaiah. Unrolling it, He located the place where it was written: (Isa. 61:1-2)

> *The Spirit of the LORD is upon Me,*
> *because He has anointed Me to preach*
>   *the gospel to the poor;*
> *He has sent Me to heal the brokenhearted,*
> *to proclaim liberty to the captives and*
>   *recovery of sight to the blind,*
> *to set at liberty those who are oppressed,*
> *to proclaim the acceptable year of the*
>   *LORD (Luke 4:19).*

Before Christ began His ministry three important things happened. First He was baptized; second, He was anointed and empowered by the Holy Spirit; and third, He was led by the Holy Spirit.[7]

Notice carefully what the Lord Jesus did *after the Holy Spirit came upon Him:*

1. He preached the Gospel.
2. He healed the brokenhearted.
3. He preached deliverance to the captives.
4. He brought sight to those in darkness.
5. He brought freedom to those who are bruised—in need of emotional healing.
6. He proclaimed that the era of salvation was *here*.

The point is so clear, isn't it? If the Savior did all these things after the Holy Spirit empowered Him, how much more we!

When the Master finished reading in the synagogue, He rolled up the scroll and gave it back to the attendant. Then, while everyone was looking at Him, the Lord said, "Today this Scripture is fulfilled in your hearing" (v. 21).

Jesus Christ as God did not need the anointing—He was, and *is,* the Source of it. But Christ the Man was fully dependent on the Holy Spirit's power. Without it He would have been helpless and ineffective in fulfilling His calling.

Let the Miracles Begin

It was only after the Lord's anointing by the Holy Spirit, His encounter with satan, and His proclamation in the synagogue that the miracles began to take place. The Lord Jesus went to Capernaum and cast a demon out of a man (Luke 4:35), healed Simon's mother-in-law who had a high fever (v. 39), and "when the sun was setting, all those who had any that were sick with various diseases brought them to Him; and He laid His hands on every one of them and healed them" (v. 40).

Jesus Christ ministered with the power of the Holy Spirit in every miracle that happened in His ministry—from turning water into wine to the cleansing of the ten lepers. Remember, there were no miracles before the Holy Spirit descended on Him at the river Jordan. As the Lord Jesus began His public ministry, great crowds followed Him, but "He warned them not to make Him known" (Matt. 12:16), so that Isaiah's prophecy might be fulfilled:

> *Behold! My Servant whom I have chosen,*
> *my Beloved in whom My soul is well pleased!*
> *I will put My Spirit upon Him, and He*
> *   will declare justice to the Gentiles.*
> *He will not quarrel nor cry out, nor will*
> *   anyone hear His voice in the streets.*
> *A bruised reed He will not break, and*
> *   smoking flax He will not quench, till He*
> *   sends forth justice to victory (vv. 18–20,*
> *   which quote from Isaiah 42:1–3).*

The Lord Jesus, filled with God's Spirit, had a specific mission to accomplish. In this first coming He was not to be a conquering king, but rather a gentle lamb.

To multiply the ministry and train His followers, the Lord Jesus sent out seventy of His disciples to heal the sick and preach the Kingdom of God. When they returned and reported that even the demons were subject to them in the name of Jesus, the Savior "rejoiced in the Spirit" (Luke 10:21). The Lord revealed the source and the meaning of this extraordinary power when He said, "If I cast out demons *by the Spirit of God,* surely *the kingdom of God* has come upon you" (Matt. 12:28). Yet the Lord Jesus was also careful to put these events into perspective for His followers when He declared, "Nevertheless do not rejoice in this, that the spirits are subject to you, but rather rejoice because your names are written in heaven" (Luke 10:20).

I will always be grateful to Dr. Oral Roberts for laying the foundation for the healing ministry in this generation. The great lesson I have learned from him is that God's Spirit is an *active* Spirit and His power is released through faith.

While it is true that God is sovereign and can do what He wishes, it is also true that God delights when we show our love by trusting Him enough to do what He says. And I don't mean by this simply mental agreement with God—I mean a faith that manifests itself in action. That's real faith, and God's loving response to this is to put His mighty resurrection power at our disposal (Eph. 1:19–23; Heb. 10:32–35).

Often in our crusades I'll tell people to touch the part of their body that they want God to heal. I'll encourage them to begin moving their afflicted arms or bending their hurting legs. These actions do nothing in themselves, but they *do* demonstrate the person has faith in God's healing power. And in the Scriptures you see again and again that when the Lord Jesus healed the sick He asked them to *do* something *before* the miracle took place.

- To the man with the withered hand, He said, "Stretch out your hand" (Matt. 12:13).
- To the paralyzed man who had been an invalid for thirty-eight years, He said, "Rise, take up your bed and walk" (John 5:8).

- To the ten lepers, He said, "Go, show yourselves to the priests" (Luke 17:14).

The apostle Peter paid eloquent tribute to this when he told everyone who would listen "how God anointed Jesus of Nazareth with the Holy Spirit and with power, who went about doing good and healing all who were oppressed by the devil, for God was with Him" (Acts 10:38).

Life with Victory

Living a life without sin seems so attractive—and so unattainable. Is it really possible to live a life without sin? The Lord Jesus did, but we cannot, for our bodies of "weakness" have yet to be raised in "power" (1 Cor. 15:43). But the promise is that one day our corruption will put on incorruption, and sin will be finally and fully defeated in our lives. In the meantime, as John says, "If we say that we have no sin, we deceive ourselves, and the truth is not in us. [But] If we confess our sins, He is faithful and just to forgive us our sins and to cleanse us from all unrighteousness." (1 John 1:8, 9). But I must say that the power to live victoriously is available to us moment by moment because of what the Lord Jesus did on Calvary's cross for you and me.

The writer of Hebrews says that "We do not have a High Priest who cannot sympathize with our weaknesses, but was in all points tempted as we are, yet without sin" (Heb. 4:15). This is the reason why you and I must go to Him continually in our moments of weakness. We will find Him always able to deliver from the "guttermost" to the uttermost. As Hebrews also declares, "He is able to save to the uttermost those who come to God through Him, since He always lives to make intercession for them" (Heb. 7:25).

The same Holy Spirit that enabled the Lord Jesus to resist the temptations of satan is ready to give us protection. The Word declares "For in that He Himself has suffered, being tempted, He is able to aid those who are tempted" (Heb. 2:18).

What should we do if we stumble? Scripture declares: "If we confess our sin, He is faithful and just to forgive us our sins and to cleanse us from all unrighteousness" (1 John 1:9). Now the word for "confess" in the Greek is *homologeo,* and it means "to say the same thing, to agree, to concede, to admit, to confess."[8] Quit justifying, qualifying, and explaining—agree with God that your sin is just that, *sin.* And if you really do agree with God about that behavior, you won't come back to it. You will have turned your back on that sin, changed your mind, and *repented.* Then you will be free to enjoy the unfettered fellowship of the Holy Spirit in your life again.

The Day the Spirit Left

It would have been impossible for Christ to endure the cross without the presence of the Holy Spirit. At Gethsemane, in anticipation of those terrible events to follow, the Lord Jesus cried, "My soul is exceedingly sorrowful, even to death" (Mark 14:34). The agony was so great that "His sweat became like great drops of blood falling down to the ground" (Luke 22:44).

Through two full days of betrayals, beatings, scourgings, trials, abandonment by both apostles and the crowds who had followed Him, and all of the other physical indignities He suffered, the Savior was physically and emotionally exhausted well before He arrived at Calvary. Without the Holy Spirit upon Him the Lord would have died prior to being hung on the cross.

By the time the Lord Jesus arrived at Calvary, His own blood, now dried and hard, covered Him from head to foot, his tongue was stuck to the roof of His mouth, He was bruised and battered, and totally without energy. Yet through the power of God the Lord Jesus still endured the agony of the crucifixion for six hours, taking the sin of the world upon Himself. During this season of severe suffering, the Lord cried out with a loud voice, "My God, My God, why have You forsaken Me?" (Mark 15:34).

Since God cannot look upon sin, the Father must have closed His eyes. In this time of great suffering, the Lord Jesus became sin for us. He "cried out with a loud voice," surrendering His spirit, "and breathed His last" (Mark 15:37; Luke 23:46).

On that night of sorrow, the body of the Lord Jesus Christ was taken down from the cross and placed in a borrowed grave. The "King of the Jews" whom the people scorned and ridiculed was removed from the face of the earth. So they thought.

Three days later, the Holy Spirit was at work again. He entered into that tomb and life began to flow through the body of the Lord Jesus. He was miraculously raised from the dead. Paul says, "If *the Spirit of Him who raised Jesus from the dead* dwells in you, He who raised Christ from the dead will also give life to your mortal bodies through His Spirit who dwells in you" (Rom. 8:11, emphasis added).

It was the same Holy Spirit who "came upon" Mary

at the conception of the Lord Jesus, who anointed Him, who led Him, and who empowered Him.

Just after the Resurrection, the disciples had locked the doors of the home they were in because they feared reprisals from the Jewish leaders. To their amazement, the Lord Jesus was standing in their midst and they were filled with great joy.

After greeting them He said, "Peace to you! As the Father has sent Me, I also send you. And when He had said this, He breathed on them, and said to them, "Receive the Holy Spirit" (John 20:21, 22).

For the first time in His ministry, the Lord Jesus imparted God's Spirit to others. As Andrew Murray wrote, "Our Lord had to die before He could baptize with the Holy Spirit."[9]

Even this was just a foretaste of what was to come after Christ ascended to heaven and the Holy Spirit would be poured out on all who would seek Him.

Who gave Him the power to endure the cross? Who raised Him from the dead? It was God's Spirit. At Bethany "He lifted up His hands and blessed them" and ascended to the Father (Luke 24:50). I can't prove it, but I believe it was the Holy Spirit who reached down and lifted Him up by His outstretched hands. In my opinion it was the Holy Spirit who took Him back to Glory.

We are talking about the Holy Spirit. The One who holds the world together (Job 34:14, 15). He's not a weak Holy Spirit. He is the mighty Holy Spirit.

The Voice We Hear

When He arose from the dead, the Lord did something that He is still doing today; He spoke by the Holy Spirit. Scripture tells us that it was "through the Holy Spirit" that the Lord Jesus "had given commandments to the apostles whom He had chosen" (Acts 1:2).

The Holy Spirit is the voice of God we hear. He is the manifestation of God to our heart.

When the Lord Jesus entered God's throne room I believe He said, "Father, the work is accomplished. And now it is time to send the Holy Spirit to earth. You allowed Him to come with me. But Father, I promised my Church that the Holy Spirit would come and be with them."

The Lord Jesus told the disciples He would send "the Spirit of truth, whom the world cannot receive, because it neither sees Him nor knows Him; but you know Him, for He dwells with you and will be in you" (John 14:17).

The Lord Jesus said "another Comforter," one like Him, would soon come and abide with us forever. He did not say, "You will see Him and then get to know Him." The Master was saying, "You *already* know Him. You're looking at Him. He's My Spirit. The same one you've walked with. We are One in the wonder of the Trinity."

The disciples knew the Lord, but now there was something new coming—a revelation of Christ's Spirit. Would the world recognize the promised Comforter? No. Because they didn't know the Lord Jesus.

Today, when the Holy Spirit walks into a life, He draws that heart and life to Jesus Christ, for He always points to Jesus. When the Holy Spirit speaks, the Lord Jesus speaks. He is the Spirit of Christ, and though they are different persons of the Trinity, you cannot divide or separate them.

Today, Christ sits at the right hand of the Father in heaven, making intercession for you and me. He is still both Son of God and Son of Man.

My friend, without the Holy Spirit, the Lord Jesus would have never entered the world. He would have never taken our sins to the cross and would have never risen from the grave.

If the Lord Jesus was so dependent on the Holy Spirit while He was on earth, can we be any less dependent?

Billy Graham says, "If we are to live a life of sanity in our modern world, if we wish to be men and women who can live victoriously, we need this two-sided gift God has offered us: first, the work of the Son of God *for* us; second, the work of the Spirit of God *in* us."[10]

The same Holy Spirit who descended upon the Lord Jesus is available to empower your life today. Simply surrender to Him, give Him full sway to empower you today.

From Sinner to Saint

**The Work
of the Spirit
in the Life
of a Sinner**

I suppose every individual who goes through
the wonderful experience of receiving Jesus
considers his testimony to be the most
unique and feels the need to share it with
others so they can also experience the unbe-
lievable joy that overcomes us. In your book,
Good Morning, Holy Spirit, you shared your
story. Kindly bear with me as I share the highlights of
mine, or perhaps I should say OUR story, since three of
us received Jesus as a result of your influence."

This was the opening paragraph of a letter I received
in late 1992 from an Associate Professor at the University of Florida. His story provides a fascinating glimpse
into the convicting work of the Holy Spirit—one which
I'll share in a moment.

Even before we come to the Lord, it is the Holy
Spirit that first draws us to Him, for the Bible says,
"And when He [the Holy Spirit] has come, He will
convict the world of sin, and of righteousness, and of
judgement" (John 16:8). For remember, the Holy Spirit
was with you even before salvation for it was He who

came to convict you of sin and to make the Lord Jesus a reality in your life. And after you trusted Christ the Holy Spirit then came in. That is why the Lord declared, "The world does not know but ye know Him for He dwelleth with you and shall be in you" (John 14:17 KJV).

The Lord also declared, "No one can come to Me unless the Father who sent Me draws him; and I will raise him up at the last day" (John 6:44). He went on to declare, "And I, if I am lifted up from the earth, will draw all peoples to Myself" (John 12:32). And how does this happen? Through the work and the power of the Holy Spirit!

After receiving thousands of letters from people who have given their hearts to the Lord, I am convinced that the Holy Spirit is creative, inventive, and imaginative in the way He draws men and women to the Savior—in a crusade, through watching our program on television, or even through reading one of my books. He is never confined or limited in how He deals with man, but deals individually and with sensitivity, gently drawing and pointing men and women to the Lord Jesus.

One example which comes to mind took place at a recent Miracle Crusade. Near the end of the service a Hindu man came to the stage and began to tell how he had come to be present in the service. He had seen a crowd gathering at the arena in the city in which he lived, and as he walked by the building, "something" seemed to draw him toward the arena (he didn't know it was Someone). He walked around the outside several times before coming inside. Inside he discovered what he had been looking for for over two years—the Lord Jesus. As he stood before me on the platform, he said through tears of joy, "Tonight I found what I have longed for. I have been looking for Jesus for so long and tonight I found Him!"

Although the Holy Spirit deals in unique ways and through different circumstances with each individual, Scripture declares that there are four specific ways the Holy Spirit moves on the heart of an unbeliever.

1. The Holy Spirit Convicts the World of Sin.

Before the Lord Jesus returned to the Father He said, "And when He (the Holy Spirit) has come, He will convict the world of sin, and of righteousness, and of judgment of sin, because they do not believe in Me . . ." (John 16:8, 9).

That's what happened to the professor who took time to write to share his story with me. In his letter he talked about a series of unexplainable events which had taken place in his life, including the miraculous disappearance of a blocked aorta in his heart only hours before his scheduled surgery. Each time something like this happened, his church-going wife would give God the credit. This infuriated him—after all he was a well-educated, logical man. "No one could 'con' me into believing such nonsense!" he said.

His letter went on to say: "My wife kept telling me of the wonderful teachings she had experienced and how much more she loved Jesus because of what she had learned. My religious experience consisted only of a vague memory of an hour-long mass occasionally and having bagels and lox with my Jewish friends on Sunday mornings while my wife went to church.

"One day she came home with *Good Morning, Holy Spirit*. Since I had just finished reading a novel and she was asleep, I thought I'd try 'Benny Hinn's fiction' for a change. I figured that by reading this book I would get some good data to use against her."

"Wham!" his letter continued. "What can I say? When I finished reading *Good Morning, Holy Spirit* I realized how shallow I'd been and how terribly I had ridiculed God, Jesus, and yes, even the Holy Spirit! I had never realized what a great sinner I had been. I went into our guest bedroom while my wife slept and I wept for hours asking Jesus for forgiveness. I felt the greatest joy of my life as I turned my life over to Jesus Christ.

"The next morning I dropped off the book at my friend's shop and suggested he read it because of his similar background from Israel. When I saw my friend the following day, he said, 'I think I want to go see this guy Benny Hinn since we both come from the same area of Israel.' "

His letter continued, "That Sunday when you invited those who wanted to accept Jesus to come forward, my friend, his wife, and I practically ran to the front of the church. The three of us received Jesus publicly that day.

"Thanks for sharing your friend, the Holy Spirit, with us. Eternity would be impossible without Him!"

The Lord said that the sin the Holy Spirit would convict the world of first is the sin of not believing in Him. As Dr. Lewis Sperry Chafer, the founder of Dallas Theological Seminary so correctly observes: "This enlightenment is not of sins. Were it of personal sins it could accomplish no more than a deepening of remorse and shame, and would provide no cure. The Holy Spirit's enlightening is respecting one sin, and that is the failure to receive Christ and His salvation."[1]

The response of the people to Peter's first sermon is the response of everyone who is convicted by the Holy Spirit: "they were cut to the heart, and said to Peter and the rest of the apostles, 'Men and brethren, what shall we do?' (Acts 2:37). And Peter said "Repent, and be baptized every one of you in the name of Jesus Christ for the remission of sins, and ye shall receive the gift of the Holy Ghost. For the promise is unto you, and to your children, and to all that are afar off, even as many as the Lord our God shall call" (Acts 2:38, 39 KJV).

2. The Holy Spirit Convicts the World of Christ's Righteousness.

How did you become aware that no matter how righteous you were, it wasn't righteous enough in God's eyes? That "$99^{44}/_{100}$ percent" righteous wasn't good enough? It was because the Holy Spirit first convicted you and showed you that only through the Lord's righteousness could you be justified. For the Lord Jesus said the Holy Spirit would convict "of righteousness, because I go to My Father and you see Me no more" (John 16:10).

It was the Holy Spirit who convicted you of the fact that your righteousness wasn't good enough to gain the Father's approval—but Christ's was! And it was the Holy Spirit who convinced you to trust what Christ did on the cross to gain the Father's favor—that you needed Christ's mighty righteousness because you didn't have enough of your own.

Peter understood this glorious truth at Pentecost, when he said that Christ, having been "exalted to the right hand of God, and having received from the Father the promise of the Holy Spirit, . . . poured out [that] which you now see and hear" (Acts 2:33). For Peter knew it was because of the work of the Holy Spirit that many were convicted when they heard the Gospel in that day "not simply with words, but also with power, with the Holy Spirit and with deep conviction" (1 Thess. 1:5 NIV).

And the Scriptures are so wonderfully clear on the righteousness of Christ. 2 Corinthians 5:21 declares "For He made Him who knew no sin *to be* sin for us, that we might become the righteousness of God in Him" (2 Cor. 5:21).

3. The Holy Spirit Convicts the World of Judgment.

People need to understand the consequences for their actions. They need to know that there is everlasting punishment prepared for those who turn their backs on Christ.

The Lord Jesus said the Holy Spirit will convict "of judgment, because the ruler of this world is judged" (John 16:11). Colossians 2:13, 14 says: "And you, being dead in your trespasses and the uncircumcision of your flesh, He has made alive together with Him, having forgiven you all trespasses having wiped out the handwriting of requirements that was against us, which was contrary to us. And He has taken it out of the way, having nailed it to the cross." And because of this, verse 15 says, "Having disarmed principalities and powers, He made a public spectacle of them, triumphing over them in it."

Man, on his own, will never be convinced that he deserves judgment. It is only the Holy Spirit that can produce such conviction. And when He does, a glorious transformation takes place.

Smidgie's Transformation As I walked down the back steps of the platform after the Cincinnati crusade, I noticed one of my associates, David Palmquist, waiting there, accompanied by a man and a woman. "This is Smidgie," David said. "Could you please pray for her, Pastor Benny?"

I gently touched her forehead as I continued to walk slowly toward my waiting car. "Touch her, Lord. Visit her life with Your power and glory! And bless her husband, too." They melted to the floor and lay there, basking in God's glory. Several months later I saw them again at a crusade where she told me a most remarkable story.

"I was born to a Jewish family and raised as a Reformed Jew. Although we did not frequent the synagogue as much as the Orthodox Jews, we observed the High Holy Days. Education and materialism were emphasized in our home. Driven by the desire to succeed, I decided to become an attorney.

"As a successful New York lawyer, I enjoyed the material lifestyle my career provided. My husband, who was not Jewish, was a general contractor who worked primarily with the upper echelon of society. I was basically content with how things were going in my life. I loved my husband, our marriage was great, and professionally, I was moving along just great climbing the ladder to the top. I always told my husband, 'I'm Jewish as far as my heritage,' but inside I was confused because I didn't feel any sense of God—the kind of safety that should come from a higher being—and that troubled me.

"I began to explore various avenues looking for satisfaction. I wound up following Hindu philosophy and eastern religion. I became a guru, which in Hindu talk means people came to see me for advice at $100-$150 an hour. I was involved in channeling, the kind some of Hollywood's current personalities brag about in their books, and transcendental meditation.

"In fact, I worked very closely with Maharishi Mahesh Yogi. I had a mantra, had one of the most advanced trainings available—I even levitated. I meditated twice a day, 1½ hours in the morning and 1½ hours at night. Transcendental meditation is supposed to bring peace and solace to your life. But I was still so empty inside that I kept looking for something that would truly satisfy.

"My search to find a higher power was going nowhere. About this time I happened to be at a friend's house who shared something with me about Christianity. I remember thinking, 'Oh, I guess I'll give my heart to the Lord. This will be neat!' But I never felt anything different. I was still searching for something to satisfy me so even that became just another road leading nowhere.

"Some time later my husband and I received a call from a man whom we knew casually. He was facing a crisis and in dire straits. Because it seemed to be a somewhat desperate situation, we decided to go and spend a few hours with him.

"When we arrived, we tried to console and encourage him. We talked for a while and eventually ended up in the kitchen. As we talked, something caught my attention in another room of the apartment. I heard this music, so different from what I had ever heard. I turned around to see where it was coming from. Then I heard this man talking. The music and the man talking made me feel so funny—almost like somebody took my heart, put their hand inside of it, and physically walked me out of the kitchen into the living room.

"There I saw this man on the television screen. I didn't know what he was saying—I'm not even sure to this day. I sat down on the couch, my eyes transfixed on the television screen. As I watched I felt like something was breaking my heart in a thousand pieces. Although I'm a very private person, I began to weep. I didn't know what was wrong, but I couldn't stop crying. Here I was, in someone's apartment that I barely knew, falling apart for no apparent reason. Through the tears I tried to rationalize what could possibly be happening. After all, I was a well-educated woman. I should be able to figure this out. Grasping at straws, I finally concluded that this man on the television screen must have reminded me of my mom who had passed away at a young age. Yes, I could see similarities. That had to be the answer.

"I regained my composure and we prepared to leave. As we were about to say good-bye, our host turned and picked up a video tape. He handed it to me and said, 'Take it home. Watch it when you get some time.'

"The following week I had a very busy schedule in court with lots of long hours. When I finally got a few hours away from the courtroom, I went home to relax. As I sat in my living room, I noticed the video tape the man had given me. Curious and home alone, I turned the video on and sat down. There was that man again and the music—and that feeling. I sat there, my heart crushed, broken. I fell to my knees, crying uncontrollably. I was all alone and so broken up. Soon I found myself on the floor, asking God to forgive me for things I didn't even remember. It went all the way back to when I was a little girl. For 2½ hours I was on the floor, sobbing and praying. And all the while this man on the video (whom I now know as Pastor Benny Hinn) kept talking.

"After 2½ hours I stopped crying. And I felt so different—as though a big, heavy burden was gone. That day I was truly born again, all alone in my living room with a video of Pastor Benny playing. But I didn't feel alone anymore. Now Jesus was with me, and somehow, I knew He would never leave."

4. The Holy Spirit Testifies of Jesus.

You may try to tell someone about the Lord again and again. Then one day they exclaim, "Oh, I finally see what you've been saying!" That realization is the work of the Holy Spirit.

Just before Christ went to the cross, He told His disciples that "When the Helper comes, whom I shall send to you from the Father, the Spirit of truth who proceeds from the Father, He will testify of Me" (John 15:26).

Paul told the Corinthians that "no one can say that Jesus is Lord except by the Holy Spirit" (1 Cor. 12:3).

Often the Holy Spirit uses the *inscripturated* (written) Word of God to convict an individual. "For the word of God is living and powerful, and sharper than any two-edged sword, piercing even to the division of soul and spirit, and of joints and marrow, and is a discerner of the thoughts and intents of the heart" (Heb. 4:12). The Holy Spirit uses the Word of God because the Holy Spirit *inspired* the Word of God: "for prophecy never came by the will of man, but holy men of God spoke *as they were* moved by the Holy Spirit (2 Peter 1:21). It is *His* Word.

Here's a note of caution. We should never forget that Scripture warns us concerning the danger of resisting the convicting power of the Holy Spirit. The Lord said, "My Spirit shall not strive with man forever" (Gen. 6:3). By constant rejection we can become so hardened to His pleading that we no longer hear His voice.

Here's another note of caution. If the Holy Spirit is prompting you to share the Gospel with someone, *always* obey His leading: "For He says: 'In an acceptable time I have heard you, and in the day of salvation I have helped you.' Behold, now is the accepted time; behold now *is* the day of salvation" (2 Cor. 6:2*b*)

The writer of Proverbs said it this way: "He who is often rebuked, and hardens his neck, will suddenly be destroyed, and that without remedy" (Prov. 29:1).

My dear friend, please don't take that chance.

Today, God's Spirit is on earth to convict our hearts of sin and prepare the way for us to receive Christ (John 16:7-11).

How do we experience the new birth? The Lord Jesus said, "For God so loved the world that He gave His only begotten Son, that whoever believes in Him should not perish but have everlasting life" (John 3:16).

As a pastor I am often asked, "Pastor Benny, how do I know if I have been born again?"

My answer is as simple as John 5:24: "Most assuredly, I say to you, he who hears My word and believes in Him who sent Me has everlasting life, and shall not come into judgment, but has passed from death into life." I help the person who lacks assurance to understand that it is the Lord Jesus who is speaking the words in this passage, and then I ask them the question, "Did you hear His word and believe in Him?" That is, "Have you trusted Christ as your personal Savior?" After explaining the Gospel to them, I ask them if they have trusted Christ. If they have not trusted Christ as their Savior, I invite them to do so right then and help them to understand the full weight of the Savior's words in John 5:24 when He said that they:

- Have everlasting life
- Shall not come into judgment
- Have passed from death into life.

Any doubts after that are the whispered deceptions of the devil, and should be immediately dismissed through the powerful name of the Lord Jesus. My dear friend, if you're not sure that you're saved, why not remove all doubt and trust Christ right now?

The Work of the Holy Spirit in the Life of the Believer

As we will discover in the next two chapters, the Holy Spirit works in our lives in a great variety of ways. At the moment of conversion, however, there are two important things He accomplishes.

1. The Holy Spirit Regenerates Us.

After we trust the Lord Jesus Christ by faith and repent of our sins, something marvelous happens. We are regenerated—"born again."

The Lord Jesus told Nicodemus, "That which is born of the flesh is flesh, and that which is born of the Spirit is spirit" (John 3:6). Titus 3:5 says that it is "not by works of righteousness which we have done, but according to His mercy He saved us, through the washing of regeneration and renewing of the Holy Spirit."

On our own, it would be totally impossible to find the solution for our dilemma. "The natural man does not receive the things of the Spirit of God, for they are foolishness to him; nor can he know them, because they are spiritually discerned" (1 Cor. 2:14).

The Holy Spirit makes conversion possible since He prepares our heart to receive the Lord. "But as many as received Him, to them He gave the right to become children of God, to those who believe in His name" (John 1:12). And Peter declared that we are no longer bound by habits of the flesh. Instead we become "partakers of the divine nature" (2 Peter 1:4).

R. A. Torrey said, "I am sometimes asked, 'Do you believe in sudden conversion?' I believe in something far more wonderful than sudden conversion. I believe in sudden regeneration. Conversion is merely an outward thing, the turning around. Regeneration goes down to the deepest depths of the inmost soul, transforming thoughts, affections, will, the whole inward man."[2]

2. The Holy Spirit Sets the Believer Free.

Because of Adam's sin, we are all born with a sin nature and under a sentence of death, absolutely powerless in ourselves to do anything about it. At the cross, Christ paid the ransom for our sin. When we accept Him by faith, that sentence is forever lifted. We are free!

Paul told the church at Rome, "There is therefore now no condemnation to those who are in Christ Jesus, who do not walk according to the flesh, but according to the Spirit. For the law of the Spirit of life in Christ Jesus has made me free from the law of sin and death.

For what the law could not do in that it was weak through the flesh, God did by sending His own Son in the likeness of sinful flesh, on account of sin: He condemned sin in the flesh, that the righteous requirement of the law might be fulfilled in us who do not walk according to the flesh but according to the Spirit" (Rom. 8:1–4).

We have been given the choice between death and life. "For if you live according to the flesh you will die; but if by the Spirit you put to death the deeds of the body, you will live" (Rom. 8:13).

In his book, *The Holy Spirit*, Billy Graham says, "When a person is born again, the process is uncomplicated from the divine perspective. The Spirit of God takes the Word of God and makes the child of God. We are born again through the operation of the Holy Spirit, who in turn uses the divinely inspired Word of God. God's Spirit brings life to men. At this point the Holy Spirit indwells a person for life. He receives *eternal* life."[3]

Just as the Spirit of the Lord was "with you" to convict you (and the rest of the world) of sin before your conversion (John 14:17), He "will be in you" (v. 17) after you trust Christ.

Seven Things That Happen When the Holy Spirit Transforms You

The transforming power of the Holy Spirit is beyond measure. And the benefits of His grace exceed our ability to describe. But here is what you can expect when the Holy Spirit becomes a part of your daily walk.

First: *He Will Turn Your Wilderness Into a Fruitful Place.*

I love to visit the Holy Land. After all, it's both my *former* home, and will be my *future* home in the Millennium. When I take people to the Holy Land they are often surprised by how much of it is desolate and barren. It can be hard to imagine how anyone could even live there, let alone fight over the land. The Scripture means just exactly what it says when it refers to much of the Holy Land as wilderness, desert, and wasteland. But as desolate as so much of that wonderful land is, Isaiah nevertheless declares, "The wilderness and the wasteland shall be glad for them, and the desert shall rejoice and blossom as the rose" (Isa. 35:1). Growing up in Israel, we could see it happening all around us—but even the blossoming of Israel today cannot compare to that future time of fruitfulness.

Isaiah also tells us that "The Spirit (will be) poured upon us from on high, and the wilderness becomes a fruitful field, and the fruitful field is counted as a forest" (Isa. 32:15).

The idea of living in a wilderness is not pleasant. It is barren; a place of snakes, scorpions, and death. But the Spirit of the Lord can change the landscape into a garden—a place of beauty and abundance.

As Christians, when we produce a harvest we extol the praises of the Lord. The Master said, "By this My Father is glorified, that you bear much fruit" (John 15:8).

It is the Holy Spirit that enriches our soil and sends the rain in preparation for a thanksgiving feast. He is the one that makes the harvest possible.

It's not your fruit, but His. That is why the Scripture calls it "the fruit of the Spirit." When we present our vessels, He fills them to overflowing.

You may say, "But I'm not living in a wilderness, my garden is already planted." That's no problem with God. He says your orchard will become so blessed that your "fruitful field is counted as a forest" (Isa. 32:15).

Second: He Will Cause You to Walk With God.

It is impossible to walk with the Lord without His Holy Spirit helping and enabling you. The Lord said through the prophet Ezekiel: "I will put My Spirit within you and cause you to walk in My statutes, and you will keep My judgments and do them" (Ezek. 36:27).

And a new Christian might look at the laws of God and say, "There is no possible way I can keep those rules and regulations!" And they are right. As Howard Hendricks has said, "The Christian life isn't difficult— it's impossible!" In your own power you will fail. For it is the Holy Spirit who will cause you to walk in God's statutes and keep His judgments. Even more, He will cause you to *do* His will.

And many years ago I too discovered that it is the power of the Holy Spirit that enables you and me to live the Christian life. For had it not been for His power I would not be where I am today as a Christian. He has been my strength, my fortress, and my high tower. And remember, without the Holy Spirit you and I cannot walk with God.

For God says it is His Holy Spirit that will "cause us to walk" so that you will not fall. And it is also the Holy Spirit's power that is "able to keep you from stumbling, and to present you faultless before the presence of His glory with exceeding joy" (Jude 1:24).

My dear friend, Dr. Bill Bright, president of Campus Crusade For Christ International, says, "When we are filled with the Holy Spirit, we are filled with Jesus Christ. We no longer think of Christ as One who helps us do some kind of Christian task but, rather, Jesus Christ does the work through us."[4]

Third: You Will Know God's Presence.

One of the great comforting passages in Scripture is found in Ezekiel 39:29, where our loving Heavenly Father says, "I will not hide My face from them anymore; for I shall have poured out My Spirit on the house of Israel."

I can't tell you how much that Scripture has meant to me over the years, especially in those times when God seemed distant, and my prayers little more than empty rattling. You see, the Holy Spirit causes the presence of the Father to be a reality in our lives, and as a result of this we feel His closeness. I can tell you from personal experience, the Holy Spirit wants to be very close to you. Just whisper "Jesus" and He will be right there.

Your prayer life will dramatically change when you feel His nearness. When I needed to experience the nearness of my heavenly Father, I would go into my bedroom and say, "Holy Spirit, help me pray."

Oh, how He responded. Instead of struggling with repetitious, empty, dead prayers for ten minutes I would commune with the Lord through the Holy Spirit for hours and hours.

Now I clear my schedule to spend time alone with the Lord every morning. I turn on a tape player with worship music and begin to read the Word and talk to God—as naturally as I converse with anyone. And I begin to feel something that I can only describe as the "moisture" of God's presence on my heart.

I say, "Holy Spirit, now help me. I can't pray, but you can. Help me." And He always responds.

Start today. Make an intentional effort to spend time in the presence of the Lord.

Fourth: You Will Understand God's Word.

One of the most exciting benefits of life with the Holy Spirit is that He makes it possible to comprehend the Word. God says, "Surely I will pour out my spirit on you; I will make my words known to you" (Prov. 1:23).

If you want the Bible to come alive, invite the Holy Spirit to read along with you. He can take the most obscure and veiled passages and make them clear.

The same Holy Spirit that rested on the Lord Jesus is indwelling you—if you have trusted Him—and the Spirit of the Lord is still producing the same things: "The Spirit of the LORD shall rest upon Him, the Spirit of wisdom and understanding, the Spirit of counsel and might, the Spirit of knowledge and of the fear of the LORD" (Isa. 11:2).

Being *acquainted* with Scripture simply isn't enough—the Holy Spirit wants to be certain that "the word of God *abides* in you" (1 John 2:14, emphasis added).

Fifth: You Will Become a New Person.

People are spending millions of dollars to transform their bodies. They try exotic diets, travel to luxury health spas, and spend hours under the knife of a plastic surgeon, all in hopes of remaking their image through such superficial things. And after they've been tucked, lifted, sucked, buffed, packed, wrapped, reduced, and augmented—what do they have? Aside from big doctor bills, not much more than the same thirsty spirits they had before, still desperately in need of the Holy Spirit.

The transformation produced by God's Spirit, however, is not cosmetic. He changes you from the inside out. It is *total*. "Therefore, if anyone is in Christ, he is a new creation; old things have passed away; behold, all things have become new" (2 Cor. 5:17).

It is through the Spirit of the Lord that you are able to "put on the new man which was created according to God, in true righteousness and holiness" (Eph. 4:24).

Everything about you becomes fresh when God takes over. "I will give you a new heart and put a new spirit within you; I will take the heart of stone out of your flesh and give you a heart of flesh" declares the Lord in His Word (Ezek. 36:26).

It was because of the Holy Spirit that Samuel was able to tell Saul that the Spirit of the Lord would come upon him and he would "be turned into another man" (1 Sam. 10:6). The same is true today: the Holy Spirit like a gentleman is standing by to transform you, free you, fill you, and empower you to achieve your full destiny in Christ.

Get ready for that great transformation!

Sixth: He Will Give You Rest.

The Spirit of the Lord doesn't lead you into stress or confusion. Instead He takes you down a path where things are peaceful and calm. "In quietness and confidence shall be your strength" (Isa. 30:15).

I've never known the Holy Spirit to cause heartache or sorrow. He is the God of beauty and rest. Always.

Isaiah describes the rest the Holy Spirit gave to the nation of Israel after leading them out of Egypt and through the wilderness to the Promised Land when he wrote, "like cattle that go down to the plain, they were given rest by the Spirit of the LORD. This is how you guided your people to make for yourself a glorious name." (Isa. 63:14 NIV).

Why do cattle like to go down to the valley? That's where the rivers flow and where they can find pasture. That is where they can find peace and rest.

> *The LORD is my shepherd;*
> *I shall not want.*
> *He makes me to lie down in green pastures;*
> *He leads me beside the still waters.*
> *He restores my soul* (Ps. 23:1–3).

So many people feel so much stress in their lives and the key to relief is not a prescription, a cruise, or learning to say, "No," it's the Holy Spirit!

Seventh: He Will Bring Excellence Into Your Life.

The Spirit of the Lord is not a craftsman of inferior or shoddy workmanship. He is the author of quality and perfection.

In the Old Testament, "Daniel distinguished himself above the governors and satraps, because an *excellent* spirit was in him; and the king gave thought to setting him over the whole realm" (Dan. 6:3, emphasis added).

The measure of comparison was not his ability in battle, or his riches—it was because of the "excellent spirit" of his heart. The word "excellent" literally means, "pre-eminent" or "surpassing." The King of

Babylon saw Daniel's attitude and wanted to give him a promotion.

Men and women who want a raise in pay or a higher position in a corporation are often disappointed when they are bypassed. The decisions are not always the result of their educational background or length of service. Instead, people most often advance or decline on the merit of their performance.

Do you remember what happened in the life of Joseph? Pharaoh recognized the Holy Spirit in his life and he was made Prime Minister (Gen. 41:38).

Every day we need to allow the Spirit of the Lord to bring quality and distinction to our Christian walk.

The Holy Spirit is a transforming power. If He can change a wilderness into a garden and change the vilest sinner from a slave of sin into a child of God, just think what He has prepared for you!

9

Changed from the Inside Out

Do you have a minute, Pastor?" David Palmquist, one of my associate pastors, asked as we left our conference room following a routine planning meeting. "I just had the most wonderful telephone call from one of our partners."

"Of course, David," I responded. "Tell me all about it."

"You remember Smidgie, the New York attorney? You first met with her and her husband in Cincinnati."

"Yes, of course," I responded. "I remember her. She and her husband are faithful partners and very dear to me."

Nodding in agreement, David continued "I just talked to her before our planning meeting began. A few months ago she called, very concerned about her father. We prayed together on the phone and asked God to perform a miracle in his life. And that's just what has happened!

"She shared such a tremendous testimony with me. She said that for years she and her father were insepara- ble. Actually, she was like his shadow. Anywhere her father went, everyone knew Smidgie was close behind.

"Her mother passed away a few years ago, and when that happened, she and her father drifted apart. From talking with her it seems that she never thought it could happen, but they were eventually more like polite strangers than father and daughter. Soon it was much more than merely drifting apart—there was a great chasm between them. The social amenities were there when they were in public, but the relationship was gone.

"Material possessions, financial success, education, and golf, according to Smidgie, became the four significant pillars in her father's life, the elements by which her Jewish father measured the value of his life. This was his identity. And even though material possessions were very important to him, he was such a generous man. Smidgie said that he wouldn't hesitate to take you and all your friends out to dinner, pay for everything, and tip the waiter so substantially that it would help put him through college.

"Although her father was religious and considered himself to be an observant Jew, he never talked much about God in their home. When she was growing up her brother was bar mitzvahed, they observed all the High Holy Days, and her father was an observant Jew (no mixing of meat and dairy products, etc.) But there was no awareness of God in their home or in their lives.

"After her wonderful conversion experience, she and her husband became partners with you, Pastor Benny," David continued. "They have faithfully supported the world-wide ministry each month, often giving much more than their original $30 monthly commitment. Their lives have been touched by the Lord in such a wonderful way that she said they wanted to do whatever they could to help you proclaim the message of God's saving and healing power to the world. They also began attending the monthly miracle crusades, taking time away from work month after month to travel to the crusades.

"Smidgie told me that although her father was aware of this, he never once said, 'Who is Pastor Benny?' or 'What are these crusades you keep going off to attend?' He showed no interest or curiosity whatsoever. And because they had no real relationship anymore, she never said much either.

"Everything began to change when on one occasion, during a brief telephone conversation, Smidgie's father said to her, 'So, are you going to another crusade, Smidgie? Well, have a good time. When will you be back?' Still in shock, she answered his questions. Smidgie said he had never even acknowledged their crusade attendance before.

"About this same time her father who is a very intelligent, aggressive, successful businessman in New York's garment district, decided to have a thorough physical. It was purely preventive—he didn't think anything was wrong. Following the routine physical he was told he was 'absolutely fine.' However, one of the doctors called him back within days and said, 'You know what? I'd like you to come back and take another chest x-ray because I missed something. I don't know how it happened.'

"Smidgie said her father was stunned by the request. 'A top physician like this and he missed something?' her father said. 'Can you believe it? What could he possibly have missed?'

"Days later her father returned to the doctor, and after the requested set of tests and related procedures, the doctor said, 'Since you've just recovered from a mild case of pneumonia, this could either be an infection in your lungs or it could be lung cancer.'

"Smidgie said her father looked at the doctor in total disbelief. 'You've got to be kidding! I'm headed for my Florida home for three weeks to play some golf and take some time off!'

"'Go ahead,' the doctor responded. 'Get away for a few weeks, get some rest, play some golf, and when you come back, we'll do one more test to see what's going on.'

"Before he left for Florida, Smidgie's father called her and said, 'Smidgie, I'm going to ask you to do something for me. Would you please pray for me?'

"Even though this was totally unexpected, she responded, 'Yes, I will,' without hesitation. They talked for a few more minutes and then he was off to Florida to enjoy some sunshine and golf.

"After he left for Florida, she and her husband decided to send him a book they had read, *Good Morning, Holy Spirit.* They said they enclosed a brief note explaining that this book was a favorite of theirs and had been written by a man whom they regarded as their pastor, even though they didn't live in Orlando. Then they left her father and the future in the Lord's hands.

"Within two days they received a telephone call from Smidgie's father, thanking them for sending the book. Then he went on to tell them how he had started reading the book, and, being unable to put it down, had finished reading the entire book. He said he had read and re-read the book until the pages were almost falling out. As he was about to close the telephone conversation, he announced to them, 'After reading the book, something wonderful has happened—I've given my heart to the Lord!'

By this time David's face was glowing with excitement as he continued with the story. "Smidgie and her husband were thrilled by the news! They packed up several of the videos you have produced and sent them off to Florida, too.

"After watching one of them her father prayed, 'Would You give me another chance, Lord? If You do, I promise to give You my life and to serve You always.'

"From that moment on, her father began to change. Not long after, he called her one night and said, 'I've got to tell you something, honey. I've missed you so much, Smidgie. I want my little girl back. How about it?'

"Their relationship has been restored and now they enjoy an even richer relationship than before they drifted apart. And now her father calls regularly, sometimes three times a day she says, just to tell her how much he loves Jesus Christ and his new Companion, the Holy Spirit, whom he talks to from morning to night, just like he read about in *Good Morning, Holy Spirit*.

"And when he returned from his three-week holiday in Florida, he went back for another series of tests as the doctor had suggested. After reviewing all the information, the doctor said, 'I don't know what we saw before, but there's nothing there now. You're absolutely fine!'

"Smidgie said that as her father left the doctor's office that day, there was a new spring in his step and his heart was bubbling with excitement at the news. As soon as he got home he called her and said, 'As I was leaving the doctor's office, I told the Holy Spirit and I told Jesus that if I had to go through this all over again—thinking I had cancer or whatever—just to know Jesus and to experience the joy and reality of His presence in my life, I would do it all over again. And now to have my little girl back and our relationship restored, too—*this is my day!*'"

Just as the Lord touched Smidgie's father and transformed his life so He will do for you, too. He will totally transform you on the inside if you will only ask Him to. And then His glorious presence and power will begin to flow through you to affect the world around you. And when this happens, everywhere you go and everyone you come in contact with will notice that there is something different about you. Are you ready?

Let's first look at how He changes you on the *inside* before He flows through you to affect the world. In the next chapter you'll learn about His *outward* and *upward* work.

We have already discussed the convicting power of the Holy Spirit in bringing you to Christ, but that's only the start. He will transform you from the inside out. Now the reason that He can transform you in this way is that He dwells in you. The Apostle Paul asked the Christians at Corinth, "Do you not know that you are the temple of God and that the Spirit of God dwells in you?" (1 Cor. 3:16). But not only is this transformation possible, it's *vitally* important.

You see, the Holy Spirit dwells in you as a direct result of the blood Jesus shed on the cross. He purchased us with His blood, our entire spirit, soul, and body. We're His—no longer enslaved to our desires, but free to follow His will.

The Spirit Brings Life Instead of Death.

Can I let you in on something—one of the main reasons I strive to continually be in the presence of the Holy Spirit is because *He is so alive.* I love to experience His life. Now when I talk about life, I mean three things.

First, we experience His life when we are born again. The Lord made that clear when He told Nicodemus in John 3: "Most assuredly, I say to you, unless one is born of water and the Spirit, he cannot enter the kingdom of God. That which is born of flesh is flesh, and that which is born of Spirit is spirit" (vv. 5, 6). Jesus added an exclamation point to this when he declared, "It is the Spirit who gives life; the flesh profits nothing. The words that I speak to you are spirit, and they are life" (John 6:63).

Second, we experience His life as we are touched by His resurrection power and are quickened. In Romans 8, Paul declares, "If the Spirit of Him who raised Jesus from the dead dwells in you, He who raised Christ from the dead will also give life to your mortal bodies through His Spirit who dwells in you" (Rom. 8:11). Hallelujah for the empty tomb!

Third, we experience His life as He touches our minds and enables us to think on the things of God. Notice this remarkable passage in Romans 8: "For those who live according to the flesh set their minds on the things of the flesh, but those who live according to the Spirit, the things of the Spirit. For to be carnally minded is death, *but to be spiritually minded is life and peace*" (vv. 5, 6). Notice that those who live according to Holy Spirit set their minds on the Holy Spirit. And what is the result of this? *Life* and *peace.*

The Holy Spirit Is Our Seal and Guarantee.

After you receive Jesus Christ as Savior, something wonderful takes place. The Bible declares: "In Him you also trusted, after you heard the word of truth, the gospel of your salvation; in whom also, having believed, you were sealed with the Holy Spirit of promise" (Eph. 1:13). This sealing guarantees three things:

- Ownership: He seals us and makes us His own
- Authenticity: He seals us to show that we are His own
- Completion: He seals us to guarantee we will be fully His own, *with* Him and *like* Him.

In the ancient world, people would mark valuable property with their personal seal so that there would be no doubt about who owned it. When we trusted Christ, God put His seal of ownership on us when He gave us the Holy Spirit. The Bible says: "Who hath also sealed us, and given the earnest of the Spirit in our hearts" (2 Cor. 1:22 KJV).

Seals also functioned as an official guarantee of the correctness of the contents of a particular thing.[1] How do you know if someone is really a Christian? The answer is simple—do they have the Holy Spirit? "Now if anyone does not have the Spirit of Christ, he is not His" (Rom. 8:9). No seal, no authenticity.

The seal of the Holy Spirit in the life of the believer is God's guarantee that He will redeem us, form Christ in us, and finally and fully free us from the power and presence of sin.

The seal of the Holy Spirit, as wonderful as it is, is only a deposit, a down payment of the wonders that are awaiting us: "having believed, you were sealed with the

Holy Spirit of promise, who is the guarantee of our inheritance until the redemption of the purchased possession,
to the praise of His glory" (Eph. 1:13, 14). But to be sure,
our experience of the Holy Spirit *is* a taste, for the full
payment will be of the same kind as the down payment.[2]

This is why Paul gives us such a solemn warning in
Ephesians 4:30. God owns us, God has authenticated
us, God has given us a foretaste of glory, and God has
committed to bring us to glory. In light of all of these
wondrous things, we must never "grieve the Holy Spirit
of God, by whom you were sealed for the day of redemption" (Eph. 4:30).

The Spirit Sanctifies.

The Lord Jesus in His Word declared that
every believer should be sanctified—set
apart unto God, both *positionally* and *practically*. Do you understand what it means to
be "set apart"? Think about this, when you're in the
grocery store and you select one box of detergent from
many that are just like it and place it in your cart, the
box you have purchased has now been "set apart," it is
devoted to your use and yours alone. And so it is when
we trust Christ, God selects us, takes us into His family,
"sets us apart," sanctifying us for His use.

And how were we "set apart?" *By the Holy Spirit.*
The Bible says: "God hath from the beginning chosen
you to salvation through sanctification of the Spirit and
belief of the truth" (2 Thess. 2:13 KJV). The moment
we were born again, we became *saints* by position in
God's sight because the righteousness of Jesus Christ
was applied to our account by the Holy Spirit. "The
Scriptures teach that the moment a man believes in
Christ he is sanctified. This is clear from the fact that

believers are called saints in the New Testament irrespective of their spiritual attainments (1 Cor. 1:2; Eph. 1:1; Col. 1:2; Heb. 10:10; Jude 3). Of the Corinthians, Paul explicitly says that they 'were sanctified' (1 Cor. 6:11), though he also declared that they were 'still fleshly' (1 Cor. 3:3).[3] In other words, even though these Corinthians didn't act particularly sanctified, the Bible declares they *were* (as far as God was concerned) sanctified.

But not only are we *positionally* sanctified at salvation, we are called to live up to our exalted position in Christ by *practically* living out our sanctification through a life of personal holiness. In this aspect of sanctification as well the Holy Spirit has a crucial role in four key areas.

- *First,* He frees us from the death grip of our sinful nature. "For the law of the Spirit of life in Christ Jesus has made me free from the law of sin and death" (Rom. 8:2).

- *Second,* He actively fights against the manifestation of the sinful nature in our lives: "For the sinful nature desires what is contrary to the Spirit, and the Spirit what is contrary to the sinful nature. They are in conflict with each other, so that you do not do what you want" (Gal. 5:17 NIV).

- *Third,* He partners with you when you determine to put the ax to the sin in your life. "For if you live according to the flesh you will die; but if you through the Spirit put to death the deeds of the body, you will live" (Rom. 8:13). He labors with us when we have the courage to take seriously God's words for us: "Pursue peace with all men, and holiness, without which no one will see the Lord" (Heb. 12:14).

- *Fourth,* He actively counteracts sin in our life. When we surrender to Him, His presence in our life naturally and actively counters our sinful nature. The manifesting of this countering work is the fruit of the Spirit (Gal. 5:22, 23). As Roy Hession said in *The Calvary Road,* "Victorious living and effective soul-winning service are not the product of our better selves and hard endeavors, but are simply the fruit of the Holy Spirit. We are not called upon to produce the fruit, but simply to bear it."[4] The Holy Spirit produces the fruit—all we have to do, then, is manifest what He's doing!

The Spirit Imparts the Character of God.

It is only through the Holy Spirit dwelling in us that we begin to grow in His ways and reflect His nature and qualities.

Not only does God dwell within us, but as we get to know Him we begin to take on His very character. The veil that separated us has been pulled back, "But we all, with unveiled face, beholding as in a mirror the glory of the Lord, are being transformed into the same image from glory to glory, just as by the Spirit of the Lord" (2 Cor. 3:18). Oh I like that!

You see, the Holy Spirit doesn't merely reform us, He *transforms* our character into the character of God ". . . with ever-increasing glory" (v. 18 NIV). As Dean Alford so wonderfully says, "The transformation is effected *by the Spirit*, the Author and Upholder of spiritual life, who 'takes of the things of Christ and *shews them* to us,' . . . who sanctifies us till we are holy as Christ is holy."[5]

The Spirit Strengthens the Inner Man.

When I was a teenager I was always self-conscious about my size. I secretly wished I was bigger.

Even after becoming a Christian, I thought, "Lord, how can you use a little fellow like me?"

When the time came for me to begin my public ministry, those thoughts didn't last long. Every time I began to proclaim God's Word I felt a giant rising up on the inside—filled with strength and authority. At times I would actually listen to myself preach and think, "Is this really me?"

Since the beginning of time, man's measuring stick has been outward appearances, but the Lord looks on the heart. His body-building program is designed to strengthen the *inside* of a man or woman, boy or girl.

The Apostle Paul's prayer in Ephesians was that the Lord would strengthen the Church with might through His Spirit in the inner man, according to the riches of His glory (Eph. 3:16). He also prayed that they would "be filled with all the fullness of God" (v. 19).

And as the Holy Spirit begins to work in the depths of your soul, He strengthens you spiritually with spiritual strength and maturity that gives you an even greater level of faith and enables you to trust God for the *impossible* and believe Him for the *invisible*. No matter what the obstacle, no matter what challenge you may face, you will say with the Psalmist: "The LORD is my light and my salvation; Whom shall I fear? The LORD is the strength of my life; Of whom shall I be afraid?" (Ps. 27:1). That strength comes from deep within as the Holy Spirit brings fearless, and sometimes even *violent* faith to your life.

The Spirit Liberates You.

"Now the Lord is the Spirit; and where the Spirit of the Lord is, there is liberty" (2 Cor. 3:17).

While the law taught us what we were supposed to do, it didn't contain in itself the ability to help us observe the law. We were enslaved to sin. But Christ, by fulfilling the law through His sinless life, vicarious death, and triumphant resurrection set the stage for the Holy Spirit to come and free us from sin, giving us the inner ability to conform to God's character and fulfill the law of the Holy Spirit. We've been liberated by the Holy Spirit *from* sin and *for* service.

I'll never forget my first meeting with my assistant, Curtis Johnson, for this is what happened to him. He was a young man whom I met almost by chance several years ago in our church parking lot, of all places! I saw him wandering around the parking lot aimlessly, as though he was lost, as I was leaving the campus. Since I did not know him, I stopped to ask him, "Are you alright?"

As we talked, I discovered that he had not eaten in three days and was a drug addict who desperately wanted to be free from this bondage. Although he had sought help on many occasions through many organizations, he was still bound by drugs. He knew his life of drugs was going nowhere and he was desperate for help.

I gave him some money and told him to go get something to eat. Then I told him to come back so we could talk some more.

Later as we talked and prayed, he was gloriously saved and delivered from every bondage in his life. He began to attend our church regularly and to grow spiritually. God touched him supernaturally and a miracle began to unfold in his life. As the weeks and months passed, he grew stronger in the things of the Lord. With his past behind him, he began to look for ways to serve the Lord and the doors began to open for him.

That was several years ago, and I am thrilled to tell you that this young man who was set free from the bondage of drugs was truly liberated to serve. He serves faithfully in every service in which I minister and has been a great blessing to me. He travels with our team, in the United States and overseas, and is present in all of our church services. He is truly a living, breathing example of what it means to be liberated from sin for service. He has a great love for the Lord Jesus and has given his life in service to the Master. To God be all the glory!

As Paul said, "the law of the Spirit of life in Christ Jesus has made me free from the law of sin and death" (Rom. 8:2).

I am always happy to tell people that Heaven is going to be filled with imperfect people who have been made perfect by the work of Christ at Calvary. This mighty work is available to us through His Spirit.

The Spirit Brings Renewal. In the fascinating book, *The Day America Told the Truth,* the authors ask Americans what they would most want to change about themselves in order to fulfill their potential as humans.[6] How would you answer this question? What would you say?

Although your answer might be the outgrowth of deep thought and soul searching, here's the top two responses of the American people:

- I want to be rich.
- I want to be thin.

Now this is certainly pathetic and shallow—but hardly a news flash, is it? This probably doesn't surprise you for as you know it's almost impossible to open a magazine or watch television without being barraged by advertisements or infomercials offering the promise of health, wealth, youth, and vitality—from weight-reduction spas to vitamin supplements to fitness equipment.

Attempting to roll back the clock on our physical condition, however, is only a temporary solution. And no matter how easy it is to buy real estate with no money down or flatten your flabby stomach, spiritual renewal is not available through an 800 number, it cannot be purchased—but it is *freely* offered to you *through the Holy Spirit.*

Who is the source of that renewal? *The blessed Holy Spirit.* It is "not by works of righteousness which we have done, but according to His mercy He saved us, through the washing of regeneration and renewing of the Holy Spirit" (Titus 3:5). Did you notice that? The Holy Spirit not only *regenerates,* He *renews.* Now renewal here doesn't mean to turn back the clock, it means a new you! A new *quality* of life. Now a tummy trimmer may make you feel better about yourself, but the Holy Spirit will give you *a whole new self,* and help you to do your "spiritual exercise." The Bible tells us to "reject profane and old wives' fables, and exercise yourself toward godliness. For bodily exercise profits a little, but godliness is profitable for all things, having promise of the life that now is and of that which is to come" (1 Tim. 4:7, 8).

The Spirit Brings You Hope.

Hope is looking forward to something with confidence or expectation.[7] Hope is based on love, that is, that the One who loves us will do what He promised because of His love, and the Bible says that the Holy Spirit gives hope when we are going through difficulties.

As God's beloved child, you can count on Him to be actively at work in those hard times to refine you. As a result: "tribulation produces perseverance; and perseverance, character; and character, hope" (Rom. 5:3, 4).

And the Bible goes on to say: "And hope does not disappoint us, because God has poured out his love into our hearts by the Holy Spirit, whom he has given us" (Rom. 5:5 NIV). The love of God, poured into our hearts by the Holy Spirit is the proof. Like the gentle rain which nurtures the plant, the Holy Spirit pours into our hearts the "rain" of spiritual refreshment and encouragement in the midst of our hard times.[8]

God gives hope, and as you trust Him in the hard times, He sends a mighty torrent of joy and peace to your heart, so much so that you can overflow with hope. How? By the power of the Holy Spirit: "Now may the God of hope fill you with all joy and peace in believing, that you may abound in hope by the power of the Holy Spirit" (Rom. 15:13).

But not only does the Spirit give hope in the midst of the difficulties of the present, He also give us hope for the joys of the future: For we through the Spirit eagerly wait for the hope of righteousness by faith" (Gal. 5:5). Are you homesick for heaven? Do you find yourself yearning for the Rapture? Do you say, "Even so, come quickly Lord Jesus"? Do you yearn for a new body and a new nature? I do. The Bible calls it "the blessed hope—the glorious appearing of our great God and Savior, Jesus Christ" (Titus 2:13 NIV). Who is the source of this hope? Galatians 5:5 declares that it is the Holy Spirit who lives within us.

The Holy Spirit Gives Comfort. The first time Jesus ever referred to the Holy Spirit as the "Comforter" was the night before He was betrayed. Responding to the sadness of His disciples because of the fact that He was leaving them, He said "I will pray the Father, and He shall give you *another Comforter,* that he may abide with you for ever" (John 14:16, emphasis added).

Now this word *comforter* is an interesting word. It is also translated by such words as "counselor" or "helper." "It is a legal term, but with a broader meaning than 'counsel for the defense' . . . . It referred to any person who helped someone in trouble with the law."[9] So then the Holy Spirit dwells within us, counseling, helping, comforting, taking up our cause when we need His help.

What did Jesus mean when He said there would be *another* (Greek: *allos*) Comforter? He meant that the coming Holy Spirit would be *just like Himself.* He was saying "one besides Me and in addition to Me but just like Me. He will do in my absence what I would do if I were physically present with you."[10] It is so clear now why the Holy Spirit can be called the "Spirit of Christ" (Rom. 8:9) and "the Spirit of His Son" (Gal. 4:6).

So the Lord Jesus promised He would send a Helper just like Himself, and on the Day of Pentecost when the Holy Spirit came the Savior delivered on His promise. The mighty work of the Holy Spirit at Pentecost resulted in thousands believing on Christ and experiencing first-hand the comforting work of the Holy Spirit. As a result, churches were established throughout Judea, Galilee, and Samaria. Even during times of persecution, those early believers walked "in the fear of the Lord and in the comfort of the Holy Spirit, [and] they were [greatly] multiplied" (Acts 9:31).

The Spirit Gives Us Assurance. One of the mountain-top passages of Scripture is Galatians 4:1–6: "Now I say that the heir, as long as he is a child, does not differ at all from a slave, though he is master of all, but is under guardians and stewards until the time appointed by the father. Even so we, when we children, were in bondage under the elements of the world. But when the fullness of the time had come, God sent forth His Son, born of a woman, born under the law, to redeem those who were under the law, that we might receive adoption as sons. And because you are sons, God has sent forth the Spirit of His Son into your hearts, crying out, 'Abba, Father!' "

Now I want those of you who have experienced the heartache of a wrenching home situation in your childhood to pay special attention. None of us *come from* perfect homes, and none of us *provide* perfect homes, no matter how hard we try. But perhaps your childhood was characterized by abuse, lack of love, insecurity, or turmoil. And beneath the anger or even the denial are deep feelings of hurt and profound questions about your worth or lovability as a person.

Believe me I can relate to you. I've lived through a war, endured the agony of a transcontinental move, changing languages, schools, friends, countries, and cultures. I've experienced the devastation of parental rejection when I was born again and trusted Jesus as Savior. When Christ found me, I was basically a destroyed person with regard to my self-image, and yet it was at these very points that the Holy Spirit provided such comfort and assurance that I was His—that I actually belonged to Jesus my Savior and God my heavenly Father.

You see, when we trust Christ, the Holy Spirit transforms us from strangers into God's children, adopting us into God's wonderful family. Now sometimes in the natural children taunt each other with the charge that they're not really the biological children of their parents, but rather have somehow been adopted, as if an adopted child is somehow inferior to a biological child. But not so in God's family. God adopts each of us into His family, making us heirs of God and joint heirs with His beloved Son, Jesus, giving us the privileges that come with this.

Whatever your background, when you trust Christ, you become a member in the best family there is. And one of the great works of the Spirit is that He "bears witness with our spirit that we are children of God" (Rom. 8:16).

Deep on the inside we receive the knowledge that we're no longer outsiders. All inferiority, the sense of not belonging, the anger—can all be gone, replaced by the gentle voice of the Holy Spirit saying, "It's behind you now, the Father loves you and you're in His family now."

And this happens at the level of our spirit—the witness is not *to* our spirit, it is witness *with* our spirit by the *Holy Spirit*. The word for "bear witness" means to confirm or testify in support of someone. This word often appears in official documents from the first century next to the signature of the person who witnessed the signing of the agreement, thus validating that the people whose names were on the agreement actually signed it.[11] Do you see the point of this word picture? The Holy Spirit is in dialog with our spirit, saying, "Yes, I was there when you trusted Christ. Yes, you've been adopted into God's family, I witnessed it. Yes, you are a full member of the family. Yes, God is your loving heavenly Father. No, you don't need to be insecure about your new family."

The Holy Spirit and the Mind of the Believer

The Holy Spirit reveals the things of God. From the first small steps of my Spirit-led walk I knew I would be lost without the revelation of the Holy Spirit. The Holy Spirit delights to make things known to us that transcend our own thinking. You see, "no one knows the things of God except the Spirit of God" (1 Cor. 2:11). And God has delighted to make His truth known to us through the Holy Spirit. The Word says God has "revealed them to us through His Spirit" (v. 10).

I have spent thousands of hours studying the Bible and reflecting on practically every word, but nothing equates to what happens when the Holy Spirit begins to make known to you the things of the Kingdom.

You can own every lexicon, concordance, and Bible dictionary ever printed and still be woefully lacking in *spiritual* knowledge. Now don't get me wrong, I have a large library and I'm a voracious reader, but only the Spirit can fully reveal God's mysteries. After all, He is the author of the Book.

The Lord showed the Apostle Paul things he would

not have discovered on his own. This is what the Greek word translated "mystery" means. For example, God told him that both the Jews and Gentiles were to make up the body of Christ. This was something "which in other ages was not made known to the sons of men, as it has now been revealed by the Spirit to His holy apostles and prophets" (Eph. 3:5).

The Bible says that what we have been given is not the spirit of the world, "but the Spirit who is from God, that we might know the things that have been freely given to us by God" (1 Cor. 2:12).

The average person can't comprehend the things of the Spirit: "they are foolishness to him; nor can he know them, because they are spiritually discerned. But he who is spiritual judges all things" (vv. 14, 15).

Those who refuse to "plug in" to the Source of spiritual wisdom will never understand what the Lord has imparted to us, regardless of how studiously they study or how diligently they investigate. What will always set us apart is that "we have the mind of Christ" (v. 16).

The Holy Spirit Brings the Works of Christ to Your Remembrance.

Jesus extended this wonderful promise about the Holy Spirit to comfort the Apostles on the eve of His arrest and crucifixion: "He will teach you all things, and bring to your remembrance all things that I said to you" (John 14:26). This same marvelous promise applies to us today as well.

During the delivery of almost every message, the Holy Spirit brings things to my remembrance about the Lord Jesus that I did not plan to say. It's the Holy Spirit doing His work. Now like any preacher of the Gospel worthy of his calling, I believe that the Lord expects me to be totally prepared for the responsibility of feeding His sheep, and I believe that part of Jesus' promise here occurs when I study. I must tell you, however, that no matter how much time I put into the preparation of a message, the Lord also has things He wants to communicate, and I want to be oh so sensitive to that.

Some people are surprised when I show them the books of sermon outlines in my office—thinking that there is some kind of conflict between preparing the message and being open to the leading of the Holy Spirit. Nothing could be further from the truth! The reality is that I rely on the Holy Spirit, both as I study and as I deliver what the Holy Spirit has led me to prepare.

The Holy Spirit teaches truth.

As Spirit-led believers, we can depend upon the Holy Spirit to reveal truth to us as well as protect us from error. This is our confidence because it is promised to those who know God. "We are of God. He who knows God hears us; he who is not of God does not hear us. By this we know the spirit of truth and the spirit of error" (1 John 4:6).

I experienced this very thing recently while browsing in a large bookstore. I came across a new release which caught my attention, and, because I had heard something about the book a few weeks earlier, I thought I'd look through it quickly.

The title brought a certain measure of curiosity to mind about the contents. Scanning the book jacket quickly revealed that the book dealt with the author's after-death experience. I continued to page through the book, reading over some chapter titles, glancing at pages here and there. As I explored the contents of the book, "something" made me pause and examine the open page before my eyes more carefully. It seemed as though an inner alarm was going off. "What's wrong?" I asked myself.

The very moment the question came to mind, my eyes came to rest upon some text which clearly explained my inner turmoil. This was a book with a New Age message! But it was well disguised and sounded like many other marvelous stories I had read about individuals who have had an after-death experience, come back to life, and shared their glorious glimpse of eternity as believers.

I quickly placed the book back on the shelf and left the bookstore. As I walked away, I thought about how subtle the devil is to hide his lies and snares between the covers of an innocent-looking book. But how glorious to know that my wonderful Companion, the Holy Spirit, never leaves me and was beside me in that bookstore. It was He who shined a light on the darkness deceptively hidden in the book.

So how can we know if something contains truth or error? We can't just make a judgment based on how we feel. The first thing I want to know is what does the book say about the Lord Jesus, for He is the Way, the Truth, and the Life (John 14:6).

Today, "it is the Spirit who bears witness, because the Spirit is truth" (1 John 5:6). The Holy Spirit is an instructor, but He's so much more than that, He is the truth. He is the teacher of what is trustworthy and reliable. He is the source of all truth.

*The Holy Spirit causes you to be
occupied with spiritual things.*

A well-respected friend of mine who is also in full-time ministry attended our 1994 Atlanta Miracle Crusade. When he arrived at the arena, he asked if he could speak to me briefly. But because the service was about to begin, it was not possible so he was ushered to his seat.

The presence of the Holy Spirit was so intense throughout that service that from the downbeat of the first song by the crusade choir the atmosphere was electric—charged with God's power and presence.

The service order was similar to most crusade services. We enjoyed such rich worship as thousands joined in unison to lift up the name of Jesus Christ. The special music by the musicians added greatly to the service and it continued to build in power and intensity.

As the anointing descended for the miraculous, the intensity of God's presence increased greatly. The anointing of the Holy Spirit was evident. The massive auditorium was charged with God's power, and miracles began happening everywhere. People in the auditorium were standing as I asked those who were healed to make their way to the front to testify of God's healing touch. There were glorious testimonies of healing and tears of joy and gratitude as one after another declared, "I've been healed!"

As the service was about to close, I invited those who wanted to ask Jesus Christ to forgive their sins and be their Lord and Savior to come forward and experience the greatest miracle—salvation. People responded immediately from everywhere. It took several minutes for them to make their way to the front. Thousands came forward.

As I prayed the sinner's prayer with those who had responded, I looked across the sea of faces before me. Some prayed fervently and with conviction, others wept uncontrollably as they repented. An eternal transformation was taking place before my eyes.

As the prayer concluded, I was about to close the service and dismiss the crowd, when suddenly a young couple standing at the crowded altar caught my attention. In the natural there was nothing which distinguished them from the rest of the crowd. Yet, my full attention was suddenly focused on them. I paused for a moment. Then, pointing in their direction, I said, "Bring this couple to the platform."

As they stood facing me, I began to speak to them with boldness. Although I had never met nor seen them before, the words I spoke seemed to touch something deep inside them. They stood there, hand in hand, trembling and crying, as I told them how they had run from God, attempting to ignore a divine calling for ministry upon their lives. As I spoke, they nodded to confirm what I was saying. I laid hands on them and asked the Lord to deliver them from every bondage which held them captive. Each word came with such force and power.

I paused briefly to ask, "Who are these people?" A guest minister who was seated on the platform stepped forward immediately. He was crying too. He walked straight toward the young couple and hugged them. I looked at the threesome, questioningly, as they stood there crying and embracing.

Finally he turned toward me and began to speak.

Wiping his tears away, he began by telling me that this young couple was his nephew and his nephew's wife. He said he had received a distressing telephone call from them the night before. "Uncle," his nephew said, "we're at the end of our rope. We can't take it any longer. The drugs, the alcohol, and so many other things in our lives have such a hold on us that we feel like there is no hope." A feeling of total despair was evident in his voice.

His nephew went on to tell how he had even taken an overdose of drugs combined with alcohol the night before in an attempt to end his life. However, his mother had somehow found him, and while praying intensely for him had gotten him medical help. His nephew's call was an obvious cry for help.

After a lengthy telephone conversation, he had finally convinced them to catch the next available flight and meet him to attend this meeting. "Just wait 24 hours," he had told them, "and let me fly you both here to meet me. I'm going to a Benny Hinn crusade tomorrow night and I want you both to go with me." Nothing to lose, they had accepted. He had provided the airline tickets and trusted God for a miracle.

And there they were, standing on the platform, their arms wrapped around each other and their uncle. Only moments ago they had been bound by sin, but now, as I looked into their faces, the transformation that had taken place deep within showed on their faces. Their countenance was now filled with hope and peace. The transforming power of God's love and forgiveness and the visible work of the Holy Spirit were evident. The greatest miracle had just happened before my eyes. It was glorious!

The miracle starts in the thought life, and the agent

is the Holy Spirit, who *can* give you the victory. "For those who live according to the flesh set their minds on the things of the flesh, but those who live according to the Spirit, the things of the Spirit. For to be carnally minded is death, but to be spiritually minded is life and peace" (Rom. 8:5, 6).

This young couple had come to the meeting with thoughts of hopelessness, but the Holy Spirit changed all that. When they left that evening, their future held life and peace.

The Holy Spirit leads and guides.

The story about the young couple is not over yet. As the three of them stood before me, arm-in-arm, tears flowing, my friend (and their uncle) began to tell me something absolutely incredible. He had arrived at the arena that evening just as the service was about to begin. His nephew and wife had been seated somewhere in the arena. Meanwhile, he had asked to speak to me briefly prior to the service, hoping to tell me of the serious need of his nephew and wife. However, because the service was about to begin, he had been taken straight to the platform where he had been seated throughout the service. He had not been able to make me aware of their presence or their need, but the Holy Spirit had!

That guidance is available today. In fact, it's not just available today, it's expected that God's children *will* follow that guidance: "For as many as are led by the Spirit of God, these are sons of God" (Rom. 8:14).

Months later I saw my friend at another meeting where he gave me an update on his nephew. He said that since their glorious experience at the Atlanta crusade, they have been attending church regularly, never missing a service, and are now in a training program in preparation for full-time ministry. To God be all the glory!

The Holy Spirit bears witness of Lord Jesus.

In every great outpouring of the Spirit, the focus has been upon the centrality of the Lord Jesus. During the historic Azusa Street revival in Los Angeles in 1906, Frank Bartleman was one of the central figures. In his chronicle of the events, He wrote, "Any work that exalts the Holy Ghost or the 'gifts' above Jesus will finally land up in fanaticism. Whatever causes us to exalt and love Jesus is well and safe. The reverse will ruin all. The Holy Ghost is a great light, but focused on Jesus always, for His revealing."[12] In every great ministry, the focus has been upon the centrality of the Lord Jesus. In every great Christian, the focus has been upon the centrality of the Lord Jesus.

Do you remember what Jesus said, "When the helper comes . . . He will testify of Me" (John 15:26)?

After Pentecost, Peter preached that God had raised up the crucified Christ, "And we are His witnesses to these things, and *so also is the Holy Spirit* whom God has given to those who obey Him." (Acts 5:32, emphasis added). Notice here then that the Holy Spirit was not merely *a* witness, He *bore* witness through the miraculous signs and wonders commencing with the resurrection right through to the ascension and extending into the very foundation of the early Church. And, I might add, right up to today.

Every time I preach the gospel, I pray that men and women will come to faith in Christ. You see, in my opinion the greatest miracle in the world today happens when a person trusts Christ as His Savior. Yet where does this confession come from? The Apostle Paul was clear when He said that "no one can say that Jesus is Lord except by the Holy Spirit." (1 Cor. 12:3). For it is the Holy Spirit who performs the greatest miracle, enabling us to say with all our heart, "Jesus is Lord of my life," and this miracle is only the beginning—it is only the introduction for what happens when He works *through* us to reach the world.

10

The Presence and the Power

You say that your Jesus heals—prove it!"
Those were the words of a crippled man who walked to the platform with his family and interrupted my message.

At the invitation of some Roman Catholic priests I was preaching in a small village called Spanish in northern Ontario. It was 1975.

Almost everyone in the audience was from a tribe of North American Indians who lived in that area. They were big people whose creased, deep-lined faces seemed chiseled in stone.

"What are these folks thinking?" I wondered as I began to minister. Their countenance showed absolutely no emotion—no nods or smiles of agreement on their stoic faces. They just stared at me.

My message was on God's power to save, heal, and fill with His Spirit. About half way through my sermon, and to my surprise, I saw a young Indian man and his family slowly walking up the aisle toward the platform. The husband had a severe limp. I thought,

"Lord, this is wonderful. They are coming to give their lives to You."

But they didn't even hesitate at the altar. Nobody stopped them as they walked up the steps of the platform and finally stood right in front of me, staring at me.

Dumbfounded, I stopped preaching and said, "Can I help you?"

The man looked at me sternly and said, "You have been telling us that Jesus is alive today. I am twenty-eight years old and I am crippled. My wife has cancer. Look! My little girl's skin is bleeding because of a severe case of eczema. No one has been able to help her. You say that your Jesus heals—prove it!"

Now the congregation was staring at me with even more intensity. I glanced at the priests and they were praying. One of them looked like an Old Testament prophet, with a beard so long it almost touched the floor. I called them over to me and said, "Gentleman, let's kneel down and call upon the Lord."

And then I prayed, "Lord Jesus, this man tells me to prove what I am preaching. But, Lord, I'm not preaching *my* gospel. I'm preaching *your* gospel. *You* prove it!"

Although I prayed with boldness, I wasn't sure what to do next. So, I waited. It seemed as though time stood still at that moment. Not a sound could be heard. I didn't know what was happening, but I wasn't about to open my eyes. I just knelt there, eyes closed, and kept praying.

Suddenly there was a loud noise and another. It startled me and I opened my eyes to see what had happened. As I looked around I saw the man, his wife, and daughter all lying on the floor. The Spirit of God had descended with such power that the man and his entire family fell backward to the floor. By this time everyone in the auditorium was looking at me, wondering what had happened. Almost suspended in time, we all waited to see what would happen next.

Finally the family members began to get up. As the father looked at his daughter, he began to shout and cry all at the same time. As he examined her arms, he shouted, "They're not bleeding any more! It's a miracle!"

As I looked at her little arms, I was astonished to find that not only had the bleeding stopped; it looked like she had new skin on her arms. Almost at the same time, her father began to run around the building, saying, "I'm healed! I'm healed." His crippled leg was restored. As his wife began to examine herself, she also found that God had touched her too.

The presence of the Holy Spirit so changed that meeting that those expressionless Indians suddenly lifted their hands and began to praise and worship the Lord. Many asked Christ to be their Savior that night.

And I realized that when God's Spirit is at work there is nothing we need to demonstrate or prove. He uses us in service, but it is His power, His presence and His proclamation that brings life.

The Holy Spirit Opens Heaven

The work of the Holy Spirit is not only *inward,* it is also *upward* and *outward.* He brings us into a new relationship with God and prepares us for service.

Every time I welcome the Holy Spirit He opens the portals of heaven and ushers me into the presence of the Father.

The Holy Spirit Brings You Into God's Presence.

"It's like heaven on earth."

That's how people describe their feelings when they enter the atmosphere of the anointing. It may happen in a large crusade, a small prayer meeting or when you are alone with God.

When the Holy Spirit begins to do His work any barriers between you and the Lord are removed. Suddenly you are *close* to Him. Some people describe it as "being lifted into the heavenlies." Others say, "I feel His presence surround me right where I am."

Because of the completed work of Christ, the Comforter is here to make heaven real. "For through Him we both have access by one Spirit to the Father" (Eph. 2:18).

It's amazing how our perspective changes when the Lord is near. Mountains become foothills. Tears become smiles. Moses was able to endure the wilderness because God told him, "My presence will go with you, and I will give you rest" (Ex. 33:14). And we can say, "In Your presence is fullness of joy" (Ps. 16:11).

The Holy Spirit Helps In Prayer.

Prayer is an awesome privilege—and an awesome responsibility. I like the way Evelyn Christenson puts it: "It is awesome to realize that at the end of our lives we will be the sum total of our responses to God's answers to our prayers, for God has chosen to be limited in His next action by our response to His previous answer. The final outcome of our lives is decided by a lifelong series of responses of God's answers to our prayers. The way we respond to God and then He, in turn, to us actually determines the directions our lives will take."[1] In this important task of praying, the Holy Spirit helps us in two ways: He helps us *when* we pray, and He helps us *by* praying for us.

There is a marvelous way to pray that's mentioned in the Word. It's called praying "in the Spirit." Really, it's the only way to pray. Jude 20 contains the command, "building yourselves up on your most holy faith, *praying in the Holy Spirit*" (Jude 20, emphasis added). To the Christians at Ephesus, Paul said they should be "praying always with *all prayer and supplication in the Spirit*" (Eph. 6:18, emphasis added). Now I enjoy praying in a heavenly language, and do so often, but praying "in the Spirit" is much more than this. It also means to pray in the realm of the Holy Spirit and in the power of the Holy Spirit. This is one of the many reasons why living in fellowship with the Holy Spirit is so important—it allows us to experience His power and His presence when we pray.

But not only does He make His power available to us *when* we pray, He also prays *for us!* Listen to the marvelous truth of Romans 8:26: "The Spirit also helps in our weaknesses. For we do not know what we should pray for as we ought, but the Spirit Himself makes inter- cession for us with groanings which cannot be uttered" (Rom. 8:26).

Let's break this down phrase by phrase. *The Spirit helps:* literally, "keeps on helping"—He doesn't help us just now and then, He continuously helps us. The word "help" is an interesting one, it pictures someone coming to the aid of another to help them carry a heavy load.[2] Isn't this wonderful? The things that capture our attention and drive us to our knees *are* heavy—too heavy to bear alone, and often too complex to express with words alone.

Notice that the Holy Spirit helps *in our weaknesses. For we do not know what we should pray for as we ought.* Actually, that word should be translated, "weakness." "He helps our entire *weakness,* but especially as it manifests itself in relation to our prayer life, and particularly in relation to knowing what to pray for at the present moment. While we wait for our full redemption [vv. 18–25] we need guidance in the particulars of prayer."[3]

The Holy Spirit helps us through *making intercession for us.* Notice actually that the text says, "the Spirit *Himself.*" No intermediaries, no agents—the Third Person of the Trinity, very God Himself, intervening in our behalf. The word "intercession" is also a picturesque word depicting "rescue by one who 'happens on' one who is in trouble" and pleads or intercedes on their behalf.[4] Don't let your circumstances, no matter how distressing, keep you from prayer. The Holy Spirit is waiting to plead your case before the Father.

The Holy Spirit intercedes with *groanings which cannot be uttered,* or "sighs that baffle words."[5] I love how Bishop Newell explains this: "expresses at once the vastness of our need, our utter ignorance and inability, and the infinite concern of the blessed indwelling Spirit for us. 'Groanings'—what a word! and to be used of the Spirit of the Almighty Himself! How shallow our appreciation of what is done, both by Christ for us, and by the Spirit within us!"[6] And what is the result of all this: *Now He who searches the hearts knows what the mind of the Spirit is, because He makes intercession for the saints according to the will of God.* The Holy Spirit takes our tangled thoughts and emotions, what we're praying for and what we *should* pray for, and with deep emotion brings the right sentiments to the Throne. Hallelujah for the intercessory work of the Holy Spirit!

J. Oswald Sanders sums it up so well: "The Spirit

links Himself with us in our praying and pours His supplications into our own. We may master the technique of prayer and understand its philosophy; we may have unlimited confidence in the veracity and validity of the promises concerning prayer. We may plead them earnestly. But if we ignore the part played by the Holy Spirit, we have failed to use the master key."[7]

The Holy Spirit Inspires Us To Worship.

One of the greatest movements of the Holy Spirit in the world today is the rebirth and revival of worship. In true worship, people meet the Lord with their intellect, will, *and* emotion. That's the difference between a cold, dead service and one that is vibrant and alive with God's presence.

If you've ever been in one of our crusades, you know how *wonderful* the sense of worship is. Occasionally people think it has something to do with me. They compliment me for leading in worship. But you know what? I don't lead in worship—the Holy Spirit does. I may be on the platform, but I'm worshipping the Lord just like everyone else. The Holy Spirit is in control, and I follow His leadings just like everyone else.

Remember, worship isn't singing *about* the Lord and praying that God will meet your needs; worship is lifting your praise *to* the Lord in love, devotion, and adoration. Jesus said, "God is Spirit, and those who worship Him must worship in spirit and truth" (John 4:24).

Who gives us the ability to really worship? The Holy Spirit: "For it is we who are the circumcision, *we who worship by the Spirit of God,* who glory in Christ Jesus, and who put no confidence in the flesh—" (Phil. 3:3 NIV, emphasis added). It is the Holy Spirit who reveals

Jesus to us. And the more we see of His beauty, His holiness, and His glory, how can we do anything else but bow before the King of Heaven to adore and magnify His name?

The Holy Spirit Leads Us To Give Thanks.

Scripture tell us to "be filled with the Spirit, speaking to one another in psalms and hymns and spiritual songs, singing and making melody in your heart to the Lord, giving thanks always for all things to God the Father in the name of our Lord Jesus Christ, submitting to one another in the fear of God" (Eph. 5:2, 21).

Did you notice the four results of being controlled by the Holy Spirit: He'll anoint your speaking, He'll anoint your singing, He'll anoint your relationships ("submitting to one another"), and He'll anoint your perspective ("giving thanks *always* for *all things*").

It is so *natural* to be ungrateful, and it's just as natural to be thankful only for the things that seem good at the time. But when the Holy Spirit has control, you'll be able to give thanks all the time, and for everything that comes your way—even the things that are not pleasant. The Word says, "In everything give thanks; for this is the will of God in Christ Jesus for you" (1 Thess. 5:18).

When you are walking with the Holy Spirit, He is constantly prompting you to say, "Thank you, Lord." You'll experience what Paul wrote about when he described his own experience of "thanking God without ceasing" (1 Thess. 2:13).

We are to give thanks at all times and in all things. But what if you don't feel like being thankful? I heard a story from a friend about this very thing. He said that one day while in prayer he just didn't *feel* like saying "thank you" to the Lord for anything. Oh yes, he knew that he had a great deal for which to be grateful, but he just didn't feel it deep within. So he began this exercise in gratitude. He looked at his toe, and moved it back and forth. As he moved it, he said, "Thank you, Lord, for my toe. Thank you that I have a toe and that I have no pain in it." Then he began to move his ankle. No pain, no stiffness, it worked perfectly. He prayed, "Thank you, Lord, for my ankle and that it works perfectly just as you created it." He looked at his foot, stood firmly on it, even standing on his tip toes. And as he did, he continued to thank the Lord. He moved on to his leg. As he moved his leg, bending his knee and standing on his foot, he said, "Thank you, Lord, for my legs. Thank you that I can stand, that I can walk, and that I have no pain in my legs." He continued on, thanking the Lord Jesus for a strong back, arms, hands, fingers, and so on. By the time he finished, he was weeping and thanking the Lord for all his blessings. His exercise of gratitude had become a prayer of thanksgiving from the depths of his soul.

It's a wonderful feeling to be able to say, "Bless the LORD, O my soul . . . And forget not all His benefits" (Ps. 103:2).

Now be very careful—even though the Third Person of the Trinity is at work in our lives, He must not become the object of our praise and thanksgiving. Instead, we are instructed to recognize the Father and the Son as the source of all good things. But we thank them *through* the Holy Spirit.

If you haven't experienced the healing that comes

from this thankfulness, don't wait another moment, let the Holy Spirit bring healing to your perspective!

Power for Service

When the Holy Spirit entered my life He did not immediately thrust me out into ministry. First He changed me on the inside and gave me a relationship with the Father and the Son. I was in His "school of the Spirit" for twelve months before I preached my first sermon in a little church in Oshawa, Ontario. Day after day He taught me from the Word and prepared me for what was ahead.

Instead of asking, "What will the Holy Spirit do for me?" we need to ask, "How will the Holy Spirit use *me* to reach my generation?" Reread that last sentence. I meant every word I said. If God can use a murderer like Paul, a meek man like Moses, and a shy, stuttering boy like Benny Hinn, *imagine what He wants to do through you!* He has called and empowered each and every one of us. Believe in that empowerment and surrender now.

The Holy Spirit Gives Us Power.

No one will have to tell you when the Holy Spirit enters your life. You will know it. You will sense and feel a sudden surge of power that is unlike anything you have ever known.

This phenomenon is not unexpected. Remember, Jesus told His disciples to tarry in the city of Jerusalem "until you are endued with power from on high" (Luke 24:49). Jesus clarified this when He promised that they would "receive power when the Holy Spirit has come upon you" (Acts 1:8).

When that mighty power arrived like wind and fire at Pentecost, people were dramatically transformed. The

Apostle Peter was changed from a coward who had denied the Lord to a fearless preacher who saw crowds of 3,000 and 5,000 come to Christ. What Doctor Luke wrote of in the book of Acts was also the experience of Paul as He took the Gospel to Thessalonica: "knowing, beloved brethren, your election by God. For our gospel did not come to you in word only, but also in power, and in the Holy Spirit and in much assurance, as you know what kind of men we were among you for your sake" (1 Thess. 1:4–5).

The history of the church is filled with all kinds of people—including timid, frail and often unprepared men and women who were changed into spiritual dynamos by the power of the Holy Spirit. I should know: I am one of them.

Paul prayed for believers to accept the fact that they would "be strengthened with might through His Spirit" (Eph. 3:16).

The Holy Spirit Performs Miracles Through Us.

We know that Jesus performed many miracles, yet He said of those who believe in Him: "Greater than these shall ye do" (John 14:12 KJV).

I wish I could explain signs, wonders, and healing, but I can't. All I know is that they did not cease with the ministry of Christ and the apostles. How can I be sure—at the very least from my own personal experience? I was born with a severe stuttering problem that completely disappeared the moment I stood up to preach my first sermon.

God confirms His Word and bears witness "with signs and wonders, with various miracles, and gifts of the Holy Spirit" (Heb. 2:4). Not just back then, but right now.

Through the ministry the Lord has entrusted to us we have heard the testimonies of thousands of people who have been delivered and healed miraculously. I believe this is only the beginning of a mighty work God is about to do in the world.

Billy Graham said that "as we approach the end of the age I believe we will see a dramatic recurrence of signs and wonders which will demonstrate the power of God to a skeptical world."[8]

The Holy Spirit Liberates Us To Love.

One of the first signs that God's Spirit is at work in your life is that you will have a great love for people—whether they be Christians or non-believers.

As you know, at the outset of my spiritual experience, my family turned against me. But my love for them only deepened until they were drawn to the cross.

The church at Colosse held a special place in Paul's heart, so much so that he said "We always thank God . . . when we pray for you" (Col. 1:3 NIV). Why? Because of their faith and love (vv. 4, 5). And where did that faith and love come from? *The Holy Spirit* (v. 8)! As Dean Alford says, "This love is emphatically a gift, and in its full reference the chief gift of the Spirit (Gal. V22; Rom. XV30), and is thus in the elemental region of the Spirit."[9]

It is this love of the Holy Spirit that empowers us to mightily intercede for others, one of the greatest expressions of love we can manifest (Rom. 15:30).

The Holy Spirit Produces The Good Harvest In Us.

The law of sowing and reaping is a well-established divine principle. What we plant determines what we will harvest—whether it is good seed or bad.

Paul somberly warned, "Do not be deceived, God is not mocked; for whatever a man sows, that he will also reap. For he who sows to his flesh will of the flesh reap corruption, but he who sows to the Spirit will of the Spirit reap everlasting life" (Gal. 6:7–8). How do we "sow to the Spirit?" *First,* by, relying on His power to reckon ourselves dead to the works of the flesh, "adultery, fornication, uncleanness, lewdness, idolatry, sorcery, hatred, contentions, jealousies, outbursts of wrath, selfish ambitions, dissensions, heresies, envy, murders, drunkenness, revelries, and the like" (Gal. 5:19–21). *Second,* by relying on the power and presence of the Holy Spirit to manifest the fruit of the Spirit.

The Holy Spirit Produces Fruit In Us.

In the New Testament, Jesus uses the image of a vine with branches to illustrate our relationship to Him. He said, "Abide in Me, and I in you. As the branch cannot bear fruit of itself, unless it abides in the vine, neither can you, unless you abide in Me" (John 15:4).

Then He added: "I am the vine, you are the branches. He who abides in Me, and I in him, bears much fruit; for without Me you can do nothing" (v. 5).

What does the Holy Spirit produce in us? Paul gave us the list. "The fruit of the Spirit is love, joy, peace, longsuffering, kindness, goodness, faithfulness, gentleness, self-control" (Gal. 5:22–23).

The first three describe our relationship to God, the next three our relationship to others, and the final three our inner self.

Notice that "fruit" is used in the singular. This is because the entire crop comes from the same "vine"— and they are all equally important, and should be equally visible. The Holy Spirit is the only source for all of the fruit.

While the gifts of the Holy Spirit are given separately, we are to evidence *all* of the fruit.

The Holy Spirit Gives Us Gifts.

I doubt that I will ever outgrow the thrill of opening a special gift on my birthday or at Christmas. At those times I'm just like a child.

God has gifts for the believer, too. And they are even more wonderful to receive. Now the order of this section and last one is important and intentional: the gifts of the Holy Spirit are meaningless without the fruit of the Holy Spirit (1 Cor. 13:1-3). The vital union with Christ that produces the fruit of the Holy Spirit is the place to start, then you can truly appreciate the marvelous variety of the gifts of the Holy Spirit mentioned in 1 Corinthians 12:8-10:

- Word of wisdom
- Word of knowledge
- Faith
- Healings
- Working of miracles
- Prophecy
- Discerning of spirits
- Tongues
- Interpretation of tongues

There are many gifts which God makes available to His children, nine of which are found in 1 Corinthians 12. What a wonder it is that God both adopts us into His family and equips us to be able to make a genuine contribution to the Savior and His Body, the Church. And make no mistake, every believer is so equipped. The Scripture tells us that "the manifestation of the Spirit is given to each one for the profit of all" (1 Cor. 12:7).[10]

What is the greatest response we can offer to the Giver of gifts? We can put the gift into action. Peter says, "As each one has received a gift, minister it to one another, as good stewards of the manifold grace of God" (1 Peter 4:10).

Don't ever insult the Holy Spirit by thinking your gift is unimportant, or your role unnecessary. He has given you *exactly* the gifts He wants you to have (1 Cor. 12:11). Pastors, help your people understand their gifts and put them to work for the Savior. In my opinion, Howard Snyder puts it so well when he says, "The function of a local church should be to expect, identify and awaken the varied gifts that sleep within the community of believers. When all gifts are affirmed under the leadership of the Holy Spirit and in the context of mutual love, each gift is important and no gift becomes an aberration."[11]

The Holy Spirit Baptizes Believers Into The Body of Christ.

There is a wonderful analogy in Paul's letter to the Christians at Corinth that compares the Church to the human body.

The apostle says that the body is a unit, though it is made up of many parts. "For by one Spirit we were all baptized into one body—whether Jews or Greeks, whether slaves or free—and have all been made to drink into one Spirit" (1 Cor. 12:13).

Even though an individual may have only one gift, they are a valuable part of the body. Even though we may come from different races, continents, and ethnic groups, the Holy Spirit marvelously melds us together into the Body of Christ for the Scripture declares that the Holy Spirit "[distributes spiritual gifts] to each one individually as He wills" (1 Cor. 12:11).

I have seen this demonstrated in such a powerful way at the Crusades. The audience which gathers at a miracle crusade is made up of people from many different denominational backgrounds, many cities from across America, many different races, many continents, and many different backgrounds. Yet, as the service begins, this gathering of thousands of individuals becomes one voice offering up praise and worship in perfect harmony and unity to the Lord Jesus. As we lift our hands and sing the glorious lyrics which exalt and magnify His name, expressing a desire to know Him more, all attention is focused on Him.

> *Fill my cup, Lord, I lift it up, Lord,*
> *Come and quench this thirsting of my soul.*
> *Bread of Heaven, feed me 'til I want no more.*
> *Here's my cup, fill it up, and make me whole.*

At that moment nothing else matters. We only long to be in His presence.

And as members together we are to "Bear one another's burdens, and so fulfill the law of Christ" (Gal. 6:2).

The Holy Spirit Appoints Us To Ministry.

The book of Acts is laden with the details of the initial work of the Holy Spirit in building and broadening the Body of Christ. Now don't be misled, this is also His concern today, and He is calling us all to a ministry to accomplish this. Be sure you're following His leading, and that you're serving where *He* has appointed you. Never force or presume on the Holy Spirit. Be sensitive like the church at Antioch, who heard the Holy Spirit say, "Separate to Me Barnabas and Saul for the work to which I have called them" (Acts 13:2). The leaders at Ephesus knew their calling, and so did everyone else. That's why Paul could say to them: "take heed to yourselves and to all the flock, among which the Holy Spirit has made you overseers" (Acts 20:28).

The old and the young experience unique pressures in ministry, as Peter outlines in 1 Peter 5:1-9:

- Older, more established ministers are to: willingly shepherd, avoid greed, lead eagerly, avoid domineering, lead by example, and concentrate on their future reward.
- Younger, rising ministers are to: submit to their elders, submit to each other, clothe themselves with humility, await God's timing, cast their anxiety on the Lord, and realize that God does care for them, even while in the background.
- All ministers are to: be sober, be vigilant, resist the devil, and remember the sufferings of other believers in the world

The Holy Spirit Gives Direction To Our Lives.

Have you ever been faced with a moment of great decision? I have. And that's when I turn to the Holy Spirit to be my compass and guide.

If you have trusted Christ as your personal Savior, you should absolutely expect His direction and be sensitive to it. After all, "For as many as are led by the Spirit of God, these are sons of God" (Rom. 8:14).

Sometimes He speaks in a whisper; at other times forcefully and with power. Then there are moments that I have an inner feeling I cannot dismiss. Regardless of *how* He speaks to me, it's vital that I hear his voice. He is always ready to clear my path and lead the way.

- He's the One who spoke to Peter at the house of Simon the Tanner and said, "Go downstairs . . . Go with them" (Acts 10:20 NIV).
- He's the One who told Saul and Barnabas *not* to travel to Asia. (Acts 16:6).

When you allow Him to guide you in the details of your daily life and service, marvelous things begin to happen. Part of the problem with the churches mentioned in the book of Revelation was that they were no longer sensitive to the direction of the Holy Spirit. Christ's use of repetition pounds the point home over and over again when He said, "He who has an ear, let him hear what the Spirit says to the churches" (Rev. 2:7, 11, 17, 29; 3:6, 13, 22). Don't be in a position where Jesus has to ask you to turn your hearing aids on!

The Holy Spirit Enables Us To Communicate In Power.

When the Holy Spirit begins to work, you will not rush out to tell the world what *you* are like; you will tell them what *Christ* is like. You'll have a revelation of Jesus. Your message will be about the mighty God, merciful Savior, and great High Priest you serve.

The power of Pentecost was given for a reason—that "you shall be witnesses to Me in Jerusalem, and in all

Judea and Samaria, and to the end of the earth" (Acts 1:8).

The gospel was not sent to earth in mere words, "but also in power, and in the Holy Spirit and in much assurance" (1 Thess. 1:5).

Paul confessed that he did not come with "excellence of speech or of wisdom declaring to you the testimony of God" (1 Cor. 2:1). He came in weakness, fear, and in much trembling. He said, "My speech and my preaching were not with persuasive words of human wisdom, but in demonstration of the Spirit and of power, that your faith should not be in the wisdom of men but in the power of God" (vv. 4,5).

The Holy Spirit Causes Us To Speak The Will Of God.

There are many gifted speakers in our world, but have you ever examined their content? Many seem more concerned with their personal experiences than with God's purposes.

When we listen to the Holy Spirit we won't be guilty of speaking our own will, but the Lord's.

You won't need to rely on yourself when the Holy Spirit is at work. The last words of David, the singer of songs, were these: "The Spirit of the LORD spoke by me, and His word was on my tongue" (2 Sam. 23:2).

Theologian Donald Guthrie writes of this enabling of the Holy Spirit, "Proclamation which is dependent on the Spirit is seen to be independent of human wisdom. This does not mean that Spirit-endowed preaching is opposed to human wisdom, but that human wisdom is not the source of the message."[12]

Mark 13:11, a special promise for those experiencing persecution, is part of this: "But when they arrest you and deliver you up, do not worry beforehand, or premeditate what you will speak. But whatever is given you in that hour, speak that; for it is not you who speak, but the Holy Spirit."

The Holy Spirit Equips You For Service.

You may know what the Holy Spirit wants you to *be,* but what does He want you to *do?* When Saul was blinded by the great light on the road to Damascus, a man by the name of Ananias was led by the Spirit to go to the house where Saul was staying.

Ananias laid his hands on him and said, "Brother Saul, the Lord Jesus, who appeared to you on the road as you came, has sent me that you may receive your sight and be filled with the Holy Spirit" (Acts 9:17).

Today, the Lord wants you to receive, function, flow, and live in His Spirit. It is not for a spiritual "high"— it is for service. Get ready! The Master is about to return. He will look deeply into your eyes and ask, "What have you done with what I have given you?"

Have your two talents become four? Have your five become ten? Or will He say, "Cast the unprofitable servant into the outer darkness" (Matt. 25:30)?

Time is running out. God is not interested in filling buildings, He is concerned with filling heaven! And He has chosen to accomplish the task by filling you with His power!

Daniel said that those who "know their God shall be strong, and carry out great exploits" (Dan. 11:32).

The Lord wants to fill you to hasten the day that the world will be transformed from a place of desolation into a land of beauty (2 Peter 3:12–14). "The wilderness will rejoice and blossom" (Isa. 35:1 NIV). And that is just the beginning. "Then the eyes of the blind shall be opened, and the ears of the deaf shall be unstopped. Then the lame shall leap like a deer, and the tongue of the dumb sing. For waters shall burst forth in the wilderness, and streams in the desert" (Isa. 35:5-6).

What a mighty visitation! And the Lord wants you to be part of it! When the fullness of God's anointing fills you, you will feel like the Psalmist when he declared, "Let God arise, let his enemies be scattered" (Ps. 68:1a).

The Holy Spirit offers you the experience of His presence and the appropriation of His power—it's time to share Him with the world!

11

The Transforming Fellowship of the Holy Spirit

I f the Book of Acts were being written today, what do you think it would include? Perhaps a testimony you have heard would be recorded in its pages.

In every part of the world the outpouring of God's Spirit is alive. Millions can document what is happening because of their fellowship with the Holy Spirit.

Every day the words of Jesus are being fulfilled: "Most assuredly, I say to you, he who believes in Me, the works that I do he will do also; and greater works than these he will do, because I go to My Father" (John 14:12).

In the mid-1970s I attended a Full Gospel Businessmen's Fellowship International Convention in Miami. In one of the services, Demos Shakarian, the founder of the organization, gave a prophecy I could not erase from my mind. He declared on God's authority: "The day will come when believers will have such an anointing on their life that they will walk through hospitals, laying hands on the sick, and the sick will be healed."

I wondered, "Would I ever see such a manifestation? Would God raise masses of people from their beds of affliction?"

I remember hearing Kathryn Kuhlman say that there would come a day when every sick saint would be healed in a service. And then she would say in her slow, deliberate style, "Might this be the service?"

Request of the Reverend Mother   In 1976 I was invited by Pastor Fred Spring to conduct a series of meetings in his Pentecostal church in Sault Sainte Marie, Ontario, Canada.

God moved mightily in that city and the church could not contain the crowds. A woman who had a secular daily television program was converted and began promoting the meetings. Plus, a large Catholic Charismatic fellowship became active participants of the crusade. In my early ministry, a group of Catholic priests from several churches sponsored most of my meetings in Northern Canada.

During the crusade I received a special invitation from the Reverend Mother of a Catholic hospital in the area. She wanted me to conduct a service for the patients—along with three other Pentecostal preachers and seven Catholic priests.

The chapel of the large hospital seated about 150. It was quite a sight that morning. There were patients present with varying types of ailments. Some were in wheelchairs. Others had been rolled right into the chapel on their beds—with intravenous feeding tubes in their arms. Some patients were too ill to be moved to the chapel. Doctors and nurses were looking on from the balcony. Many could not attend because of the limited space.

After ministering I announced, "If there is anyone

who would like to be anointed with oil and prayed for, please come forward."

After a minute of awkward silence, a man slowly walked to the front for prayer. I thought, "Lord, we have made all of this effort and only one person wants to receive a healing."

After praying for the man, I called all of the guest ministers to the front. I announced that we were going to pray for everyone present and invite them to come forward, section by section. And they did just that. While they were coming forward, some small containers of anointing oil were located for each of us to use.

On one side of the chapel the three Pentecostal preachers began to pray for the patients, one at a time. As they anointed each one with oil and laid their hands on the patients, they prayed aloud, asking the Lord Jesus to touch and heal every sick body. On the other side of the chapel the Catholic priests carefully anointed each patient, making the sign of the cross on their forehead while praying in almost inaudible tones. I stood at the front of the chapel, watching this lesson in contrasts. It was apparent that the Pentecostal preachers were very comfortable with the way in which they were ministering, while the Catholic priests seemed to be equally at ease as they anointed each person and prayed for them.

"What Do I Do?"

There was one priest who seemed reluctant to participate. When I announced that we were going to pray for every person in the chapel, he just stood there. Because he was rather short and unimposing, I didn't notice immediately that he had not joined the other priests. I turned to him and said, "Father, come on up and help us."

He replied, "No . . . I'm fine."

I asked again and he declined again, shaking his head from side to side to confirm his words. I waited for a moment, and finally went over and placed a container of oil in his hand and said, "Here, take one of these and help us. Please!"

He looked at me rather sheepishly and said, "Well, I have never done this before. What am I supposed to do?"

"Just anoint them with oil and pray for them like the others are doing," I quickly replied. Up to that point, it had been a rather uneventful service.

The little priest glanced quickly in the direction of the other priests, observing their technique. Then he stepped forward, rubbed some oil on his finger, and touched the first man. Wham! The patient fell backward to the floor under the power of the Holy Spirit.

If I live to be 120 I will *never* forget that moment!

The priest was standing there with his finger frozen in mid-air, staring at the patient lying on the floor. On his face was a look of pure fright. He just stood there, motionless, staring straight ahead. Finally he turned to me and asked, "What happened?"

I said, "He's under the power."

He replied, "My God! What power?"

I tried to re-assure him that everything was all right and encouraged him to continue praying for the patients. Reluctantly, and still with a bewildered look on his face, he moved on. Well, the next person he touched hit the floor, too. And the next. Every person he anointed went down under God's power.

Suddenly, all across the room, the Spirit of the Lord

descended mightily. Patients began to receive instant healing. One by one, they began to testify of miracles that were taking place.

After the service in the chapel, the Reverend Mother asked, "Oh, this is wonderful! Would you mind coming now and laying hands on all the patients in the rooms who could not come to the service?"

She asked all those who wanted to minister with us to follow along. More than fifty doctors, nurses, Pentecostal preachers, priests and nuns joined this "Miracle Invasion" team as we headed for those hospital rooms. As we walked down the hallway, I turned around and saw the priest who had been so reluctant to pray just minutes ago, now walking close behind me. And guess what . . . he still had his finger in the air!

I said, "Excuse me, Father, but you can put your hand down."

"Oh, no!" he protested. "It may drain out!"

He spoke with such deep conviction that I didn't make any more suggestions.

As we walked down the halls of the hospital that day you could feel God's Spirit all over the building. Within a few minutes the hospital looked almost like it had been hit by an earthquake. People were under the power of the Holy Spirit up and down the hallways as well as in the rooms. The sounds of praise were coming from every direction.

While I was praying, the prophecy of Demos Shakarian flashed before me. It was true! And it was happening before my eyes! We were walking through a hospital and people were being healed!

As we continued down the corridors of the hospital, we passed a visitor's lounge filled with people. Some were sitting there smoking, some were talking, and some were watching the "Phil Donahue Show." My friend, the priest (who still had his finger up in the air), looked at me and nodded toward the lounge area, indicating he thought we shouldn't overlook these people. Obviously, they had no idea who we were, although it was apparent that something was happening. We entered the lounge and began to anoint each of the visitors. One by one, they fell under the power. In fact, as we began to pray for one gentleman who was smoking, he fell under the power with a lit cigarette still in his mouth!

Pastor Fred Spring, who is now a minister on our staff, says "The revival at the hospital was a taste of heaven itself. It was a demonstration of what can happen when people get in tune with the Spirit of God."

When I think about this, I realize what a wonderful sense of humor God has. He chose to use that priest who really did not know what he was doing or understand what was happening. Yet, God used him in such a mighty way that day. This is just another example which so clearly shows me that God will use any one of us, but only if we are available. Always remember that it's not ability but our *availability* that matters to God. When we make ourselves available to Him for service, we become a channel which He can anoint to bring His healing power and presence to the lives of others.

The same thing takes place in the miracle crusades. Those glorious miracles don't happen because of any ability I possess. I couldn't even heal an ant! Before I ever take one step onto the platform I always invite the Holy Spirit to walk out with me. As I make myself available to God, He anoints me for service. And as His power and presence flow through me in that service, it's not anything I possess that touches the people; it's the Lord. Much like a garden hose carries water to thirsty, wilting plants growing in parched soil, I'm just the channel He anoints and uses to bring God's healing power and presence to the hurting and spiritually hungry. I make myself available and He does the rest!

What I feel when that anointing of the Holy Spirit comes upon me is beyond description—it's glorious! Absolutely nothing can compare with the fellowship of the Holy Spirit. His sovereign work will revolutionize your life. Scripture records so many instances of how a visitation of the Holy Spirit changed the speech, the worship, and even the appearance, of people in Bible times.

Every chapter of the Book of Acts is a record of the dramatic change that happened to the Apostles because of the fellowship of the Holy Spirit. When you welcome the Holy Spirit, the same thing can happen to you.

You'll Be Changed

Acts 1: He'll change the way you hear.

Just before Jesus returned to heaven, He told His apostles not to leave Jerusalem, but to wait for the Promise of the Father of whom they had heard Him speak (Acts 1:4). He said "for John truly baptized with water, but you shall be baptized with the Holy Spirit not many days from now" (Acts 1:5).

The Lord's instructions were somewhat difficult to understand. They knew the fellowship of Jesus, but had no concept of what it meant to be baptized with the Spirit.

They not only heard with their *ears,* they listened

with their *heart*. One hundred and twenty Christians gathered in the Upper Room and began to pray.

Acts 2: He'll change the way you speak.

When the Holy Spirit came, their speech was different. They began "to speak with other tongues, as the Spirit gave them utterance" (Acts 2:4).

With the power he received at Pentecost, Peter declared the message of Christ, and three thousand people were added to the church.

Episcopalian Dennis Bennett, in his inspiring book, *The Holy Spirit and You,* makes this observation: "He overflowed from them out into the world around, inspiring them to praise and glorify God, not only in their own tongues, but in the new languages, and in so doing, tamed their tongues to His use, freed their spirits, renewed their minds, refreshed their bodies, and brought power to witness."[1]

Acts 3: He'll change your appearance.

Here's what I notice about people with a strong anointing on their life. They look young, regardless of their age. Their eyes sparkle, and they have physical strength.

Allow me to tell you about a minister I knew years ago whose countenance radiated with the Lord. He was so alive and preached with such power and authority. I knew him for years and he had a great anointing of the Spirit upon his life and ministry. During his ministry, however, a major problem surfaced in his life. Rather than deal with it, he chose to ignore it, and the presence of God left him. It was only a few months later that I saw him and I was shocked! He didn't even look like himself. His appearance was that of a haggard old man. The sparkle was gone. The zeal for life had vanished. He had "aged" instantly.

After they were filled with the Holy Spirit, Peter and John went to the temple gate and were asked for money from a beggar. They told him, "Look at us" (Acts 3:4) for a look of power and boldness had come upon them because of God's presence.

Instead of giving him money, Peter said, "Silver and gold I do not have, but what I do have I give you: In the name of Jesus Christ of Nazareth, rise up and walk" (v. 6).

The crippled beggar jumped to his feet and began running, leaping and praising God. When the people saw what had occurred, "they were filled with wonder and amazement at what had happened to him" (v. 10).

Acts 4: He'll change your behavior.

It is so difficult to fully describe what I experience during a service when the anointing comes upon me. Every ounce of fear and apprehension disappears. I become bold against satan and all his forces. I become fearless. I become a different man, all because of God's wonderful anointing.

And because of the Holy Spirit, the behavior of Peter and John was drastically changed after the Day of Pentecost. Instead of fearing the Jews, they were proclaiming the message of the gospel with confidence. "When they saw the boldness of Peter and John, and perceived that they were uneducated and untrained men, they marveled. And they realized that they had been with Jesus (Acts 4:13).

Fellowship with the Holy Spirit gives you

- Boldness to come before God.
- Boldness with men.
- Boldness against satan.

What gave David the courage to do battle against Goliath? What gave Paul the nerve to stand before King Agrippa and insist that Jesus is still alive? It was God's Holy Spirit.

He is still in the business of changing behavior.

Acts 5: He'll change your experience of the Holy Spirit.

Peter had a new friend who may have been invisible to others but was a reality to him. He told the Sanhedrin, the supreme Jewish court, "We are His witnesses to these things, and so also is the Holy Spirit whom God has given to those who obey Him" (Acts 5:32).

The disciples did not say, "We are His witnesses and so is Mary Magdalene." Or, "So are the soldiers who were there." The Holy Spirit was real to them, and the evidence of His presence in their life was there for all to see. "God also bearing them witness, both with signs and wonders, and with divers miracles, and gifts of the Holy Ghost, according to his own will" (Heb. 2:4 KJV). This was part of the power that Jesus had promised to them before He ascended into heaven (Acts 1:8).

Oh, how wonderful it is to have the Holy Spirit as your Friend and Companion and to experience His reality each and every moment.

Acts 6: He'll change your position.

It is impossible to predict where your walk with the Holy Spirit will lead. The story of Stephen, as recorded in

Acts, is a good example. He was not an apostle and before becoming a deacon, he held no high office. Stephen was simply active in the church of Jerusalem, a man full of the Holy Spirit and faith (Acts 6:5).

It is apparent that the Holy Spirit was moving in a great and powerful way, touching not only the preachers but also the laymen, for the Bible says, "Stephen, full of faith and power, did great wonders and signs among the people" (v. 8).

How did he move from a position as a layman to a position in ministry as an usher or administrator ("waiting on tables" [v. 2]) to an evangelist? It was because of His fellowship with the Holy Spirit. And because of this fellowship, the Holy Spirit gave him great authority and changed his position.

When members of the synagogue began to argue with Stephen, "They were not able to resist the wisdom and the Spirit by which he spoke" (v. 10). He had a new position, and new authority in ministry.

Acts 7: He'll change your vision.

A relationship with the Holy Spirit will change what you see. Instead of looking down, you'll start looking up— where the horizon is much brighter.

Stephen was about to be bound and carried through the streets of Jerusalem and stoned for his faith, but the Holy Spirit gave him a glorious vision. The Bible says, "Being full of the Holy Spirit, [he] gazed into heaven and saw the glory of God, and Jesus standing at the right hand of God" (Acts 7:55).

To get a new perspective, follow the advice of Paul: "Set your mind on things above, not on things on the earth" (Col. 3:2).

Acts 8: He'll change your discernment.

Have you ever met a Christian who had no tact or wisdom when dealing with those who didn't know the Lord? I have. God is concerned with "timing."

When it was the perfect moment to witness to an Ethiopian, "The Spirit said to Philip, 'Go near and overtake this chariot.' So Philip ran" (Acts 8:29, 30).

He knew the voice of God so well that when the Spirit said, "Now," Philip responded instantly. He didn't want to miss the opportunity.

During the journeys of Paul, he did not witness to people until they were ready for it. Once, when he was on a ship headed for Rome, they were in a violent storm. If he had witnessed to them when there was no tempest in their life they probably would have turned a deaf ear. Paul had the right words—but he was sensitive to discern the right time. He told them about "an angel of the God to whom he belonged and serfed, saying, 'Do not be afraid' " (Acts 27:24). He told them that God promised to protect all who sailed with him.

Don't trust your own judgment. Allow the Holy Spirit to give you discernment.

Acts 9: He'll change your attitude.

Saul who later was called Paul is a prime example of how the Holy Spirit can transform your walk. Can you imagine calling someone who is a blasphemer, a persecutor, and a murderer, "Brother"?

In the natural it sounds impossible. But that's what the Holy Spirit can do. When God told Ananias to go and pray for Saul, he argued: "Lord, I have heard from many about this man, how much harm he has done to Your saints in Jerusalem (Acts 9:13).

Nevertheless, Ananias obeyed God and went to pray for Saul. The moment Ananias met him, he laid his hands on him and said, "Brother Saul, the Lord Jesus, who appeared to you on the road as you came, has sent me that you may receive your sight and be filled with the Holy Spirit" (Acts 9:17).

Even the apostles didn't want to associate with Saul. They were not convinced of his conversion. As far as they knew he was on his way to Jerusalem to kill them for they had seen no evidence to the contrary. It took Barnabas to change their attitude. He brought Saul before them and explained "how he had seen the Lord on the road, and that He had spoken to him, and how he had preached boldly at Damascus in the name of Jesus" (Acts 9:26, 27).

When the apostles saw the transformation that had taken place in Paul, they were amazed. This man who had once been a threat to their own personal safety and to the message they preached now went about proclaiming "Christ in the synagogues, that he is the Son of God" (v. 20).

If the Holy Spirit can transform Saul into Paul, totally re-orchestrating his life and the purpose for his very existence, imagine how he could transform you and me. Just one touch of His presence can change the course of our life so that we will walk in His ways to accomplish His will and not our own.

Acts 10: He'll change your tradition.

My hometown of Jaffa, Israel, had the ancient Greek name of Joppa in Bible times. As a boy I have climbed to the Citadel, a lighthouse on the highest spot overlooking the harbor. Near this lighthouse is the house of Simon the Tanner where the apostle Peter had an experience that changed the world.

Peter's vision on the rooftop was of God lowering four-footed animals, reptiles and birds in a giant sheet. God told Peter to kill and eat them. Peter, a man bound by tradition, said "Not so, Lord! For I have never eaten anything common or unclean" (Acts 10:14).

The Lord answered, "What God has cleansed you must not call common" (v. 15).

While Peter thought on the vision, the Holy Spirit told him to go downstairs and meet three men who were looking for him. Furthermore, God said he should "go with them, doubting nothing; for I have sent them" (v. 20).

Peter despised Gentiles. He was so bound by his Jewishness that before this moment he would not talk to them. But because of the vision he had seen, Peter discarded his tradition and had a great ministry to the Gentile world.

Only the Holy Spirit can produce such a radical transformation.

Acts 11: He'll change your outlook.

At times the Holy Spirit will reveal the future in preparation for trials and struggles coming your way. We find one instance of that in verse 28.

"And there stood up one of them named Agabus, and signified by the Spirit that there should be great dearth throughout all the world: which came to pass in the days of Claudius Caesar" (KJV).

When this kind of revelation occurs, there is no natural explanation for it. However, there is an inward knowing that what has been revealed to your heart will take place and that because of God's grace, He is preparing you. Through prayer you can be prepared for what is ahead.

Acts 12: *He'll change your prayer life.*

It would have been totally impossible for me to develop a prayer life without first becoming acquainted with the Holy Spirit. It flows so naturally when you know Him, yet apart from Him it is impossible.

When the believers heard that Peter was in prison, "constant prayer was offered to God for him by the church" (Acts 12:5). They learned what it meant to pray without ceasing.

This continual prayer was offered until the answer came for Peter and he was delivered from Herod's prison by an angel. The chains fell off and he walked out of the prison.

In fact, this divine intervention by God on Peter's behalf was so miraculous and out of the ordinary that Peter wasn't even sure whether or not it was happening. He thought he was having a vision. Just moments before his liberation, Peter had been sleeping, chained between two soldiers. Then suddenly a bright light appeared in the prison, and an angel of the Lord woke him and said, "Get up quickly, Peter." And with that, his chains fell off! Then the angel of the Lord told him to put his sandals on, wrap his garment around him and follow him. Not until he was outside the prison walking on the streets did he realize what had really happened!

The believers in the Book of Acts were able to pray without ceasing for Peter because of the presence of the Holy Spirit for prayer without ceasing is impossible without the help and assistance of the Holy Spirit. Ask Him today to develop that in you and He will. Psalm 80:18 declares, "Quicken us, and we will call upon thy name" (KJV). Ask Him to quicken you daily and He will do it.

Acts 13: He'll change your calling.

Since the moment the Holy Spirit called me to preach His Word there has never been a moment of doubt concerning my calling. It was not an occupation chosen by trial and error or a decision that was self-motivated. God directed and I said, "Yes."

On every page of the Book of Acts you will meet people who were called by God for a specific task. During a service at the church at Antioch, the Holy Spirit said, "Now separate to Me Barnabas and Saul for the work to which I have called them" (Acts 13:2).

The church fasted, prayed, and laid their hands on them before sending the evangelists away. Scripture tells us they were "sent out by the Holy Spirit" to the island of Cyprus (v. 4).

There is only one way to know God's direction and leadership for your life. Continue to seek the Holy Spirit until He makes your calling sure—and remember, the Holy Spirit speaks through the Scriptures and through godly people as well as directly.

Acts 14: He'll change your authority.

As Paul and Barnabas ministered from city to city, there was a power in their preaching, an authority and confirmation to their words and deeds.

When they came to Lystra, a man crippled from birth who had never walked heard them. And as Paul spoke, the man's faith came alive and Paul perceiving "that he had faith to be healed" said with a loud voice, "Stand upright on thy feet." And the crippled man leaped to his feet and began to walk.

Paul was watching the man while he preached but waited to speak until the man was ready for his miracle. The Holy Spirit gave Paul that perception to know when the time for that miracle was right.

Acts 15: He'll be your partner in decision making.

One of the greatest benefits of walking with the Holy Spirit is that I don't have to make decisions alone. I have a Teacher, a Guide, and a Counselor to help me every step of the way. He is more than an advisor. He is a partner in settling every issue.

When the church at Jerusalem sent a letter to the Gentile believers at Antioch they wrote something of profound importance. They said, "It seemed good to the Holy Spirit, and to us" (Acts 15:28).

Allow the Spirit of God to become more than a Companion. Allow Him to participate in your decision making.

Acts 16: He'll change your direction.

More than once we have made detailed plans for a major crusade when the Holy Spirit has clearly warned me, "Don't go." I can't explain it and I certainly don't understand it, but I have to obey His leading.

When Paul and Silas traveled through the region of Galatia, "they were forbidden by the Holy Spirit to preach the word in Asia. After they had come to Mysia, they tried to go into Bithynia, but the Spirit did not permit them" (Acts 16:6, 7).

That is when the Holy Spirit gave Paul a vision of a man from Macedonia, pleading, "Come over to Macedonia and help us" (Acts 16:9).

It's a cliché, but a good one: "When God shuts one door, He always opens another."

When you let God chart your course, you will be on the right path. Remember, the Holy Spirit never makes a mistake. Trust Him to lead and He will do so with perfection.

Acts 17: He'll change your world.

At Thessalonica, Paul and Silas were involved in a near-riot, but it really wasn't their fault. The Jews were so jealous at the crowds who were listening to Paul explain scripture that they rounded up some unsavory characters at the marketplace, formed a mob and started a riot in the city (Acts 17:1–5).

The throng shouted to the rulers of the city, "These who have turned the world upside down have come here too" (Acts 17:6).

Their reputation preceded them and news of their activities spread quickly. Almost everywhere they went they saw a revival. People were turning to Christ, healings were taking place, and the Spirit of God was at work.

And he wants to do the same through you today.

Years ago, someone told me "Benny, the quickest way to turn your world upside down is to turn yourself right-side up." It was good advice.

Acts 18: He'll change your understanding.

You will begin to know the ways of God more perfectly. I feel fortunate to be surrounded in ministry with people who have a deep dedication to the task God has asked of them. I am grateful for the sensitivity with which they minister as they serve Him. It is a result of their relationship with the Holy Spirit.

"And he began to speak boldly in the synagogue: whom when Aquila and Priscilla had heard, they took him unto them, and expounded unto him the way of God more perfectly" (v. 26 KJV).

Acts 19: He'll change you as His presence lingers upon you.

When Paul came to Ephesus, he found "certain disciples," and said to them, "Have ye received the Holy Ghost since ye believed?"

The disciples to whom he spoke answered, "We have not so much as heard whether there be any Holy Ghost."

We find that Paul taught them about the Holy Spirit and then laid hands upon them, and "the Holy Ghost came on them."

Later in this same chapter we find that "God wrought special miracles by the hands of Paul: so that from his body were brought unto the sick handkerchiefs or aprons, and the diseases departed from them, and the evil spirits went out of them (v. 11, 12 KJV). The presence of God was so strong on Paul that the anointing could be transferred by the laying on of hands and upon handkerchiefs. The sick were healed and evil spirits were cast out because the anointing of the Holy Spirit lingered in such a great way upon Paul.

Paul was greatly opposed in Ephesus by both the Jewish establishment and the followers of pagan religions (vv. 9 and 23–41).

And never forget that the greater the opposition, the

greater the power. In this difficult and dangerous city, "God worked unusual (literally, "extraordinary") miracles" (19:11, 12). The Holy Spirit wants to do the same today, only if we are willing to pay the price which is total yieldedness to Him.

Acts 20: He'll change your leadership.

God did not send His Spirit to earth so that we could neglect our duties. As a Counselor and Guide, He shows us how to take responsibility for God's work and empowers us to do it with supernatural results giving us a place of responsibility and influence in the kingdom.

Paul's farewell message to the Ephesian elders after three years of ministry came straight from his heart. His objective was to have *them* accept the mantle of leadership. He told them with great emotion, "Therefore take heed to yourselves and to all the flock, among which the Holy Spirit has made you overseers, to shepherd the church of God which He purchased with His own blood" (Acts 20:28).

Paul issued this challenge with great confidence because he knew the Holy Spirit would give them all they needed to succeed in spiritual leadership. He also knew that after his departure, "savage wolves will come in among you, not sparing the flock" (v. 29). They would be determined to distort the truth and deceive the disciples.

God took Moses, "a very humble man, more humble than anyone else on the face of the earth" (Numbers 12:3 NIV) and made him into a great leader. And He wants to do the same for you and through you today.

Acts 21: He'll change your insight.

At times God has given me a specific word of prophecy for someone. Sometimes this will happen as an individual stands before me on the platform in the crusades or at my church. So far, however, the Lord has never asked of me what He asked of Agabus. When He gave him a word from God for Paul—the Billy Graham of his day— he did not shrink from delivering it. At Caesarea, Agabus walked up to the apostle, took Paul's belt and bound it around his own hands and feet. Then he said, "Thus says the Holy Spirit, 'So shall the Jews at Jerusalem bind the man who owns this belt, and deliver him into the hands of the Gentiles'" (Acts 21:11).

It took a man who had a strong relationship with the Lord to make such a declaration.

The prophecy of Agabus gave Paul insight as to the difficult days ahead. He responded, "What do you mean by weeping and breaking my heart? For I am ready not only to be bound, but also to die at Jerusalem for the name of the Lord Jesus" (v. 13).

When we receive insight, it makes us bold and loyal, even unto death. Paul said, "I am ready not to be bound only, but also to die at Jerusalem for the name of the Lord Jesus." When you know the Holy Spirit, you will see beyond the temporal, and not even death will frighten you.

Acts 22: He'll change your commission.

Do you remember the moment you gave your heart to Christ? Paul's experience on the Damascus road was one he certainly could not forget. Like so many people, Paul was sincere—but sincerely wrong. Paul had no use for Jesus or His followers. Although Paul took his opposition of Christ to an extreme, he was not unlike many of us in the days before we met the Master.

And met the Master he did! He gave his testimony of being blinded by a bright light, and how his night turned to day. Paul had seen the resurrected Christ, and that convinced him of the truth of the Gospel. From a changed *recognition* came a changed *commission:* "The God of our fathers has chosen you that you should know His will, and see the Just One, and hear the voice of His mouth. For you will be His witness to all men of what you have seen and heard" (vv. 14, 15).

Paul's story is mine too. I was blind, but now I can see. Hallelujah!

Acts 23: He'll increase your influence.

People continue to ask, "Does the Lord really speak to people?" My answer is an unqualified "yes!" Not only because of my personal experience, but because of God's Word.

The city of Jerusalem was in such an uproar over Paul that the commander of the prison thought the mobs would take him away by force. In the midst of that crisis, Scripture says, "the Lord stood by him and said, 'Be of good cheer, Paul; for as you have testified for Me in Jerusalem, so you must also bear witness at Rome'" (Acts 23:11).

Because of God's power on his life, Paul was brought before Caesar and testified for his Master. And as Paul demonstrated, God opened doors supernaturally for him and brought him into a greater dimension of influence before men of power and authority for the glory of God.

Acts 24: He'll establish your eternal hope.

The Lord continues to remind me of my primary mission in life. It is *to bring people into the presence of the Lord so that they can receive from Him.* If you attend any of our crusades or watch our television ministry, you understand that clearly.

Paul, too, was on a mission. No matter in what circumstances he found himself, he presented the Gospel. And Paul, too, was supernaturally aided to do what he did and nothing could shake his commitment.

As Paul stood accused before the governor he said, "But this I confess unto thee, that after the way which they call heresy, so worship I the God of my fathers, believing all things which are written in the law and in the prophets: And have hope toward God, which they themselves also allow, that there shall be a resurrection of the dead, both of the just and the unjust" (v. 14, 15 KJV). Here Paul declares that he was given hope—hope given only by the Holy Spirit, even in the presence of our enemies.

Acts 25: He'll give you great confidence.

Paul's reliance on the Lord never wavered. In the face of the Jews who hated him and the Romans who were baffled by him, he remained not only confident, but *feisty!*

He boldly maintained that "I have done no wrong, *as you very well know* . . . I appeal to Caesar" (vv. 10, 11). Now make no mistake, the Romans had heard Paul's message—even if they didn't quite understand it yet. The Roman official noted his understanding that Paul's message was about "Jesus, who had died, whom Paul affirmed to be alive" (Acts 25:19). What baffled them was that Paul not only affirmed it, he was totally convinced.

How did Paul know Christ was alive in the loneliness of a prison cell, the pain of a flogging, or the desolation of a shipwreck? Through his never-ending companionship with the Holy Spirit. Jesus not only promised to send the Comforter, but He delivered on that commitment.

Acts 26: He'll change your witness.

Before God healed my stuttering tongue I would use every trick in the book to avoid speaking. Even as a young Christian, I would never volunteer to read the Scripture in public or give a short testimony.

But what a change took place when God healed me as I preached my first sermon on Pearl Harbor Day, December 7, 1974. My tongue was loosed, and it seems I have not stopped talking since.

Paul took every opportunity to present his testimony, too, and to bring deliverance to the captive. His defense before King Agrippa was so strong it has been a model of study for legal scholars. There was strength in his witness and power in his words. When he was finished, Agrippa said, "You almost persuade me to become a Christian" (Acts 26:28).

Almost anyone can produce a speech, but only the Spirit can produce a testimony.

Acts 27: He'll change your chaos into peace.

On his final journey to Rome, Paul was a prisoner on a ship with 276 passengers. After two weeks of storm-tossed seas, the apostle was the only person who knew the meaning of peace. As day was about to dawn, "Paul implored them all to take food, saying, 'Today is the fourteenth day you have waited and continued without food, and eaten nothing'" (Acts 27:33).

He not only urged them to eat for survival, but reassured them, "Not a hair will fall from the head of any of you" (v. 34).

In a time of testing it is only peace from above that can calm the storm.

I know what it is like to be near the point of death.

In 1983, flying with six passengers in a Cessna aircraft at 11,000 feet, we ran out of fuel near Avon Park, Florida. I was asleep, but not for long. "We're in trouble. Pray! Pray!" were the first words I heard from our pilot, Don.

Everyone began crying out in fear. But suddenly a great peace came over me. I said, "Don, it's going to be all right. No one will be killed."

God used those words to calm the passengers. "Please don't cry," I told them. "Just relax. God isn't through with me."

We crash landed in a field and there were some injuries, but I did not have a scratch. Deep within my spirit I had the assurance, "It's going to be all right."

He turned chaos into peace.

Acts 28: He'll change your conflict into victory.

Paul was shipwrecked off the island of Malta, and every passenger reached land in safety. But as they were building a fire for warmth, a viper came out of the heat and fastened itself on to Paul's hand.

When the island natives saw the snake hanging from his hand, they said to each other, "No doubt this man is a murderer, whom, though he has escaped the sea, yet justice does not allow to live" (Acts 28:4).

Instead of screaming, "I'm going to die! Get me some medicine!" he simply shook the serpent off and sustained no ill effects.

The islanders expected him to die instantly. After a while, when they realized he was going to live, "they changed their minds and said that he was a god" (v. 6).

Only the Holy Spirit can turn your conflict into victory.

The message of the Book of Acts is that nothing can replace a personal relationship with the Holy Spirit. He works so mightily in the lives of people attuned to Him. The Upper Room experience is wonderful, but it's only the first step on a road of ever-increasing fellowship.

Allow Him to change your hearing, your speech, your vision, your actions, and every part of your being. Start now to practice the presence of the Holy Spirit.

CHAPTER

12

Removing the Barriers to Blessing

I n 1991, I was in Virginia Beach, Virginia, to appear on the "700 Club" with Pat Robertson. Following the program I was asked to speak to the entire staff of The Christian Broadcasting Network and Regent University.

When I concluded my message on God's anointing, I gave the microphone to Pat. As he began to pray to close the service, I felt a tremendous anointing. Suddenly I heard him praying for me and as he continued to pray I began to weep.

To this day he does not know the impact his prayer had on me. I was going through an extremely difficult period in my life.

I had just written *Good Morning, Holy Spirit* and I was under attack from many sides. The book was selling 50,000 copies a week. Our television ministry and crusades were exploding.

The Danger Ahead   Just before I flew to Virginia Beach, Suzanne and I had a lengthy conversation. We were beginning to comprehend the magnitude of our growing ministry and realizing all it would entail. The idea of moving into such a high-profile arena was becoming frightening.

"Benny, do we really, really want this?" she asked me. "Do you really want this ministry to grow, for with the growth there is danger. Other ministers couldn't handle the growth of their ministries and they fell, will you fall too?"

"What are you talking about?" I queried. But I knew exactly what she meant.

Suzanne wanted my assurance that when the pressure became intense I would remain strong and focused on the Lord Jesus. She said, "I would rather have you stop right now than do something that would disgrace us." It was before our fourth child was born.

Without knowing the struggle I was going through, Pat Robertson began to pray: "Dear Lord, Your Word declares that you are able to keep us from falling and present us before your throne with exceeding joy.

"We are kept by your power and not by our strength. We are sustained by the Living Water and Bread of Life and we will never be thirsty or hungry. You will preserve and protect so that we may be able to stand before you without spot or wrinkle."

When Pat finished his prayer I lifted my hands and made a vow before God that nothing in my life would bring a reproach on the gospel. Then the Lord said to me, "Benny, *Go! I* will be with you. *I* will keep you from falling. Just keep your eyes on Me."

When I returned home I assured Suzanne, "Don't worry, honey. The Lord has us in the palm of His hand.

He is going to lead us, bless us, and protect us. And by God's grace I will always follow His leading."

Oral's Advice

I am not a golfer, but when Dr. Oral Roberts asked me to play a round with him I thought I'd give it a try. We were in Boca Raton, Florida, as guests of Bill Swad, a great soul winner who built one of America's largest automotive empires in Columbus, Ohio.

I told Oral, "I really don't know how to play this game."

"Don't worry. I'll teach you," the evangelist replied.

What I learned that day, however, was much more than how to use a putter or get out of a sand trap. We talked at length about the working of the Holy Spirit.

Riding in his electric cart I said, "Oral, I want you to give me some advice."

"On what topic?" he inquired.

"Well, you have been in the healing ministry all of these years. Others have fallen by the wayside. How have you kept yourself?"

Oral laughed and said, "Benny. I haven't kept myself; the Lord has." He said, "Listen, I've made my share of mistakes—but remember, the Lord does not give up on His saints easily. He holds on to us. He is very long-suffering." Then Oral said, "And as long as you walk with Him, He will hold you better than you can hold Him."

The great evangelist reminded me that Moses saw the Messiah rather than "the treasures in Egypt; for he looked to the reward" (Heb. 11:26). He said, "Benny, you're going to face many struggles, but never take your eyes off of the Master."

Barriers to Blessing

Through the years, I have felt the Spirit of the Lord at work in my life—leading me, shaping me, and even convicting me.

Not long ago I began to realize that our television audience consists not only of Christians who love and support our television ministry, but the world as well. The Lord cautioned me, "Benny, if you are not careful, you could offend some of these people for eternity."

I also knew that someday I would stand before God for my actions.

During the past few years the Lord has sent Godly men into my life for the purpose of accountability. One of them is Jack Hayford, the well-known pastor of Church on the Way, in Van Nuys, California.

Like a father, Pastor Hayford told me, "Benny, we have always realized that the touch of God was on your life. No one has ever really questioned that. But you have been doing some distracting things that have caused us to question, 'Does Benny Hinn know what he's doing?'"

The Lord had been dealing with me for two years on these issues. I was not comfortable with some of the things that were taking place in our services.

Jack Hayford was right. Some of my actions were distracting. For example, once, several years ago, the Lord specifically directed me to take off my coat and lay it on someone who had come to the platform for prayer. To be quite honest, when the Lord told me to do this I really struggled with it.

What confirmed to me that that was what He wanted me to do were the many Scriptural accounts of the Lord doing things in what to us may seem unusual ways. For instance, Elijah used his cloak to work a miracle: "Elijah took his cloak, rolled it up and struck the water with it. The water divided to the right and to the left, and the two of them crossed over on dry ground" (2 Kings 2:8 NIV). The Lord even worked a miracle through the *bones* of Elisha: "Once while some Israelites were burying a man, suddenly they saw a band of raiders; so they threw the man's body into Elisha's tomb. When the body touched Elisha's bones, the man came to life and stood up on his feet" (2 Kings 13:21 NIV).

In fact, all someone had to do was touch the hem of the Savior's garment to be healed: "And wherever he went—into villages, towns or countryside—they placed the sick in the marketplaces. They begged him to let them touch even the edge of his cloak, and all who touched him were healed" (Mark 6:56 NIV).

In the early church, God was again at work healing people using methods that can be surprising to the modern reader: "God did extraordinary miracles through Paul, so that even handkerchiefs and aprons that had touched him were taken to the sick, and their illnesses were cured and the evil spirits left them" (Acts 19:11, 12 NIV). These miracles, far from being distracting, resulted in great confidence in the Lord and His power: "As a result, people brought the sick into the streets and laid them on beds and mats so that at least Peter's shadow might fall on some of them as he passed by" (Acts 5:15 NIV).

After thinking about all these things, I followed the Lord's direction and just as you might expect, He moved mightily in that service.

Then next week I did it again. And again, even throwing my coat sometimes. Before long it became a habit. People were coming to the crusades *expecting* to see me take off my coat and use it as a means of bringing the anointing to those present.

What was sacred at first had become a distraction—and I was deeply troubled when I realized that people were looking at a *method* rather than the *Master*. Finally I said, "No, I can't continue doing this. I serve a Lord of class and quality, and this is not a dignified way to present Him."

Today, in our services, the power of the Holy Spirit has not diminished. In fact, it has become much stronger.

I have discovered that just because the Lord directs us to do something once does not mean we are expected to make it the major theme of our life or ministry. When the Lord Jesus was about to pray for a man with no sight, He spat on the ground and made clay with the saliva; and He anointed the eyes of the blind man with the clay" (John 9:6).

Does that mean we are to establish "Mud Ministries, Inc." and run around the world rubbing clay in everyone's face? No. We need to be sensitive to the Holy Spirit and do what He directs.

A genuine anointing is priceless. When it is present there is such beauty. People's lives are touched and changed.

Don't get me wrong. If the Holy Spirit directs me to do something, even something unusual, I will always be responsive to His leading.

On the Mountain

While God was "reshaping" my ministry, I spent a great amount of time studying the Lord's Sermon on the Mount. Based on what He said, I taught a series of messages titled: "What is a true Christian?"

- "Blessed are the meek, for they shall inherit the earth" (Matt. 5:5).
- "Blessed are the pure in heart, for they shall see God" (v. 8).
- "Agree with your adversary quickly" (v. 25).
- "Do not do your charitable deeds before men, to be seen by them" (Matt. 6:1).
- "Do not lay up for yourselves treasures on earth" (v. 19).

Just before the Master concluded His message, He gave a stern warning: "Not everyone who says to Me, 'Lord, Lord,' shall enter the kingdom of heaven, but he who does the will of My Father in heaven. Many will say to Me in that day, 'Lord, Lord, have we not prophesied in Your name, cast out demons in Your name, and done many wonders in Your name?' And then I will declare to them, 'I never knew you; depart from Me'" (Matt. 7:21–23).

When I read those words I fell before the Lord and prayed, "Lord, please help me to do the will of the Father. Lord, help me be more like You." And while in prayer, the Holy Spirit assured me that my calling was to bring God's people into His presence and to point people to the Savior. And when God's people come into His presence and see the Lord Jesus, it is then that miracles happen.

From Sadness to Joy

The Spirit of the Lord is creative and unique. He's always doing the unexpected, manifesting His presence in ways that are often surprising, but always refreshing. To me, "holy laughter" falls into that category.

The first time I ministered in Portugal, at a Sunday afternoon meeting, a woman dressed totally in black approached the platform.

She had a very sad countenance on her face. My first thought was that perhaps she was in mourning for her husband's death.

The moment I touched this sorrowful woman, something remarkable took place. She broke into the most incredible laughter I'd ever seen, and she fell to the floor under God's power. The joy of the Lord came over her and she went from sadness to gladness in seconds.

As some of the ushers were about to pick her up I said, "Wait. I want to watch this." It was the first time something like this had happened in one of my meetings. I had heard Kathryn Kuhlman speak of "Holy Laughter," but I had never personally seen it. There was pure ecstasy on the woman's face. It was magnificent and beautiful. There was nothing offensive about it. Her face was just beaming.

The woman's son came up to the platform, worried about his mother. Obviously, he had never encountered anything like this before. Neither had I.

The son seemed to be angry with me. He thought I had done something to his mother. When he reached down and tried to pull her up, he fell to the floor laughing—just like his mother.

Then a friend of the woman came to the platform. She was also dressed in black—from her dress to her scarf and shoes.

She was biting her nails and her brow was furrowed. It was a concerned look of, "What has happened to my friend?" But when she reached over to offer help, the same power hit her and she began to giggle like a little child.

When the Spirit of laughter subsided and they stood on their feet, I spoke with them through an interpreter. "Please tell me what happened to you. What is it? Describe it."

They could not even talk. It was one of the most holy and most beautiful things I had ever seen. It was unusual, but did not seem out of order.

But never forget that any fresh and unique manifestations of the Holy Spirit can tragically become common and distracting. When people start to seek the *manifestation* rather than the *Master,* it is then that the presence of God lifts. And then all that remains is the form but not the power. But when the Holy Spirit is present and in control, you'll always find perfection, and God's power displayed will always glorify and magnify the Lord Jesus. And you will walk away overwhelmed not with the *method,* but with the *Master.*

Is It Real?   The New Testament is filled with stories of the miracle-working power of the Holy Spirit. But not one time will you find where people said, "That's not real." Instead, they were *angry* with the reality.

The Pharisees may have said, "It is of the devil," but never did they conclude it was phony.

When people looked at the works of the Apostles they did not accuse them of conducting a sham or a fraud. Instead, they said, "Don't you dare do it in Jesus' name." They knew how real it was.

Today, if those who are acquainted with the gifts of the Spirit are offended by our actions, we need to take a closer look. The Holy Spirit is a first-class Person who presents the Lord Jesus to the world with dignity, respect, and honor.

The Holy Spirit, however, is sovereign and can express Himself in a number of ways. Richard Foster, in his book, *Celebration of Discipline,* says, "In many worship experiences I have seen, at any given moment, people sitting, standing, kneeling, and lying prostrate, and the Spirit of God [always] resting on them all."[1]

God does not condone disorder. If you attend one of our services there are not ten things taking place all at once. You will find the meeting to be focused on the Lord Jesus and in order. For the Lord we serve is not a God of confusion, disorder, or disturbance, He's the God of perfection, for the Bible says, "his works are perfect, and all his ways are just" (Deut. 32:4 NIV). And make no mistake about it, God's saving, healing, and delivering power *is* available today.

It Happened to Dave

Let me tell you about David Delgado. Since 1986 he has been with me regularly—on the platform as part of the ministry team and behind the scenes taking care of hundreds of details.

Dave strayed as far from God as any person I know, but the Holy Spirit would never let him go. The Holy Spirit loved Dave too much to let him remain under the bondage of drugs.

Delgado was raised on 47th Street in Brooklyn, New York, where his father was pastor of a large Spanish Pentecostal church. His parents were from Puerto Rico.

"Dad was very strict," he told me. "As a boy we had no television. Comic books were a sin and I wasn't even allowed to go to the beach." While Dave's friends were out sowing their wild oats, he was in church at least four or five nights a week.

"I grew to resent it," he recalls. "By the time I was in the seventh grade my life was like a pendulum, swinging from one extreme to the other. I would smoke pot with my friends and then come back to the church."

In the ninth grade he was "getting high" almost every day and became physically hooked on heroin. "It broke my parents' heart," he told me. "I was sent to a counseling program, a psychiatrist, a methadone clinic, and even to a Teen Challenge center."

Three different times Dave was able to break his drug addiction, but the satanic power of narcotics continued to pull him back. Says Dave, "In the mid-1970s I had a major habit and became a dealer so that I could get my own uncut drugs and prepare them for myself in higher concentrations."

"Change Me!"

Strange as it may seem, Dave Delgado always had a love for the things of God, and in particular he was drawn to the miraculous manifestations of God's healing and delivering power. Even though he was not living for the Lord, he made it a priority to attend Kathryn Kuhlman's meetings every time she was in New York City. "In the services I felt great conviction, and gave my heart to the Lord again and again, but I could never seem to get the victory over sin. The problem was that I wanted *both* God and the world. I wanted to serve Him, I really did, but I also enjoyed getting high. I couldn't seem to lose the desire."

Dave's drug involvement grew to the point that he was involved in major narcotics trafficking in three states. "I had twenty guys working for me and was handling tons of cash," he told me.

With federal agents about to close in, Dave hurriedly shut down his activities and started life again in Birmingham, Alabama. "I kicked the habit, and stayed clean for two years before the same demons of drugs pulled me back again," he sadly recalls.

David says, "I was doing 1200 milligrams of Demerol every day and taking Dilaudid, a class-A narcotic we called "hospital heroin" back in New York."

During this time Dave married, divorced and married again. "I began to embezzle from banks, steal money from night depositories, and was arrested for buying and selling stolen property."

But back in New York City, his faithful mother never stopped praying for her prodigal son.

Delgado finally told his wife, "If we are ever going to have a chance for a new start we have to move to Florida." His wife, who had so faithfully stuck by him and prayed for him, agreed to go. Anything for a fresh start.

Dave found work in Orlando installing drywall. But tragically he was also sinking deeper and deeper into drugs. "With increasing frequency I would shoot myself up with a quarter-ounce of coke and afterwards drink a glass of vodka and orange juice to take the edge off. This would cause me to fall into a coma-like stupor. It was not long until I was bleeding through my nose and looked as if I was in the last stages of cancer."

Dave's wife soon began attending our church, praying earnestly for her emaciated husband. She experienced God's miraculous healing power during a service when God healed a deteriorating disc in her back.

On a Sunday morning in 1986, he joined her in church. Dave was immediately struck by how similar the ministry was to Kathryn's. When I gave the altar call, Dave rushed to the front of the sanctuary. He began to cry out, "Lord I want to serve You but I can't. You know that I love to do drugs too, and the desire is too great for me to stop. I know Your Word says that You made me and that You know every cell in my body and every hair on my head. If You don't change every cell in my body and take away this desire, I'll never be able to serve You."

In that moment of desperation, Dave raised his hands toward heaven and he fell under the power of God. Those around him picked him up and again he fell under the power of God. In that holy moment the Holy Spirit began to do a work in him that was nothing short of a miracle. When he stood to his feet Dave Delgado was a brand new man, he knew it, and his wife knew it.

Recalling that day, Dave smiles and says, "I was *totally* set free and have never had the *slightest* desire to touch drugs again."

God's precious Holy Spirit restored his health, his home, and has given him a ministry—and God isn't finished with him yet. Like John Mark, "he is helpful to me in my ministry" (2 Tim. 4:11 NIV).

The Same Power

Who is the Holy Spirit we welcome today?

- He's the same Spirit who came upon a boy named David and caused him to slay a lion, a bear, and a giant named Goliath (1 Sam. 17).
- He's the same Spirit who gave Elijah the power to outrun the chariot of Ahab (1 Kings 18:46).

- He's the same Spirit who gave the Apostle Paul the strength to preach after he had been stoned and left for dead (Acts 14:19-28).

The Holy Spirit I have come to know is the One who turned ordinary people into spiritual giants. They subdued kingdoms, wrought righteousness and obtained promises. They escaped the sword and turned the enemies of God to flight (Hebrews 11:33, 34).

The Holy Spirit empowered the Lord Jesus to walk into the Temple one day and throw countless people into the streets. That could not happen in human strength. Only the Holy Spirit can operate with such might (Matt. 21:12-17).

The same resurrection power that raised Jesus Christ from the dead "will also give life to your mortal bodies through His Spirit who dwells in you" (Rom. 8:11).

When you look for Him with expectation, He will come. The historic Welsh revival of 1904-05 was a direct result of Evan Roberts' submission to the Spirit of the Lord. At the start of the great outpouring he preached, "Now do not say 'Perhaps the Spirit will come,' or 'We hope the Spirit will come," but 'We *believe* He will come.'"[2]

Over 100,000 people came to the Lord in Wales, and the revival spread throughout the World. Author Eifion Evans, documents that "Convictions for drunkenness in Glamorgan fell from 10,528 in 1903 to 5,490 in 1906."[3] Three months of revival had done more to sober the country than the temperance movement of many years.

Forever! The Holy Spirit promised by the Lord Jesus was not only for today. He came to "abide with you forever" (John 14:16).

I believe the Second Coming of the Lord is on the horizon. The Bible says it will happen "in a moment, in the twinkling of an eye, at the last trumpet. For the trumpet will sound, and the dead will be raised incorruptible, and we shall be changed." (1 Cor. 15:52).

"For the Lord Himself will descend from heaven with a shout, with the voice of an archangel, and with the trumpet of God. And the dead in Christ will rise first. Then we who are alive and remain shall be caught up together with them in the clouds to meet the Lord in the air. And thus we shall always be with the Lord." (1 Thess. 4:16, 17).

It won't be long before we see the Lord, and He will welcome us into eternity. What a day that will be! And I know just like me, you too are looking for that glorious day, for we are not looking for the *under*taker, we're looking for the *upper*taker.

On that great day there will be no more tears. No more pain and sorrow. We're going to look into the face of the Master and hear Him say, "Welcome!"

Will the work of our Teacher and Guide end when we enter heaven? I don't believe so. The Holy Spirit will be there. Forever. Billions of years from now we'll still be filled with His presence. In eternity we will know even more. It will be a place of eternal revelation.

The Holy Spirit's information superhighway is limitless. It stretches from here to heaven—and beyond. He has much more to give than we can fathom.

Have you ever wondered why the angels cry "Holy, Holy, Holy?" I believe it is because our triune God is continually revealing Himself in Heaven and with each new discovery, they cry, "Holy."[4]

Make Him Welcome

The cry of my heart is that of the Apostle Paul. He desired "that the God of our Lord Jesus Christ, the Father of glory, may give to you the Spirit of wisdom and revelation in the knowledge of Him, the eyes of your understanding being enlightened; that you may know what is the hope of His calling, what are the riches of the glory of His inheritance in the saints" (Eph. 1:17, 18).

Will you allow me to pray with you today?

> *Holy Spirit, we welcome You right now.*
>
> *Come and magnify Jesus through every one of us and use us to declare Him to the world. May Your Word live in our hearts, enlightening our understanding and imparting Your truth. Enrich our prayer life with Your presence and power, and shine through us that people everywhere will be drawn to the cross of Calvary, and glorify Jesus Christ always in us and through us. In Jesus' name. Amen.*

The Holy Spirit is standing at your door. Like any visitor, He will not enter unless He is invited.

Along with me, will you say?

> *Holy Spirit, you are welcome in this place.*
> *Holy Spirit, you are welcome in this place.*
> *Omnipotent Father, of mercy and grace,*
> *You are welcome in this place.*

Welcome, Holy Spirit!

Endnotes

Chapter 2

1. Paul Yonggi Cho, *Successful Home Cell Groups* (Plainfield, NJ: Logos International, 1981), p. 124.
2. R.A. Torrey, *The Best of R.A. Torrey*, (Grand Rapids, Baker: Reprinted 1990), pp. 23, 24.
3. J. Rodman Williams, *Renewal Theology, Vol. I: God, the World & Redemption* (Grand Rapids, MI: Academic Books, Zondervan Corp., 1990), p. 154.
4. R.A. Torrey, *The Person and Work of the Holy Spirit* (Grand Rapids: Zondervan: Revised Edition—1974), p. 12.
5. *NIV Study Bible,* General Editor: Kenneth Barker (Grand Rapids: Zondervan, 1985), pp. 1459, 1498.
6. "Fairest Lord Jesus" From Münster Gesangbuch to the tune of the Crusaders' Hymn. From *Hymns for the Family of God,* Fred Bock, editor. (Nashville: Paragon Associates, Inc., 1976), Hymn 240, verse 4.
7. For more on Claudio Freidzon, and the wonderful work of the Holy Spirit in the great nation of Argentina, be sure to read, "Revival in Argentina: A New Surge in Spiritual Power," by Don Exley and Brad Walz in the October 1993 issue of "Mountain Movers."
8. Ibid., p. 7.

9. R.A. Torrey, *The Person and Work of the Holy Spirit,* p. 9.
10. Billy Graham, *The Holy Spirit* (Waco, TX: Word Books, 1978), p. 23.
11. Lewis Sperry Chafer, *Systematic Theology,* Volume VI "Pneumatology," p. 24. Emphasis added.
12. John F. Walvoord and Roy B. Zuck, editors, *The Bible Knowledge Commentary, Old Testament.* Allen Ross wrote the commentary section on Genesis. (Wheaton: Victor Books, 1985), p. 28.

Chapter 3

1. *Encyclopaedia Britannica,* 15th Edition Vol. 4, p. 381. "Edwards, Jonathan."
2. Fritz Rienecker, *A Linguistic Key to the Greek New Testament,* translated, with additions and revisions, from the German Sprachlicher Schluessel Zum Griechischen Neuen Testament, edited by Cleon L. Rogers, Jr. (Grand Rapids: Zondervan, 1982) One volume edition, p. 217.
3. John Rea, *The Holy Spirit in the Bible* (Lake Mary, FL: Creation House, 1990), p. 172.
4. Rea, p. 167.
5. Rea, p. 167.
6. A. J. Gordon, *The Ministry of the Spirit,* (Minneapolis, MN: Bethany House Publishers, 1985), p. 23.
7. "Satan has a hold on people because of their fallen state. Since Christ was sinless, Satan could have no hold on him." *NIV Study Bible,* p. 1626.

Chapter 4

1. *NIV Study Bible,* General Editor: Kenneth Barker (Grand Rapids: Zondervan, 1985), p. 1670.
2. Chafer, Volume 7, p. 188.
3. Walvoord, *The Doctrine of the Holy Spirit,* as quoted in Chafer, Vol. 7, p. 20.
4. *Discipleship Journal* #36, p. 11.

Chapter 5

1. *Discipleship Journal, #36,* p. 7.
2. Joseph Bayly, *Decision Magazine,* May 1978.
3. R. Laird Harris, Gleason L. Archer, Jr. and Bruce K. Waltke, *Theological Wordbook of the Old Testament* (Chicago: Moody, 1980) Vol. 1, p. 304.
4. *Theological Wordbook of the OT,* vol. 1, p. 103.
5. *The Autobiography of Bertrand Russell* (Little and Brown, 1967).
6. Walvoord and Zuck, *Bible Knowledge Commentary OT,* p. 1056.
7. Don Meredith, *Who Says Get Married* (Nashville, TN: Thomas Nelson) p. 42.
8. *Single Adult Ministries Newsletter.,* Vol. 17, No. 5, March 1990, p. 1.
9. Robert Hanna, *A Grammatical Aid to the Greek New Testament* (Grand Rapids: Baker, 1983), p. 348.
10. *Grammatical Aid,* p. 176.
11. Chafer, Vol. 7, p. 23.

Chapter 6

1. J. Rodman Williams, *Renewal Theology, Vol. I: God, the World & Redemption* (Grand Rapids, MI: Academie Books, Zondervan Corporation, 1990), p. 210.
2. Dwight L. Moody, quoted in *Great Quotes and Illustrations,* (Waco, TX: Word Publishing, 1985), p. 139.
3. "Whether God was referring to wind, physical breath, the principle of life, or the Holy Spirit is uncertain. However, the results were obvious. God gave life to these dead bones." John R Walvoord and Roy B. Zuck, editors, *The Bible Knowledge Commentary, Old Testament.* Charles H. Dyer is the contributing author for the book of Ezekiel, (Wheaton: Victor, 1985), p. 1298.

Chapter 7

1. *Bible Knowledge Commentary,* p. 20.
2. R. A. Torrey, *The Person and Work of the Holy Spirit* (Grand Rapids, MI: Zondervan, 1974), p. 171.
3. *Person and Work,* p. 172.
4. *Bible Knowledge Commentary,* p. 25.
5. John F. Walvoord and Roy B. Zuck, *The Bible Knowledge Commentary, New Testament.* Louis Barbieri wrote the section on the Gospel of Matthew. (Wheaton: Victor Books, 1983), p. 25.
6. *Bible Knowledge Commentary NT.* Grassmick wrote the section on the Gospel of Mark, p. 106.
7. For more on the wonderful anointing of the Holy Spirit and what it can mean to you, be sure to read my book, *The Anointing,* published by Thomas Nelson, and available in your local Christian bookstore.
8. *Linguistic Key to the Greek New Testament,* p. 786.
9. Andrew Murray, *The Blood of the Cross* (Springdale, PA: Whitaker House, 1981), p. 13.
10. Billy Graham, *The Holy Spirit* (Waco, TX: Word Books, 1978), p. 11.

Chapter 8

1. Lewis Sperry Chafer, *Systematic Theology,* Vol. VI "Pneumatology" (Dallas: Dallas Seminary Press, 1948), p. 95.
2. R. A. Torrey, *The Person & Work of the Holy Spirit* (Grand Rapids, MI: Zondervan, 1974), p. 90.
3. Billy Graham, *The Holy Spirit* (Waco, TX: Word Books, 1978), p. 86.
4. Bill Bright, *The Christian and the Holy Spirit* (Orlando, FL: New Life Publications, 1994), p. 24.

Chapter 9

1. Rienecker and Rogers, p. 454.
2. Thiessen, p. 289.

3. Rienecker and Rogers, p. 523.
4. Roy Hession, *The Calvary Road,* as quoted in *Christianity Today,* September 22, 1989, p. 35.
5. Henry Alford, *The New Testament for English Readers* (Chicago: Moody) p. 1105.
6. James Patterson, *The Day America Told the Truth* (Prentice Hall Press, 1991), chapter 5.
7. American Heritage Dictionary from CompuServe.
8. Rienecker and Rogers, p. 359.
9. *NIV Study Bible,* p. 1625.
10. *Spirit-Filled Life Bible,* p. 1603.
11. Rienecker and Rogers, p. 366.
12. Frank Bartleman, quoted in William Menzies, *Anointed to Serve* (Springfield, MO: Gospel Publishing House, 1971), p. 55.

Chapter 10

1. Evelyn Christianson in *My Heart Sings* as quoted in *Christianity Today,* November 19, 1990, p. 46.
2. Zuck & Walvoord, *Bible Knowledge Commentary,* John Witmer wrote the section on Romans. p. 473.
3. Charles C. Ryrie, *The Holy Spirit* (Chicago: Moody, 1965) p. 106.
4. Rienecker & Rogers, p. 367.
5. A.T. Robertson, *Word Pictures in the New Testament,* (New York: Harper & Brothers, 1930).
6. W.R. Newell in *Romans Verse By Verse,* pp. 326, 327 as quoted in Chafer, *Systematic Theology,* vol. 6, p. 44.
7. J. Oswald Sanders, *Spiritual Leadership* in *Navigator 2:7 Series,* Course 2, p. 82.
8. Billy Graham, *The Holy Spirit* (Waco, TX: Word Books, 1978), p. 166.
9. Henry Alford, *The New Testament for English Readers,* (Chicago: Moody), p. 1283,

10. For more on the gifts of the Holy Spirit, be on the lookout for my next book from Thomas Nelson, which will be on gifts of the Holy Spirit. And be sure to take a look at what my good friend Professor J. Rodman Williams has said in his *Renewal Theology*, especially Volume 2, pp. 323–325. (Don't forget the footnotes in this section, either).

11. Howard Snyder, *The Problem of Wineskins* (Downers Grove, IL: Inter-Varsity Press, 1975), p. 135.

12. Donald Guthrie, *New Testament Theology* (Downers Grove, IL: Inter-Varsity Press, 1981), p. 550.

Chapter 11

1. Dennis Bennett, *The Holy Spirit and You* (Plainfield, NJ: Logos International, 1971), p. 28.

Chapter 12

1. Richard Foster, *Celebration of Discipline* (New York: Harper Collins, 1988), p. 170.

2. Eifion Evans, *The Welsh Revival of 1904* (Bridgend, Wales: Evangelical Press of Wales, 1969), p. 89.

3. Evans, p. 161.

4. Henry Clarence Thiessen, *Lectures in Systematic Theology*, Revised by Vernon D. Doerksen, Revised Edition copyright 1979, (Grand Rapids: Eerdmans, 1979), p. 91.